Writing Creatively

WRITING CREATIVELY

J. N. HOOK

Professor of English and Counselor in the Teaching of English
The University of Illinois

Second Edition

D. C. HEATH AND COMPANY
Lexington, Massachusetts

Preface

Since the first edition of *Writing Creatively* appeared in 1963, teachers of English in both high schools and colleges have become increasingly aware of the dangers of almost exclusive attention to expository writing. Articles in the *English Journal, College Composition and Communication, Clearing House,* and other professional publications, as well as countless speeches and discussions in professional gatherings, have stressed the fact that the ability to write with vigor as well as clarity, and with color as well as precision, an ability fostered by creative writing, is not only a worthy objective in itself but is also of value in improving exposition.

The second edition of *Writing Creatively,* like the first, attempts to provide for students stimulating information about how to write anything that transcends the composition on "How to Make a Kite" or "My Summer Vacation"—and how to make even that kind of composition better. Through its hundreds of hints and scores of exercise items, it suggests takeoff points for the student who through imaginative use of the language can make a guided flight into the wild blue yonder. It pays as much attention, however, to the earthbound mortal who only walks but can be taught to walk more seemingly and more gracefully.

This book is intended for use in either of two situations: in a course called by some such name as "Creative Writing" or in a "regular" English class whose students can profit from instruction in vigorous and colorful writing. For the first situation it provides enough basic material for a one-semester course or, if supplemented by approximate literary readings, for a full year. For the regular class it offers provocative assignments that may be alternated with other work for one or more years.

Although schools are probably wise in stressing expository writing (because that is the kind of writing that most people do most often), those schools may be unwise that almost completely exclude the composition of poetry, short stories, personal essays, plays, and the like. Such writing has these values, among others:

1. It helps to open the floodgates of expression. When a student may occasionally write on a subject that does not tie him down to the ordering of facts, when he may sometimes write about what he *feels* and not just what he *knows*, when he can experiment and play with the language, he relaxes. Barriers to expression lift, and first a trickle emerges, then a brook, and possibly at last a torrent.

2. It often leads to improvement in the mechanics and structure of writing, as several studies have shown. Perhaps this improvement is attributable partly to increased interest, partly to reduced tension.

3. It results in greater awareness of words and hence in more precise diction. A student becomes word-conscious when he has tried to describe exactly a blossom-laden apple orchard or to find for a poem the only words that will reveal how he felt when in imagination one battle-gray dawn *he* was Francis Scott Key.

4. It leads to more acute understanding of literature. The student who has tried to play a musical instrument has a greater appreciation of Beethoven or of Hindemith than has the musically illiterate, but the student who has tried, however amateurishly, to compose music has still larger appreciation. The analogy with writing and literature is obvious.

A few features of *Writing Creatively* need special mention. One is that many types of expository writing—themes, articles, letters, journalistic accounts—are treated in some detail, on the assumption that all these can be written more effectively than they usually are. A second is that emphasis is constantly placed on helping the student to draw upon his own experience and on showing him that his experience is richer than he may suppose. Third, Chapters 15-17, entitled "From Manuscript into Print," "Work Habits of Professional Writers," and "Writing as a Profession," give hard-to-get information that any literate American should have and that young would-be writers find especially thought-provoking.

This second edition stresses the fact that writing that is creative should not be permitted to be sloppy in sentence structure and mechanics. A creative-writing fad existed in many secondary schools in the late 1920's and the 1930's, with too exclusive emphasis on color, imagination, and emotion. As a result, some students failed to learn important basic facts about sentences, usage, punctuation, capitalization, and the like. Those students had trouble in college English classes in which disciplined writing was required. The work in creativity had released their minds and increased their fluency, but they were hampered in college by their lack of attention to the common "decencies" of expression. Both a released mind and a control of the medium of expression are important. The two are not incompatible, as the work of almost any professional writer proves. The title of the Commission on English book, *Freedom and Discipline in English*, suggests the necessity for the combination of freedom and discipline in the entire English program.

In keeping with the insistence upon such discipline, the new *Writing Creatively* includes a "Style Index for Quick Reference," so that each student will have available a handy and brief guide to punctuation, sentence structure, and other mechanical matters. Teachers may want to use the marginal symbols in that index as they mark student papers for revision. I do not imply that evaluation should degenerate into a picayune error hunt, but I do insist that the student is done a disservice if the teacher pays no attention to observance of the generally accepted conventions. Freedom, yes; discipline, yes. The pairing is essential.

Grateful appreciation is expressed to the publishers and authors who grant permission to include the following:

An excerpt from *Manhattan Transfer* by John Dos Passos, published by Houghton Mifflin Company, is reprinted by permission of the author.

An excerpt from *Autobiography of Lincoln Steffens* is reprinted by permission of Harcourt, Brace & World, Inc.

"Calculating Machine" from *The Second Tree from the Corner* by E. B. White, copyright 1941 by E. B. White, appeared originally in the *New Yorker* and is reprinted by permission of Harper & Row, publishers.

An excerpt from *The Way West*, by A. B. Guthrie, is reprinted by permission of Houghton Mifflin Company.

Poems by Illinois high school students, from the *Illinois English Bulletin*, are reprinted by permission of Wilmer Lamar, editor, and the Illinois Association of Teachers of English.

"That Greek Dog," by MacKinlay Kantor, copyright 1941 by MacKinlay Kantor, is reprinted by permission of the author.

"Who Is the Beauty? Who Are the Beasts?" by Jeannette Miller, originally published in *Seventeen*, is reprinted by permission of the author.

"Oasis," from "Talk of the Town," *New Yorker*, December 5, 1960, is reprinted by permission of New Yorker Magazine, Inc.

An excerpt from "Golden Wedding," by Ruth Suckow, is reprinted by permission of Ferner Nuhn, Literary Executor, Estate of Ruth Suckow Nuhn.

An excerpt from "A Cold Day," by William Saroyan, from *The Daring Young Man on the Flying Trapeze*, is reprinted by permission of the author.

An excerpt from "Robert Frost: Master Conversationalist at Work," by John Ciardi, is reprinted by permission of Saturday Review, Inc.

The review of *The Hands of Cormac Joyce*, by Margaret Hurley, is reprinted by permission of Saturday Review, Inc.

Excerpts from *Writers at Work*, edited by Malcolm Cowley, are reprinted by permission of The Viking Press, Inc.

The excerpt from "After the Storm" (copyright 1932 Ernest Hemingway; renewal copyright © 1960) is reprinted with the permission of Charles Scribner's Sons from *Winner Take Nothing* by Ernest Hemingway.

Excerpts from *Modern Writers at Work*, by Josephine K. Piercy, are reprinted by permission of the author.

An excerpt from *Characters Make Your Story*, by Maren Elwood, is reprinted by permission of The Writer, publishers.

J.N.H.

Urbana, Illinois

Contents

Introduction

What Does Writing Creatively Mean?

CONFLICTING POINTS OF VIEW

All writing is creative.
No writing is creative.
Some writing is creative.

EACH of those beliefs is held by many teachers and students of writing. Let's look quickly at reasons for each.

All writing is creative. Some persons declare that whenever anyone puts his own words on paper, he is creating. It makes no difference whether what he writes is a novel, an answer to an examination question, or a grocery list. He is bringing into existence something that did not exist before, and hence is creating. An epic poem is a creation, these persons say, but so is a business letter or a simple paragraph written as a class exercise.

No writing is creative. Those who argue in this second way say that *any* creation is impossible. One of the fundamental laws of matter is that no new matter may be created, no old matter destroyed. Everything in the universe already exists and cannot be added to. Therefore any piece of writing is only a collection of old thoughts, old emotions, and old images, stated in old words arranged in old grammatical patterns. There is nothing new under the sun or beyond it.

Some writing is creative. In George Orwell's *Animal Farm*, the ruling pigs add to the slogan "All animals are equal" the clause "but some animals are more equal than others." Persons who say that some writing is creative would

1

not argue very vigorously against the contention that "all writing is creative"; however, they would add, "but some writing is more creative than other writing." They would say that the grocery list or the routine class exercise or the usual business letter is so slightly creative that it hardly deserves the adjective, but that writing which reveals imagination, an unusual grasp of relationships, a personal way of looking at a subject, an emotional reaction, and exquisite care with words, is strongly creative. Therefore a letter ordering a yellow blouse scores about zero on a scale of creativity, but Homer's *Odyssey* or Shakespeare's *Hamlet* is close to the top.

THE POINT OF VIEW OF THIS BOOK

The author of *Writing Creatively* accepts all three of the conflicting beliefs. Impossible? The German philosopher Hegel believed that conflicts or apparent contradictions could often be resolved by looking at the evidence in a new light. Let us see whether we can throw new light on the three contradictory statements.

First, let us admit that nothing absolutely new can be created. Even when a scientist transmutes one element into another, he is only rearranging the minute particles of matter. When a composer writes a symphony, he makes use of ageless types of sound as well as the experiences of thousands of earlier composers. When an author writes the most imaginative novel he can conceive, he is still incorporating his acquired knowledge of lasting truths, and is still using in his own fashion a language that millions before him have spoken and written.

The fact that nothing completely new can be created should not be disheartening. The scientist is not saddened because he cannot make new matter out of nothing. He accepts the physical law, which he calls the law of conservation of matter, just as he accepts the principle of gravity or any other physical fact. It is only one of the limitations, the boundaries, within which he must do his work.

Even though a creation cannot be completely new, everything that is not copied directly from something else is partly new. The newness comes from the rearrangement of the old parts. The scientist may rearrange molecules. The composer rearranges the notes that symbolize sounds. The novelist rearranges the words that call to a reader's mind a new grouping of pictures, emotions, ideas. Even the woman who this week writes a grocery list puts down an arrangement of items different from that of last week, so she too is a creator.

The creative act, then, consists of finding effective new combinations. The painter uses a palette, paints, brushes, and canvas similar to what others have used, and perhaps depicts the same kind of subject matter. But he in effect looks at the subject from a different angle, sees something in it that others have not seen, spaces the sections of his painting differently and makes different use of lights and shadows, spreads his paints thicker or thinner, acquires varying degrees of richness in color. If he is a true artist, the painting that results is unmistakably his. It is a creation and can be respected as such, even though it is but an individual's new arrangement of what already existed. It is the individual that makes the art. And what is true of creation in painting is equally true of all other kinds of creativity.

The amount and variety of rearrangement differ considerably, however. When Susie washes dishes, she changes the position of food particles, transferring them to the sink and thence to the sewers. She is creative, for she is creating clean dishes in place of dirty ones, and—although she never thinks of this—she is making the contents of the city's sewers a little different. Eventually her dishwashing will affect slightly not only the entire sewage disposal system but also the whole water system of the city, the state, the nation, and the world, just as when one tosses a pebble or

takes a step he moves the center of the universe. But Susie's
dishwashing is hardly as creative as the scientist's transmu-
tation of elements, because the scientist is doing something
less common and more significant.

Similarly, Susie's mother's grocery list is less creative
than the newest cookbook in the bookstore, and much less
creative than John Steinbeck's *The Grapes of Wrath.* All
three of these pieces of writing are creative because each
represents a rearrangement. But the novel is the least common, the most personalized, and the most significant of the
three. Steinbeck wove into his story love and hate and fear
and sadness and laughter, an attack on injustice and on
man's inhumanity to man, believable but colorful human
beings, accurate descriptive passages, vivid language, and a
suspenseful plot. Most of these ingredients are usually missing in cookbooks or grocery lists.

The point of view of this book, then, may be summarized
in this way:

1. Creativity is derived from new ways of looking at
relatively familiar things, from new arrangements of what
is already known.

2. Any piece of original writing is somewhat creative,
but some writing is more creative than other writing.

IMPLICATIONS

This book is not intended just for the would-be professional writer. Creativity is useful in most kinds of writing.
Freshness of thought and diction makes some persons' letters joys to receive. An unusual approach in a sales letter
may bring best results. A vividly written term paper in a
college course (other things being equal) is most likely
to bring a high grade. The attitudes and skills that a high
school student acquires in a creative writing course will not

necessarily lead to a career in writing, but they should help to brighten and make more effective almost everything he writes during the rest of his life.

If you accept the definition of creativity as being essentially an act of arrangement, and if you want to be a creative writer, the biggest implication is that you must be willing to rearrange. To do so, you will have to think, and thinking is notoriously hard work. You can't create just by using your prettiest words to write down the commonplace things that everybody in your school knows or believes. Pretty words aren't an adequate measure of good writing. You can't create much by idle dreaming. The creator is a thinker, a feeler, a doer. He is not a conformist. Above all, he is a questioner. He constantly asks *why*.

Why does our school have this regulation? Why are sunsets usually more colorful than sunrises? Why did Jim act as he did when the team lost? Why don't the other students like and respect that girl? Why do some animals hibernate, but not others? Why do many students try to be so much alike? Why do we say that one person is original but that another is eccentric? The list of *why's* is endless, and the creator keeps asking and trying to answer both the answerable and the unanswerable *why's*.

And he tries to see the relationships among all the things that he experiences or that he learns indirectly. The creative mind is constantly assembling, reassembling, adding to, re-arranging. It is able

> To see a world in a grain of sand,
> And a heaven in a wild flower.

It sees the end in every beginning, the beginning in every ending. It can become aware of unsuspected relationships between a polar bear and a bird of paradise, between courage and despair, between the wind and the sun and a lonely star and a girl just turned seventeen.

So thinking is essential to creation, but so is sensitivity. Not the kind of sensitivity that makes some people hide their heads in a pillow during a thunderstorm, or the kind that ohs and ahs over the first crocus. Rather, the creative person feels deeply and wants to feel more deeply and wants to understand what he feels. He doesn't hide his head when he hears thunder, but he looks out at the lightning, and he asks and finds out about what causes thunder and lightning, and he wonders how wild creatures react to violent weather, and he recalls Ben Franklin's dangerous experiment with the kite in the thunderstorm, and he relates lightning to the electricity that illuminates his room, and he recalls that physicists say that all matter is electricity, and he asks himself only half facetiously, "Does that mean that I am a lightning bolt?" He is sensitive to the beauty of the first crocus and its contrast to its wintry surroundings, but he recognizes beauty also in those surroundings, and in bumpy city streets, a gaudy neon sign, a church spire aspiring, a rainbow in a thin film of oil, a book with a tattered cover, a baby smiling through tears, an old man with creases of life in his face. His sensitivity alerts him to the beautiful, and to the beautiful in the ugly, and to the ugly in the beautiful, and to the patterns that run through all.

The creative person, finally, seeks the perfect medium to express to others the emotions he has felt, the relationships he has discovered, the endless kaleidoscopic patterns. For some the medium is sound: music; for some it is sight: painting or sculpture or ceramics or architecture; for some it may even be taste or smell: a chocolate cake or the aroma of bacon and coffee and a morning campfire. For many, words represent the perfect medium: exact words, meticulously chosen and precisely fitted together. No medium is best for all, and none is easy to master. The sculptor's or the chef's years of apprenticeship are long, and so, usually, are the other creators' years. And nobody finds the perfection that his mind envisions. But in the search, many brighten their lives and the lives of those who sympathize with the attempt.

EXERCISE

1. Discuss the following questions. (In all discussions suggested in this book, you should not merely repeat what the book says. Think for yourself, provide original examples, and feel free to disagree—courteously, of course—with the author and with one another.)

a. How would you support the belief that all writing is creative? What kinds of classroom exercises have you prepared or observed that were creative? Can a textbook be creative? An answer on an examination? Answers in grammar exercises?

b. Defend or attack the belief that no writing can be creative.

c. Assuming that there are degrees of creativity, from your own reading rate the following items on a scale from Probably Least Creative to Probably Most Creative: (1) a science textbook, (2) a poem about spring, (3) an index, (4) a science fiction short story, (5) a poem about an oak tree that survived a war, (6) a magazine article about the next Presidential election, (7) a newspaper story about a murder, (8) a "horror comic" book, (9) a novel based on personal experience in a war, (10) instructions for building a small boat. In what circumstances might items you ranked low be made creative? In what circumstances might items you ranked high be only slightly creative?

2. As your teacher directs, write one or more paragraphs on "What I Think Creative Writing Is" or "The Qualities a Creative Writer Should Possess."

Section A

GENERAL PRINCIPLES

1
Something to Write About: Subject and Theme

2
Observation and Sensory Words

3
Description and Imagery

Section A

GENERAL PRINCIPLES

1

Something to Write About: Subject and Theme

THE selection of a subject is to the author what choice of position is to the general—once skilfully determined, the battle is already half won.—Bovee

A nation's literature is always the biography of its humanity.
                                        —Robert, Lord Lytton

EXERCISE ONE

Read the first quotation at the head of this chapter. (Such introductory quotations are called *epigraphs*.) Answer for yourself and be ready to discuss in class these questions:

1. Why is position important to a general? (If you are interested in military strategy, you may want to read in *Fifteen Decisive Battles of the World*, or in any of the numerous military histories of the Civil War. In Garrett Mattingly's *The Armada*, note in Chapters XXIII–XXVIII how the opposing admirals maneuvered for position.)

2. Why is choice of subject important to a writer? Why is the battle "half won" when a good subject is selected?

Now read the second epigraph.

3. What is meant by "the biography of its humanity"?

4. What kinds of subjects does this epigraph suggest are worth writing about? Does it imply that literature should mainly concern famous persons? Does it mean that fantasy, fiction, or poetry is not truly part of a nation's literature?

WRITE WHAT YOU KNOW

The major purpose of this chapter is to help you find in your own experience material to write about. As your experiences widen and deepen, you will of course have richer subject matter. But even now you have lived enough, seen and heard and read enough, felt enough to write something worth sharing.

The tendency of too many high school writers is to choose subjects they know little or nothing about. They set their stories in Afghanistan or on the planet Venus, although they have never been in either place. The rural student writes an imaginative story about Times Square, and the New Yorker writes a rural idyll. The subject of death is a favorite, even among students who have never suffered a personal loss. Of course literature has room for fancy or fantasy, but not for stories that are factually inaccurate or untrue to life.

In spite of what you have just read, though, it is sometimes stimulating to unfetter your imagination completely and write on the most fantastic and unbelievable subject that occurs to you and in the most individualistic style possible. Such experiments may be artistic failures, but the exercises may help to limber your mind and make you more creative when you do turn back to more fact-oriented subjects.

EXERCISE TWO

1. If you know anything about science fiction, show by examples that it is ordinarily based on the author's knowledge of science, which he then extends into the unknown by means of his imagination.

2. In what sense are fantasies such as *Alice in Wonderland* or the fairy tales of Grimm or Andersen based on truth? Choose a particular incident or a single story to illustrate.

3. How do you account for the fact that much high school creative writing concerns topics that the writers know little about?

4. Why, in your opinion, is it better to write on a subject that you know reasonably well? Why is it also good to write occasionally a completely fanciful story?

5. In a magazine or book that gives brief biographical data about its authors, try to discover how each author was qualified to write about the topic he chose.

6. Write one or more paragraphs, as your teacher directs, in answer to one of the first five questions.

WELL, WHAT *DO* YOU KNOW?

You will now prepare a seven-part inventory, consisting of answers to about fifty questions, intended to call to your mind some of the things you know enough to write on.

Why seven parts? Almost all our knowledge is based on experiences with (1) family, (2) other persons, (3) school, (4) travel, (5) work, and (6) reading. (Some of these may overlap a little, but let's not worry about that.) Then, running through all the other six, are (7) emotional experiences, a necessary ingredient in all good writing. Our inventory, which is intended to be suggestive rather than complete, will take up each of these seven areas in turn.

The answers to the inventory are to be written on seven separate sheets of paper. Some questions may be answered in only a word or two, but others you may want to reply to in a paragraph. Some of the things you write later may be discussed by the whole class, but this inventory is intended mainly for your eyes and your teacher's. Starred questions, though, are good for class discussion.

Please either type or write with a ball-point pen, and make a carbon copy so that both you and your teacher will have a copy for reference.

EXERCISE THREE

Inventory: Part I—Family

1. Your name and age.

2. Are both your parents living? One parent? Occupation or occupations?

3. Are you living with both parents? With one? If not, with whom?

4. Have you any living brothers or sisters? Ages?

5. Choose the three words that you believe best characterize (a) your father, (b) your mother, (c) each living brother or sister. If you are not living with your family, choose three words to characterize each person in the household where you live.

*6. What is your earliest recollection?

7. What is the most pleasant day you can remember when your family, or some members of your family, were together?

8. Which member of your household can you best imagine in a story? Why?

*9. What are three events in the life of your household that might be of interest if written up well? (These may be simple events of the sort Clarence Day wrote about in *Life with Father* or Kathryn Forbes in *Mama's Bank Account*.)

Part II—Acquaintances

1. Who was your best friend when you were six years old? Twelve? Today?

2. Which of your acquaintances of about your own age has led the most exciting life? What made it exciting?

*3. Which adult of your acquaintance has led the most exciting life? Why do you say so? Which adult whom you know has perhaps been of greatest service to humanity? Why?

*4. If you were to write an article on "The Most Unforgettable Person I Ever Knew," whom would you write about and why? (Exclude members of your family.)

*5. Name five qualities that you most admire in a person your age, and five you most dislike.

°6. For years people have argued about whether heredity or environment is more influential in a person's life. Write a sentence or so about an acquaintance who seems to have been affected more by one than the other.

7. People react differently to the same situation. Imagine that three of your acquaintances have failed in an important examination. How would each probably react?

8. Name a situation that might test whether a person is a true friend.

°9. Read your answers to the preceding eight questions, and choose one as a "story seed." Summarize in one or two sentences the story, play, or article that might grow from this seed.

Part III—School

1. How many schools have you attended? Where were they? What are the biggest differences you have noticed between schools, or between two grades, or between elementary and high school?

2. What is your favorite subject in school? Have you always had the same favorite? If not, how do you account for the change?

3. In a sentence or two, summarize the most amusing incident you remember from your school days.

°4. Stories are based on conflicts. List five kinds of conflicts found in school life. These may be conflicts between persons, between a person and a fact of life, or within a person.

°5. What is the most dramatic moment you recall in any extracurricular activity?

Part IV—Travel

1. In how many of the states have you been? In which foreign countries, if any?

°2. If you have not been in more than five states, list three arguments you would use in a paper on "Authors Should Know One Place Well." If you have been in more than five, list three arguments to prove that "Travel Increases an Author's Understanding."

°3. What place that you have seen would provide the best

background for a murder mystery? A spy story? A love story?
A sports story?

*4. From your observations of people in various places, do
you conclude that differences between people of various lo-
calities are slight or considerable?

*5. Think of any city or town you know fairly well. List five
ways in which a story set in that place in 1900 would differ from
a story set there today. (Try to be specific. Don't list such gen-
eralities as "Clothing" and "Transportation." Say instead, "Horse-
drawn streetcars.")

Part V—Work

1. Knowledge of various kinds of work is useful to an author.
Tell why.

*2. List three or more books that could not have been
written if their authors had not known details of the work
described. (E.g., Melville could not have written *Moby Dick*
if he had not known sailors' work.)

3. What kinds of work have you done, either at home or
away from home?

4. What other kinds of work are you familiar with, through
observing workmen or through hearing about the jobs from
parents or friends?

5. What other kinds of work do you know enough about
to use as background, even though you lack detailed information?

Part VI—Reading

1. "Reading enriches, but is no substitute for experience."
Think of an example to illustrate that statement.

2. Name two or more *places* that you have become well
acquainted with through reading.

3. Same as 2, only this time it's *occupations*.

*4. What three *persons* (real or fictional) have you come
to know most thoroughly through your reading?

*5. List two or more truths about human nature that you
have found vividly illustrated in literature.

Part VII—Emotional Experiences

1. Do you prefer to spend more time alone, or with a group of congenial people your age?

2. What makes you most happy?

3. What makes you most sad?

4. What makes you most angry?

5. What makes you most afraid?

6. Have you ever thought yourself deeply in love? Often? How long, on the average, does each "love" last?

*7. William Wordsworth said that a poem results from "emotion recollected in tranquillity." Name two or more literary works in which the author's dramatization of an emotion is central.

8. Select one of your answers to Questions 2–6, and in a sentence summarize a story or a poem that could grow out of that answer.

INSPIRATION IS AN ILLUSION

"I can write only when I have inspiration," many young authors say. Professional writers know that inspiration is largely an illusion. In the sixteenth century Sir Philip Sidney, in the first of his sonnets called *Astrophel and Stella*, tells how he struggled to write these love poems. He chewed on his quill pen, read in other authors "to see if thence would flow / Some fresh and fruitful showers upon my sunburned brain," and waited for inspiration to strike. Finally, " 'Fool!' said my muse to me, 'look in thy heart, and write.' "

As we shall see in a later chapter, most professional writers set aside regular times for their writing, and they *make* themselves write. They do not wait for some mysterious visitation, a rosy cloud, or a spirit to guide the pen. They write, and if what they write seems bad, they throw it away, but keep on writing. Often the act of writing is like getting catsup out of a bottle: it comes hard as each fresh bottle is opened, but then it gushes forth. Merely sitting and looking at the bottle won't start the flow.

Thomas A. Edison, the inventive genius, attributed one per cent of his success to inspiration and ninety-nine per cent to perspiration, and an unknown writer explained that writing consists mainly of applying the seat of one's trousers to the seat of one's chair.

EXERCISE FOUR

Here are some snatches of ordinary conversation overheard in a high school corridor between classes. Choose any one of them and write a brief account of the incident it suggests to you. Write as well as you can, but use only about thirty minutes. The point of this exercise is to prove to yourself that a simple idea may generate a creative effort, and that one need not wait for a heaven-sent inspiration.

1. ". . . and his socks didn't match."
2. "We were already ten points behind."
3. "That's what made me angry."
4. "I burned them to a crisp."
5. "I don't know whether Shakespeare or somebody else said it."
6. ". . . but x can't equal 6!"
7. ". . . and he said, 'What color are your eyes?' "
8. "Then Mom said I'd be on telephone probation."
9. "No more blind dates for me!"
10. "But why did he call you an idiot?"

WHAT A THEME IS

Beneath the surface of almost every piece of writing—or sometimes lumped obtrusively on top—is a guiding idea, or theme. Remember the story of Cinderella? The Cinderella theme, that a deserving young person can rise rapidly from the depths to the heights, has been repeated thousands of times in fiction; almost all the heroes of Thomas B. Costain's historical novels, for example, are male Cinderellas. The theme of nearly every Western or crime story is that good triumphs over bad. A biographer usually tries to reveal the courage, the shrewdness, the ingenuity, the complexity, or some other dominating characteristic of the biographee; this point of view determines the theme. A poet in each poem reveals a theme, sometimes the same one again and again: the futility of war, the power of love, the strength or the pity of old age, and so on.

Theme may be defined as an underlying idea. It is an attempt to show what the author believes to be a lasting truth. It is not usually the same thing as a *moral,* for a moral is a guide to conduct whereas a theme does not necessarily refer to conduct at all.

Herman Melville, in *Moby Dick,* said, "To produce a mighty book you must choose a mighty theme," and asked for "a condor's quill" to write with and "Vesuvius' crater for an inkstand" in order to do justice to the theme of his story. Poet John Ciardi, however, has said that a great theme does not guarantee a great work. Both observations are correct, for a masterpiece results from the combination of a mighty theme with superb technical execution.

The theme is ordinarily not stated directly. Intelligent readers can usually discover themes for themselves and may even be a little annoyed when a writer says that his theme is thus and so. Besides, the purpose of literature is to picture, illuminate, reveal, dramatize, not to preach or make bald assertions.

WHY A THEME IS NEEDED

One reason for having a theme has already been suggested: authors dramatize truths in what they write, and these truths are their themes. Without such truths as a base, writing lacks significance.

A second reason is that the presence of a theme assists in the attainment of unity. Unity is oneness—sticking to one subject instead of hopping around aimlessly like a catbird in a pear tree. One high school writer, discussing five or six neighbors of his family, put down a few facts about each and handed in his paper. When his teacher criticized it for lack of unity, he said, "Why, it's all about one subject—our neighbors." The difficulty, though, was that there was no theme to hold together the random observations. The student might have chosen to show the friendliness of the neighbors, their nosiness, their interest or lack of interest in caring for their property, or any one of a number of other qualities. Stressing this one characteristic, while not excluding others, would have provided a simple theme to hold the entire composition together.

EXERCISE FIVE

1. Choose three or more of the following general subjects, limiting each in any way you wish. Write two or more possible statements of theme for each general subject you select. Each statement should be only one sentence long, and preferably should not be excessively obvious. Compare your statements of theme with those of your classmates.

Our neighbors	Ambition
War	Proverbs
High school diplomas	Friendship
Choosing a career	Fame
Wealth	Purpose of college
The value of literature	Going steady
Basketball	Beauty
A small child	Superstition
Younger brothers or sisters	Authorship
Automobiles and grades	Music

2. Choose one or more of the statements of theme you wrote for Question 1. If you were planning to develop that theme

as an essay, what points would you include? If you were going to develop it as a short story, what characters might you use, and in general what might the plot be about?

EXERCISE SIX

Recall poems, short stories, essays, or books that you have read either as an individual or as a class. Try to decide the theme of each. Do you accept the theme as a statement of truth? Can you find any contradictory themes? How do you account for such contradictions?

SUGGESTED CLASS PROJECTS

Your class, with the advice of your teacher, may want to choose one of the following projects to extend through much of the semester or the year. All members will be able to help.

1. A class in Evansville, Indiana, invented a city, prepared a map of it, imagined many of its citizens, and wrote about them all through the course. You may want to do something similar, with essays, stories, poems, and plays based on the lives of the imaginary people in a city or town you create. Thornton Wilder's play *Our Town* and some of the poems in Edgar Lee Masters' *Spoon River Anthology* may give you ideas.

2. Use newspaper stories as the bases for a number of writing experiences. One technique is to take a story about a number of persons—for instance, "Plane Crash Kills 34" or "Six Million Children Enter First Grade"—and pick out *one* of the persons involved and write an imaginary story or an article about him. The best of these may be collected in book form.

3. Another book project: Prepare an anthology of poetry written by the class, with each student choosing one or two of his best poems and finding suitable illustrations.

4. Individual journals are popular in some schools. Each student, besides regular assignments, is required to write for his journal at least one paragraph each day, on any subject he wishes. He marks any entries he wants no one but the teacher

to see. Students and the teacher may agree on some of the best entries by each student, and gather them as a book.

5. "Our Class Calendar" can contain student writing about the seasons, and simultaneously serve to recall events of the school year associated with the seasons. Student photographers may furnish illustrations.

6. The group-written short story or play is a lively activity for a few weeks. One method of procedure is for each student to describe a setting; a committee chooses the five best, and the class chooses the one or two of these five it would like to use. Then each student invents a character to act in the chosen setting, and several of these characters are picked for the story. Next, each student creates a plot in which all the selected characters have a part, and the class selects the most interesting plot. Each student writes the story, or small groups of students may collaborate.

7. A monthly or bimonthly publication may be prepared, with copies mimeographed and distributed or sold in the school. In Atlanta, Georgia, the *Brown Book* has had issues on "Interesting People," "Travel," "Science Fiction and Fantasy," "Arts," "School," "The Community," "History," and "Sports."

2

Observation and
Sensory Words

WHERE is the use of eyesight and articulate speech if a man cannot observe and recollect? . . . Cultivate this art in future. . . . You may find it of momentous service.—Robert Louis Stevenson

TRAINING YOURSELF TO OBSERVE

In some branches of the military services, part of the instruction consists of asking questions of a squad or two of men riding in an open truck. The instructor asks individuals such questions as "Was anyone at home in the last farmhouse? Does it have a telephone? Electricity? A basement? How many cows were in that pasture? Which direction were they facing? Why? Which direction is the wind coming from? About what is the wind velocity? In the third farmhouse back, were the windowshades up, down, or halfway up?"

In traditional warfare, practice in observing such details may save lives. In peace, observation may not have such dramatic value, but it may add infinitely to the riches of our daily living. Too many of us go through life with our senses so lacking in alertness that we are little better than vegetables. We plod unseeing, unhearing, unfeeling. One day is like all other days, one street like other streets, one joy like other joys, caviar like hamburger, a rose no different from a gardenia. So we live and so we die, with death only a little unlike life, for in our living we noticed little to make the living worth while.

If you have never learned to observe, what can you do? If to you a kitten is only a young cat, if your nostrils send to your brain no pleasant message of burning leaves, if food is food and that's the end of it, if the noises of city streets do not change subtly as the day wears on, if the old newspaper vendor on the corner is merely an old man, you will probably never be able to write anything that will excite anyone except your mother.

The habit of observing, like other habits, must be acquired through constant practice. Two famous French novelists of the nineteenth century, the Goncourt brothers, kept notebooks in which they recorded the details of whatever they saw, choosing carefully the words to recreate each sight, each sound, each emotion. Their word pictures of Paris are consequently among the richest and most accurate descriptions of that much-described city.

The small child learns early to observe. To him a bubble is a miracle, and though he does not know the word *iridescence*, he knows the thing itself, for the bubble has taught him. He may crawl on hands and knees for an hour behind an ant, his curiosity impelling him to learn all he can about the marvelous creature. But then he grows older, and blasé, and he stops observing closely, and nothing seems marvelous any more; his curiosity dwindles; he is excited only by physical contests or by incidents of much personal significance to him. He is dying at age fifteen, though he may not be counted dead for three or four score more years. For him to start living again, he would have to re-create his child's habit of looking, examining, reveling in the small and the great, discovering the unfamiliar in the familiar and the familiar in the strange. Probably every writer who has gained lasting fame has been able to do so. With Walt Whitman those who can observe say,

As to me I know of nothing else but miracles,
Whether I walk the streets of Manhattan,
Or dart my sight over the roofs of houses toward the sky,

Or wade with naked feet along the beach just in the edge of
the water, . . .
Or look at strangers opposite me riding in the car,
Or watch honeybees busy around the hive of a summer fore-
noon. . . .
To me every hour of the light and dark is a miracle,
Every cubic inch of space is a miracle,
Every square yard of the surface of the earth is spread with
the same,
Every foot of the interior swarms with the same.

EXERCISE ONE

1. Why did Stevenson (quoted in the epigraph of this chapter) value observation and the ability to describe what had
been observed? Think of examples to show that observation
may be "of momentous service." If you have read anything that
Stevenson wrote, such as *Treasure Island, Kidnapped, Travels
with a Donkey,* or *A Child's Garden of Verses,* show that he
himself possessed the ability to observe and describe.

2. Stevenson mentions only eyesight as a means of observation. How else may we observe?

3. How, in your opinion, can the art of observation be cul-
tivated?

4. Here are some simple tests of your present habits of observing.

　　a. Name three things you saw on the way to school this
morning that you do not remember seeing before.

　　b. Name three sounds you *consciously* heard on your
way to school.

　　c. Name two pleasant odors you were *consciously* aware
of on your way to school.

　　d. Give the height and the color of the eyes of the person sitting behind you. If no one is behind you, choose someone else whom you cannot see. Arrange to check your recollection.

　　e. Draw a rough diagram of another classroom in your
school. Include the correct number of desks, tables, chairs,

cabinets, bookshelves, other furniture, chalkboards, and windows and doors.

USING NOUNS TO DESCRIBE

When students think of describing anything, most of
them think in terms of adjectives. Professional authors,
though, tend to work their nouns and verbs harder than
they do adjectives or adverbs. Nouns are useful in description because when a reader sees the name of something
he knows, he can picture it in his mind.

The word *lily*, for example, causes the reader to see a
flower that can hardly be confused with a rose or a mari-
gold. *Lily*, however, creates a less definite picture than
Easter lily, tiger lily, or *lily of the valley*. Most names of
physical things occupy a place in a list that may be arranged from general to very specific:

General	Less general	Fairly specific	Specific	Very specific
vegetation	plant	flower	lily	tiger lily

Any of the five nouns in that sample list may be useful
at times. For instance, you may want to refer to the "rich
vegetation" of a tropic area without naming specific plants.
Or you may have occasion merely to mention "plants and
animals" or "flowers and trees." If you have need to describe, though, you will often need specific nouns. "Mother
grows flowers in her garden" is not nearly so descriptive as
"Mother grows verbenas, phlox, and geraniums."

Nouns are not merely sight words. In describing taste
or odor, and sometimes in describing sound or feeling, you
need nouns for the simple reason that no appropriate adjectives exist. For example, no adjectives exist to reveal
adequately the taste of coffee, of olives, or of cinnamon, or
the odor of apple-wood smoke or freshly cut hay. But you
can say "It tasted like coffee," or "The odor reminded me

of apple-wood smoke," and most of your readers will understand.

EXERCISE TWO

1. Place the following items in a five-heading list ranging from General to Very specific (like the list on page 26). Then fill in as many of the other four headings in each group as you can.

fauna   hovel   boat   infant

2. Choose a descriptive passage from any book you have been reading recently. Be prepared to discuss in class the author's use of nouns as aids to his description.

3. If you were writing a detailed description of your English classroom, what are twenty nouns you might want to include?

4. Write a brief description of any place you have recently seen or can see now. Use no descriptive adjectives, but choose your nouns with special care.

5. Recall a recent experience in which you tasted something unfamiliar to you or smelled an unusual odor. Try to describe the taste or the odor.

USING VERBS TO DESCRIBE

In "Song of the Chattahoochee" Sidney Lanier's gay little river says:

> I *hurry* amain to *reach* the plain,
> *Run* the rapid and *leap* the fall,
> *Split* at the rock and together again,
> *Accept* my bed, or narrow or wide,
> And *flee* from folly on every side.

The rushes *cry*, the dewberry *dips*, the reeds *sigh*, the white quartz *shines*, "the smooth brook-stone did *bar* me of passage," the dry fields *burn*, and flowers *yearn*.

Suppose that instead of choosing such verbs Lanier had written something like this:

I *make* my way down to the plain, *going* through rapids and over waterfalls. Sometimes a rock *gets* in my way, but I *ignore* interruptions and *take* whatever comes, *paying* no attention to foolish distractions. I *see* rushes, dewberries, and quartz, and *hear* the sound of reeds, as I *pass* over smooth brook-stones on my way to *assist* dry fields and flowers.

The meaning is about the same, but the effect is lost. Lanier's poem owes much of its lasting popularity to its vigorous verbs.

Obviously a few verbs must perform our language chores most frequently: *be, have, say, see, hear,* and the like. We cannot always have something *splitting, shrieking, roaring, catapulting,* or *dipping,* because to do so would be untrue to life. In all writing, the best verbs are the truest ones. Lanier's verbs are truest for his purpose because the Chattahoochee really does hurry, run, leap, and split, and the rushes and the reeds which cried and sighed "Abide, abide," really do impede the movement of the water.

When you are writing description, then, choose the verbs that say what you mean. Avoid both the Scylla of weak understatement (e.g., "I make my way down toward the plain") and the Charybdis of unbelievable exaggeration (e.g., "I plunge toward the plain").

A minor but still important caution: Distrust the verb *seem.* Lanier's Chattahoochee does not *seem* to split at the rock; it *splits.*

EXERCISE THREE

1. Although verbs are more difficult than nouns to arrange from General to Very specific, some are clearly more specific than others. Make a list like this:

General	Fairly specific	Very specific
go	walk	saunter

Try to find five or more additional trios of verbs for your list. Compare your results with your classmates'.

2. Choose a descriptive passage from a story or poem. Especially useful is one that involves movement of some kind. Observe the author's choice of verbs. Try to decide whether substituting different verbs would strengthen or weaken the passage.

3. As a class, draw up a list of one hundred or more verbs that can be used in place of *go,* and one hundred or more that can take the place of *say.* Be able to define all verbs in the list and to think of a situation in which each might be appropriate.

4. Think of verbs (participles if you wish) that could be used accurately in describing each of these.

An eighty-yard run by a swift, elusive halfback
A small, agile player bringing a basketball down the court
A large river in time of flood
A savage windstorm
A gentle wind on a pleasant day in the country
A squirrel
Traffic during rush hour
An airplane taking off
An experiment in a chemistry laboratory (no explosion, please!)
A dance or dance step

5. Using one of the subjects in Number 4, write a descriptive passage in which you pay particular attention to verbs.

USING ADJECTIVES TO DESCRIBE

Joseph Conrad, born in Poland, became a British sailor and, after he was a grown man, learned the English language. He learned it so well that he became known as one of the greatest literary craftsmen of the British Isles. "My task," he wrote, "is, by the power of the written word, to make you hear, to make you feel—it is, before all, to make you *see*." In words he tried to convey the best features of other arts: the "plasticity of sculpture," the "color of painting," and the "magic suggestiveness of music."

To attain his effects, Conrad studied sentence rhythms, sought precise nouns and potent but exact verbs, and piled up adjectives and adverbs which he then ruthlessly sorted out, throwing away all but those that would really make the reader hear, feel, and see.

In his autobiographical *Mirror of the Sea* Conrad has a long section dealing with the east and west winds so important to men in sailing vessels. He thinks of them as kings:

[The King of the West] is a barbarian, of a northern type. Violent without craftiness and furious without malice, one may imagine him seated masterfully, with a double-edged sword on his knees, upon the painted and gilt clouds of the sunset, bowing his shock head of golden locks, a flaming beard over his breast, imposing, colossal, mighty limbed, with a thundering voice, distended cheeks, and fierce blue eyes, urging the speed of his gales. The other, the East King, the king of blood-red sunrises, I represent to myself as a spare Southerner, with clear-cut features, black-browed and dark-eyed, gray-robed, upright in sunshine, resting a smooth-shaven cheek in the palm of his hand, impenetrable, secret, full of wiles, fine-drawn, keen—meditating aggression.

This passage is more filled with descriptive adjectives than most of Conrad's writing, but each adjective serves a purpose; Conrad wastes few words. That is the lesson to be learned about using adjectives: each must have a reason for existence, or out it must go. It must add to the picture in the reader's mind, it must enhance his understanding, it must help him to feel what the author felt, or it must be thrown, still glittering, into the ash can.

EXERCISE FOUR

1. Some adjectives are more specific than others. *Hot,* for instance, is a rather general word; to indicate variations of the hotness we may prefer the more specific *torrid, fiery, warm, tepid, lukewarm,* or even, on some occasions, *volcanic* or *plutonic.* Think of more specific adjectives for each of the following:

cold	insensible	gray	bubbly	windy
dry	wet	good	bad	interesting

2. Reread the quotation from Conrad's *Mirror of the Sea.* List all the descriptive adjectives, as well as the descriptive phrases (such as "with a thundering voice"). In class, talk about what each item in your list contributes to Conrad's description of the kings of the wind.

3. As a class, select about ten pictures in a news-picture magazine such as *Life.* The subjects of the pictures should be varied, with people, places, and things all represented. Some of the pictures may be in advertisements. Independently, write one or two adjectives that in your opinion best describe what is shown in each picture. Avoid general adjectives such as *pretty* or *interesting.* Be prepared to tell the class why you chose the words you did. The class may want to vote on which adjectives are best.

4. Choose one of the same pictures you worked with in Number 3, and write a careful description of what you see in it.

USING ADVERBS TO DESCRIBE

The adverb is less valuable as a descriptive word than is the noun, the verb, or the adjective. In description it modifies a verb, and if the verb is chosen carefully, it may not require modification. However, when the verb alone cannot convey the precise meaning, an adverb may help.

For example, think of the verb *disappeared.* In what manner may a person or a thing disappear? Among the adverbs that come to mind are *abruptly, quietly, slowly, rapidly, smilingly, wistfully,* and *angrily.* Any of these adds something, perhaps something essential, to the simple meaning of the verb. But none should be used unless it does contribute effectively.

EXERCISE FIVE

1. Think of several adverbs that in some circumstances may add to the meaning of each of these verbs:

gallop	bloom	chuckle	plead	grieve
spend	sell	give	sail	appear

2. In a page or two of a short story find all the descriptive adverbs and decide why each is used and whether it could be omitted without damaging the story.

3. Write a paragraph suggested by one of the subjects named below. Be ready to justify any descriptive adverbs you use.

A high hurdles race
A school band's marching performance between halves of a game
A popular singer performing a hit song
Yourself getting up in the morning
A small child having a tantrum
A hunter stalking game
Birds building a nest
A rainstorm
Starting a balky lawn mower
An awkward student learning to dance

Description and Imagery

IN any kind of writing it is frequently necessary to describe —that is, tell about the physical appearance of something. Description often gives only essential facts, as you might do in a letter to a friend telling him about your new coat or your new school building. Sometimes, though, opinions or interpretations are included with the facts, and on occasion description involves a quick, impressionistic comparison rather than a detailed treatment.

In twentieth-century writing, description tends to be more concise than in earlier years. The modern writer usually selects only the most revealing details, avoiding long paragraphs of the sort that readers are inclined to skip. Descriptive bits are common in short stories, novels, and other types of writing, but they are likely to be scattered throughout the work instead of being concentrated in a few places.

FACTUAL DESCRIPTION

Here is a catalogue description of an electric ice cream freezer:

Ideal for picnics or parties—makes 1 pt. to 4 qts. in 20 minutes! Mixes while it freezes—assures smooth texture. Deluxe natural cedar tub, lacquered copper reinforcements. Rustproof metal cream can, durable paddle and scrapers. 12-in. diam., 20 in. high, 6 ft. cord.

Notice that this description gives an adequate word pic· ture of the freezer and answers the questions a prospective buyer would be most likely to ask. It is not imaginative or literary, nor should it be, because its purpose is only to inform. It includes little of the writer's personal opinion, although the first five words are less factual than the rest.

Now here is another largely factual paragraph, a description of playwright George Bernard Shaw, written by one of his biographers, Archibald Henderson:

In Mr. Shaw I encountered one of the most delightful and genial of men. He spoke perfect English, with a delightful Irish accent, and we were soon upon the most unceremonious terms. I found Mr. Shaw to be slightly over six feet tall, with carroty red hair and beard, slightly tinged with gray, jocular-looking eyebrows, one cocking madly upward, the other preserving the level of true gravity, and steel-blue eyes, now dancing with mirth, now flashing with baleful fire of the reformer. His forehead, of marble whiteness, was extraordinarily high, and the conformation was an elongated rectangle, ready-made to the pencil of the cartoonist. Mr. Shaw's movements were quick, nervous, and springy; and I soon learned that he was genuinely fond of boxing, cycling, and swimming, in all of which he excelled.

Mr. Henderson also presents factual information, but does so with more color and imagination than a catalogue usually does. Note as examples such phrases as "cocking madly upward," "dancing with mirth," "baleful fire," "marble whiteness," "an elongated rectangle." The opening sentence is interpretive rather than purely factual.

The purpose of description is to give a clear impression of the physical appearance of a thing, person, or place. Purely factual description, which is rare except in scientific reports, avoids any personal opinion. Modified factual description, like the two examples, appears frequently in almost all types of writing.

EXERCISE ONE

1. Choose the sweater, shoes, or something else you are wearing, and write a purely factual description of it suitable for use

in a catalogue. Be sure to answer all likely questions about such things as material, style, color choices, and range of sizes. Write clearly, but not necessarily in complete sentences.

2. Now rewrite the description prepared for Number 1. This time include some words or phrases intended to persuade the catalogue user to buy the item.

3. Describe factually a musical instrument you know well, a piece of apparatus in the science laboratory, or a tool with which you are familiar.

4. Write a description of a classmate without naming him or her. Restrict yourself to observable physical features; do not include comments on personality, character, and the like. Avoid opinion words such as *pretty* or *handsome*. See whether the other students can identify the person.

5. Describe factually a room or some other place you know well.

INTERPRETIVE DESCRIPTION

Factual description has as its primary purpose the presentation of facts about whatever is being described, although as we have seen it is often shaded by some elements of opinion. When the chief purpose of description is to present opinion, it becomes interpretive. That is, the writer draws conclusions or interprets the meaning of the physical characteristics.

As an example, here is a student's description of a woman's smile:

Her smile, if it can be called a smile, was not contagious; if it were, the world would have far less humor and mirth. Her smile was a momentary lengthening of her thin lips into a straight line as though she had jerked strings attached to each corner. It would be difficult to determine whether she cut it short to make it look less a sneer, or whether she was unwilling to waste any of her precious cheerfulness on anyone.

The author says in effect that the smiling woman was actually a gloomy, cheerless sort of person whom one would probably not like as a friend. A merely factual description of the smile would have avoided any such inference, perhaps consisting only of the first fourteen words of the second sentence.

Ralph Waldo Emerson wrote this paragraph about the catbird:

Always a good singer, he sometimes nearly equals the brown thrush, and has the merit of keeping up his music later in the evening than any bird of my familiar acquaintance. . . . The catbird is as shy as the robin is vulgarly familiar. Only when his nest or his fledglings are approached does he become noisy and almost aggressive. I have known him to station his young in a thick cornel-bush on the edge of the raspberry-bed, after the fruit began to ripen, and feed them there for a week or more. In such cases he shows none of that conscious guilt that makes the robin contemptible. On the contrary, he will maintain his post in the thicket, and sharply scold the intruder who ventures to steal *his* berries. After all, his claim is only for tithes, while the robin will bag your entire crop if he gets a chance.

Emerson interprets in this description by showing clearly that he respects, admires, even loves the catbird, and that he believes the robin to be a relatively unlikable bird.

Professional writers, when they find description necessary, decide whether they need to present only the facts or also to interpret the facts. If interpretation is necessary, they usually present it indirectly, as Emerson does. That is, they do not come out openly and say "I like catbirds better than robins," but they let their choice of words and details reflect their opinion.

EXERCISE TWO

1. In Exercise One (3) you were asked to describe factually a musical instrument, a piece of scientific apparatus, or a tool. Rewrite that description, revealing indirectly your attitude toward the object.

2. In Exercise One (5) you were asked to describe factually a

room or some other place. Rewrite that description, making it clear that you consider the place (a) bleak, (b) ugly, (c) picturesque, (d) beautiful, (e) colorful, (f) useful but unattractive, or (g) cozy.

3. Describe a person who is unknown to your classmates. Through your choice of details and words, show that the person is not very likable. Then, using different details and words, rewrite the description to present a favorable impression of the same person.

FIGURATIVE DESCRIPTION

Interpretive description often makes use of figurative language, especially comparisons. The purpose of such description is not to provide a full, detailed picture but rather to flash before the reader a quick image which will leave a definite impression. Here are several brief examples:

In her snowsuit she looked like a duck dressed in rompers.
(STUDENT)

The round dome of the auditorium looked like a huge fruit bowl turned upside down. (STUDENT)

The only clouds were a few feathers, clinging lightly to the concave blue roof of the world. (STUDENT)

> And what is so rare as a day in June?
> Then, if ever, come perfect days;
> Then Heaven tries earth if it be in tune,
> And over it softly her warm ear lays;
> Whether we look, or whether we listen,
> We hear life murmur, or see it glisten;
> Every clod feels a stir of might,
> An instinct within it that reaches and towers,
> And groping blindly above it for light,
> Climbs to a soul in grass and flowers.
> (JAMES RUSSELL LOWELL)

So quietly did the little stream dip and ripple its way through the cañon that it spoke only in faint and occasional gurgles. The voice of the stream was a drowsy whisper, ever interrupted by dozings and silences, ever lifted again in the awakenings. (JACK LONDON)

Dark presses tight the steaming asphalt city, crushes the fretwork of windows and lettered signs and chimneys and watertanks and ventilators and fire-escapes and moldings and patterns and corrugations and eyes and hands and neckties into blue chunks, with black enormous blocks. Under the rolling heavier heavier pressure windows blunt light. Night crushes bright milk out of arclights, squeezes the sullen blocks until they drip red, yellow, green, into streets resounding with feet. All the asphalt oozes light. Light spurts from lettering on roofs, mills dizzily among wheels, stains rolling tons of sleep.

(JOHN DOS PASSOS)

EXERCISE THREE

1. In the three examples given above from student writing, what things are compared? What impression do you receive of the thing being described? How would factual description differ from the figurative type used by the students?

2. In the lines from Lowell's "The Vision of Sir Launfal," to what is Heaven compared? Try rewriting the lines in factual prose. Why is Lowell's version more effective and memorable?

3. To what does London compare the little stream?

4. In the paragraph from Dos Passos, the dark is comparable to an all-powerful giant. What are the two major things that the dark accomplishes? Rewrite the paragraph factually, beginning in this way: "When darkness arrives, many things in the city are no longer visible."

5. Choose several of the following, and attempt to describe each briefly with a quick comparison that reveals your attitude:

a band formation at a football game
a television set
a locker room
a brightly lighted swimming pool on a hot summer night
a tree in early autumn

a beggar
a field of young corn
a deserted beach
a stream or lake you know well
dark clouds
a busy street at night, as seen from a tall building
a gallery in a museum
a large, busy office
a cornpicker or a combine at work
a tractor bogged down in a muddy field
a flock of wild geese
a drunk lying on the sidewalk
cheerleaders in action
books in a lawyer's office
a huge crowd leaving a sporting event

TYPES OF FIGURES OF SPEECH

Most figures of speech involve a comparison between two unlike things. Thus "He is as tall as his brother" is not figurative, because *he* and *brother* are both human beings. But in the song "Oh, What a Beautiful Morning" we are told that "the corn is as high as an elephant's eye"; this is figurative, for corn and elephants are not alike.

Inexperienced writers think of figures of speech as mere decorations, used mainly by poets. Actually we all use scores of figures every day, generally unconsciously. When we refer to the arms or legs of a chair, for example, we are unthinkingly comparing the chair to a person. We often repeat old comparisons that our parents and grandparents and their parents and grandparents used: hot as fire, quick as a flash, sharp as a tack, etc. The comparison of something unknown to something known results in clarity that otherwise might be hard to attain. For instance, if we are told that the Eiffel Tower is 984 feet tall, most of us cannot visualize that height, but if we are told that the Eiffel

Tower is as tall as fifty two-story houses piled on top of one another, we have a clearer conception. Figures of speech, in other words, are useful, not just decorative.

The most common figure of speech is not usually even recognized as figurative. This is sometimes called a *trope*. A trope, as we shall define it here, is a word or phrase that makes a rapid comparison without using such a word as *like* or *as* and without saying that one thing *is* another. Thus if we say that someone has "a wolfish appetite" or that he "wolfs his food," we are comparing his appetite or his manner of eating to that of a wolf. If we refer to "a piercing stare," we are implying that the stare is sharp and penetrating like a needle or a knife. Other common examples: peaches and cream complexion, melodious voice, a purring engine, dogged my footsteps, pumped information from him.

The two figures most often studied in school are the *simile* and the *metaphor*. The simile generally uses *like* or *as* in making the comparison, although such terms as *as if, as when, similar to,* or *resembles* may be substituted. The metaphor more boldly says that one thing *is* another.

Similes:

True courage is like a kite: a contrary wind raises it higher.
(J. PETIT-SENN)

Cruel as death and hungry as the grave.
(JAMES THOMSON)

Eyes that droop like summer flowers.   (LETITIA LANDON)

As the sun breaks through the darkest clouds, so honor peereth in the meanest habit.   (WILLIAM SHAKESPEARE)

The schoolroom was as quiet as a church on a Monday morning.   (STUDENT)

Metaphors:

Courage is fire, and bullying is smoke.
(BENJAMIN DISRAELI)

Death is the quiet haven of us all.   (WILLIAM WORDSWORTH)

The eyes are the windows of a woman's heart.

(EUGENE SUE)

Unblemished honor is the flower of virtue.

(JAMES THOMSON)

The strong pipe smoke was a cockleburr on his tongue.

(STUDENT)

Analogy is another form of comparison, sometimes developed at considerable length. It is highly useful in explanations, and is sometimes employed in debate. Henry David Thoreau, for instance, in explaining the shape of Cape Cod, drew an analogy with a bended arm. A debater who was forecasting an unsatisfactory future for television argued from the analogy that neither the motion pictures nor the radio had ever reached the level of public service predicted for them and that therefore television was unlikely to do so.

Personification is less used now than formerly. It attributes human qualities to inanimate or abstract things. A statue of Justice, portrayed as a woman with a blindfold over her eyes and balance scales in her hand, exemplifies a sculptor's use of personification. A writer who says that the skies wept or that thunder rolled in anger is also personifying.

A relatively unimportant figure is *antonomasia*. If you call a man a Scrooge, a Nero, or a Franklin, you are in effect making a comparison, and you are using antonomasia.

A few figures of speech do not normally involve comparisons. Among them are these:

Onomatopoeia. Using words that sound like what is being described: *bang, clatter, shriek, purr*

Metonymy and *synecdoche.* Using a symbol instead of the precise name: The *pen* (i.e., literary power) is mightier than the *sword* (i.e., military power); *Washington* (i.e.,

the federal government); reading *Shakespeare* (i.e., Shakespeare's writings); a remarkable *canvas* (i.e., painting)

Irony. Saying the reverse of what is meant: That is a
beautiful song (spoken ironically of a singing commercial)

Hyperbole. Intentional exaggeration: She cried a *gallon*
of tears.

Litotes. Understatement, the opposite of exaggeration:
A million dollars is *no small* amount.

Apostrophe. Addressing an absent person or an abstraction, as poets used to address a Muse or Spring, etc.

EXERCISE FOUR

1. Find in a magazine or a literature book several examples
of tropes as defined on page 40, or think of some of your own.

2. Explain the meaning of the similes and metaphors quoted
on pages 40–41. Find a few additional examples.

3. Find or think of additional examples of analogy, personification, and antonomasia.

4. As a class, list twenty or more words that illustrate onomatopoeia.

5. Find or think of several additional examples of metonymy
or synecdoche.

FINDING GOOD FIGURES OF SPEECH

A few persons think habitually in figurative language.
They constantly see similarities and differences in everything they discuss. To them such an ordinary object as
a filing cabinet may be a repository of defeated dreams or
a symbol of a civilization that has lost touch with reality.
Those who steadily express themselves in figures are the
born poets; young Shakespeare was probably one of them.

But most of us must search for the comparisons that
will clarify and enlighten our writing. Occasionally a happy
similarity will appear unbidden, but more often we must

ask ourselves what comparison will be most effective and true.

A minor American poet, Henry Cuyler Bunner, may illustrate this point. He liked to write, but finding suitable imagery was difficult for him. He loved trees, and wanted to write a poem about a tree. But what could he say about a tree that a thousand others hadn't already said? What is a tree? he asked himself. It must be a friendly thing, a lover of sunshine; it waves flaglike in the wind; it aspires upward, reaching its slender arms high. He put his thoughts down in this well-known verse:

> What does he plant who plants a tree?
> He plants the friend of sun and sky;
> He plants the flag of breezes free;
> The shaft of beauty towering high.

When the figures do not come easily, ask yourself, "What is this like? What real thing is it like?" List possibilities. Think of objects related closely or distantly to this, or like it in one way though not in others. Mere waiting for inspiration will not help; you must search aggressively.

Three kinds of figures are to be avoided. One is the trite (overused) comparison: sweet as honey, slick as ice, silence reigned supreme. Another is the excessively far-fetched or incongruous: The examination was hard as a diamond. The third is the mixed figure, in which several unlike images are close together. The following concocted paragraph is an exaggerated illustration of both trite and mixed figures:

He plunged into his climb up the ladder of success, refusing to act like a bump on a log. He swallowed his pride and worked like a dog, and even when skies were black as pitch and it was raining pitchforks, he kept cool as a cucumber, cut through the red tape, and was the last one on earth to bark up the wrong tree even though it made him as mad as a hornet, and he continued to hit on all cylinders.

EXERCISE FIVE

Try to think of picturesque comparisons to describe several of these:

> a batter waiting for a pitch
> a catcher crouched behind home plate
> a small girl in a heavy rain, wearing a too-large raincoat
> a row of telephone poles
> a small sailboat barely visible from the shore
> a freighter on the horizon
> a traffic tangle
> small children watching a Western on television
> a dignified businessman chasing his hat
> a department store on Dollar Day
> the line in the school cafeteria
> football lines waiting for the snap
> the face of the man opposite you in the football line
> paperback books in the drugstore racks
> a freight train at a distance
> an assignment in your least favored subject
> the sounds in a mill, factory, or office
> an untidy room
> a spick and span kitchen
> a broken chair
> night noises
> a town or city seen from an airplane
> a river seen from the air
> a baby's early attempt to walk
> a school corridor scene just before the class bell

Section B

WRITING FACTS

4
Bringing Compositions to Life

5
Letters

6
Autobiographies and Biographies

7
Articles and Essays

8
Journalistic Writing

4

Bringing Compositions to Life

WHY COMPOSITIONS?

IN elementary and high school and again in college, students are often asked to write what are variously called compositions, papers, essays, themes, reports, and term papers. Length may range from a sentence or two in the lower grades to several thousand words in college. Here we are concerned with a composition of intermediate length —say two hundred to five or six hundred words. In the chapter on articles and essays, we shall deal with longer compositions.

Why do schools throughout the United States, as well as in other parts of the world, require frequent writing of compositions?

The first reason is that learning to write well takes practice. No amount of isolated drill in grammar, usage, spelling, and punctuation will assure good writing. A man may be able to saw a board, hammer a nail, and wield a paintbrush, but he cannot successfully design and build a house unless he has had practice in designing and building smaller objects and in combining his varied skills. Similarly a student may know about pronouns and clauses and semicolons, but he cannot successfully write a college paper or a detailed report for an employer unless he has had practice in writing compositions in which he may combine the separate skills and bits of knowledge.

Secondly, many compositions are not intended solely for the student's practice and the teacher's perusal. Rather, they are planned to present information, experiences, ideas, opinions, beliefs, and feelings to one's classmates for their enlightenment or reactions. We learn by exchanging. Although a class of twenty-five students will have had many overlapping experiences, each member will know some things that no one else in the room knows. Sharing multiplies by twenty-five the class's opportunity to grow mentally, emotionally, and even spiritually.

Unfortunately some students look upon compositions and composition writing as dull. They may be. Compositions are dull if they are the products of a dull or lazy mind. They are dull if the writer concentrates more on commas than on content, for both mechanical accuracy and something worth saying are important. They are dull if the words crawl along like caterpillars unaware that they can ever be butterflies.

But composition writing can be interesting and compositions can be exciting if the writer sets himself the task of conveying clearly and effectively to his readers something that they do not know.

EXERCISE ONE

As a class or as individuals compile two lists. Give one the heading "Dead," the other the heading "Alive." Under the first heading list the characteristics of a dead, dull piece of writing; under the second, those of a lively one. Do not restrict yourself to the hints you have read in the preceding paragraphs.

Do not read the next part of this chapter until you have prepared these lists. Then use them to help you to decide which of the three students' compositions in the next section is dead, and what makes the other two alive.

THREE COMPOSITIONS

A teacher assigned a class the topic "Words That Confuse Me." Here are three of the results. All three are accurate in spelling, punctuation, and grammatical usage. Two would be given high grades in most high school English classes or college freshman English classes. The other would be given an average or below-average grade in many high school English classes, and a failing or barely passing grade in most college classes.

See whether you can tell which composition is the poorest and what makes the other two much better.

1. Words That Confuse Me

When I was a small child, I thought that pears should grow in pairs, or that at least the trees should be in pairs. I also wondered why Daddy said he was dressing a chicken when he was really undressing it, and why Mama said she was putting dressing into the chicken when she wasn't putting in what Daddy had taken off. A little later I assumed that a bazaar was called that because the church bazaars that I knew about certainly sold some bizarre items, such as the green porcelain tree trunk that my mother brought home for an umbrella stand. (You insert the umbrellas in the knotholes.) As a high school freshman I confused *obtuse* and *abstruse;* since geometry was difficult for me, maybe it almost made sense when I referred to an obtuse angle as an abstruse angle. Incidentally, I've never seen an angle that I could honestly call "a cute angle." And why *priceless* and *worthless* should be opposite in meaning, I'll never know.

Oh, I could write a book about words that confuse me! Of late, though, I have been most depressed by my failures with words that start with *in-*.

For example, I know that *insecure* means "not secure" and that *incapable* means "not capable." But I get into trouble when I use *invaluable* to mean "not valuable," I've found that an *infamous* person is famous (in a way), and I once read about a man who didn't live to realize his mistake when he struck a match beside a sign that read INFLAMMABLE. I've discovered that *in-* sometimes shows up as *im-*, as in *improbable*, but the difficulties remain. Last week I described a quiet, sisterly hug as "an impassionate embrace," thinking that *impassionate* means "not passionate." It doesn't.

If *insane* means "not sane," then *inane* should mean "not ane," but people look curiously at me when I say "that was a very ane remark." I used to be inept at tennis, but now I am rather ept, only the language won't let me say it. If I write a letter with an indelible pencil, the words can't be erased or deleted; my desk dictionary, though, doesn't tell me that if I use an ordinary pencil the words are delible.

Why should *ingenious* mean "clever" but *ingenuous* mean almost the opposite? Why, in history class, did everybody laugh when I defined indentures as "inside false teeth"? Grandma wears *dentures,* and *in dentures* should mean inside 'em. And what word do you use to describe a person who cannot be put into a hospital? Alas, I tried *inhospitable!*

I could include, indite, or invoke innumerable indications of my incomprehension of *in-*, as well as my other indiscretions of indiscrimination, but instead of indulging indefinitely, and inextricably incriminating myself, I shall interrupt these introversions before you throw them—or me—outuendo.

2. Words That Confuse Me

There are a great many words in the English language that confuse me. For that matter, there are a great many words in the French language, which I am studying in school, that confuse me, too. I often do not know whether I should use one form or another of a French verb, or just where I ought to put some of the words in a sentence.

Spelling confuses me a great deal. I read somewhere that the sound of "sh" in the English language can be spelled over a dozen ways, and that there are many thousands of ways possible for putting letters together in such a way that the letters could be pronounced "Shakespeare." I have trouble with many spelling words, and I think that the fault is partly mine and partly that of the language. Don't you?

I am often unsure about pronunciation. When I was a child, my mother often corrected my mispronunciations. Now sometimes my teachers or my friends do so even today, because I still mispronounce some words. Sometimes I have to look a word up in the dictionary. Most students no doubt do. My French pronunciation is even worse than my English because I have not studied it so long. I never know whether I should pronounce silent letters or not. Sometimes the French leave out letters when they are pronouncing, and sometimes they do not leave them out in the spoken form of the language, and I am confused because I do not know when they do and when they do not. English pronunciation has its peculiarities, too, as I am sure everyone realizes.

I wish I had a bigger vocabulary because then I would know more words, and if I knew more words I would not have to use the ones I am unsure about but could substitute the ones I know especially well. Then if I did not know a spelling or pronunciation I could just use a different word, and no one would be aware that I did not know the other word.

3. Words That Confused Me

I have taken the liberty of changing the tense of the verb in the title because, as an amateur botanist, I was once confused by the popular names of flowers and could see no pattern in their derivation. The sources of the names of a few flowers, such as *larkspur* and *jack-in-the-pulpit*, were easy for me to discover because the blossom looks like the thing that is named. But where did the other names originate? The dictionary and a couple of books on word origins have helped to unconfuse me. They have revealed two main sources of the names and have shown me that poetic feeling has often played a part.

A number of flowers, I discovered, were named for persons or for mythological characters. Probably the names of Mr. Zinn, a German botanist of the eighteenth century, and of Mr. Wistar, a Pennsylvania professor of "anatomy, midwifery, and surgery," would be forgotten today had they not had the foresight to have the zinnia and the wisteria (or wistaria) named for them. John Robert Poinsett, who was Martin Van Buren's Secretary of War, brought some spectacular flowers back from Mexico; obviously, they should be called *poinsettias*. The begonia was named for a French governor of Santo Domingo, the camellia for a traveler called Kamel who brought the flower from the Orient to Europe, the magnolia and the lobelia for French and Flemish botanists called Magnol and de Lobel, and the gentian for a King Gentius of Illyria, who lived over two thousand years ago.

In Greek mythology Narcissus was a youth whom the goddess of vengeance made so conceited that he looked all day at his reflection in the water. Finally a pitying god changed him into the flower that bears his name. Iris was originally the Greek goddess of the rainbow. The name *anemone,* also called a *windflower* because its Greek original meant "wind," is tied to the story of the handsome Adonis. He was loved by the goddess of love and beauty herself; when he was killed on a hunt, flowers sprang from his blood. The hyacinth is named for another handsome youth, Hyacinthus, who was a good friend of Apollo, god of the sun, and of Zephyrus, god of the west wind.

By far the greatest number of flower names, though, were borrowed by the English from common words in foreign languages. *Tulip,* for instance, goes back to a Turkish word for "turban," because the flower somewhat resembles a turban. *Lilac* comes from the Persian *nilak,* meaning "bluish," which became the Arabic *laylak. Petunia* is based on the Brazilian Indian word for "tobacco," though the resemblance between petunias and tobacco plants seems slight. *Belladonna* is Italian for "beautiful woman"; supposedly the petals are textured like the skin you'd love to touch. The face on the pansy must be a thoughtful one, for the name is derived from French *pensée,* meaning "thought" or "thoughtful." The nasturtium has an odor that inspired its name, which comes from Latin words meaning "nose twister." The Greek language has been especially generous, giving us these names, among others:

crocus: "saffron"; most crocuses are yellow, like saffron.
heliotrope: "turning toward the sun"; the flower does so.
hydrangea: "water capsule"; the seed capsule resembles a cup.
philodendron: "tree-loving"; some of these plants climb trees.
phlox: "flame."
chrysanthemum: "gold flower."
alyssum: "not madness"; supposedly the flower cured insanity.

Of all the flower names, however, the one I like best is of English origin: *daisy*. In Old English, as I found out while I was getting unconfused, the name was spelled dægeseage, which means "day's-eye," the eye of the day, the golden sun with rays of light extending from it. Surely no name could better suggest the poetic urge and the vivid imagination of many of those persons who gave names to flowers.

EXERCISE TWO

If possible, discuss these questions in class. Look back at the three compositions as often as necessary.

1. From which of the three compositions did you learn most? Least?

2. Which composition has the most interest-rousing opening? Least?

3. Which has the liveliest style? The dullest? Quote sentences as examples.

4. Which composition includes the greatest number of specific details and examples? The smallest number? In Chapter 2 you read about the value of concrete, image-making words. In which composition do you find the most such words? The fewest?

5. What meaning was attached to the word *theme* in Chapter 1 of this book? Try to state in your own words the theme of each of the three compositions, using a single appropriate sentence for each. How do these brief statements of theme help to indicate one reason for the weakness of the poorest composition? How did the writers of the other two compositions limit their subject in order to make the theme specific?

6. Indicate briefly the main point of each paragraph in each composition. For which composition is this most difficult to do? Why? What is the significance of this fact?

7. The points you jotted down for Question 6 give you a brief outline of each composition. Which outline seems most orderly? Least?

8. Which composition ends most cleverly? Most forcefully?

Most dully? Which ending best ties the whole composition together?

9. The first composition is light, whimsical, and sometimes witty. The other two are comparatively serious. Can a good composition be either light or serious? In the first composition what hints of underlying seriousness do you find?

10. Which of the compositions is the poor one? Summarize the reasons for your choice, showing clearly why it is inferior to the other two.

PREVISION

In the week before each college football game, the coaching staff and the team prepare specifically for that game. They analyze what they know about the opponents, and they develop counterstrategy. They plan plays that will capitalize on their own strengths and their opponents' known weaknesses. When the game actually starts, they may have to alter some of their plans somewhat, but they have a greater chance of success than they would have if they entered the contest blindly.

Such preparation has been called *prevision*, which means "looking ahead." Prevision is no less useful in writing than in football. The subject that you write on may be compared to an opponent. You analyze it and develop your strategy for attacking it. You consider what knowledge and skills you have that will help you to break the resistance of the topic. You work out a fairly definite plan of attack. In the actual writing you may have to change the plan to some extent, but you are more likely to write well because you are not writing at random.

The method of prevision depends partly upon the amount of time available. If time is very limited, perhaps all you can do is to use two or three minutes to decide upon the main idea, jot down the chief points, and determine which should be treated first, which second, and so on.

If more time is available, the steps are essentially the same, but each can be considered more carefully. To illustrate, let us consider the steps that the writer of "Words That Confused Me" (pages 51–53) may have gone through before he commenced writing. We shall call the writer Mac.

In assigning the topic "Words That Confuse Me" the teacher had suggested that each student limit the topic to suit himself, since it would be impossible to write about all confusing words. Mac noted several ways in which he might limit the topic:

> *lay* and *lie*
> homonyms
> how flowers got their names
> mathematical terms

Mac was interested in all these, and no doubt a good composition could be written on any one of them. He reasoned, though, that he really wouldn't have enough to say about *lay* and *lie* unless he resorted to a humorous treatment, and he didn't consider himself a humorist. He eliminated homonyms (words like *to, too,* and *two*) because the English language has a tremendous number of them; besides, he was seldom confused by them. Because of his interest in botany, he liked the idea of writing about flower names, and he thought that perhaps he could stretch the word *confuse* to cover his former lack of knowledge of the subject. He dismissed mathematical terms because, he decided, it was mathematical concepts rather than terms that actually confused him.

Having decided upon names of flowers, he began recalling what he already knew about the subject. He listed the names of thirty or forty flowers with which he was familiar, and with a word or two showed the origin of each. Sometimes he needed to check his dictionary or a book on word origins. Then he looked over the list to see whether the sources had anything in common. He found some names based on persons' names, some on mythological characters, and some on words from Greek, Latin, and about ten other languages.

Should he have, then, a paragraph on each of these—about a dozen paragraphs in all? He wisely decided against this, for he knew that many short paragraphs would produce a choppy effect. He thought it would be best to devote two paragraphs to persons' names and mythological characters, and another one to flower names from common nouns in foreign languages.

This prevision gave Mac the basic framework for his composition. During the writing he made two changes, just as a football team may shift some of its tactics during a game. He decided that he needed an opening paragraph that would show the relationship of flower names to the assigned topic, and that he needed a concluding paragraph to tie the whole composition together. He had observed previously that many names of flowers are rather poetic, and to reinforce that point he chose to write about one previously unmentioned flower whose name helped to prove it.

The steps that Mac took during prevision may be summarized in this way:

1. deciding how the topic should be limited;
2. noting what points should be included;
3. grouping the points under a very few headings, each of which makes its contribution to the topic as limited;
4. deciding the order in which the small number of items should be presented.

EXERCISE THREE

1. What evidence is there that the author of Composition 1 (page 49) followed a procedure similar to Mac's? What makes

you think that the author of Composition 2 (page 50) used little prevision? How can prevision reduce the period of anguished pencil biting that precedes the writing of many students?

2. What do you do before you start to write a composition? Do you see any ways in which prevision may help you to write better and perhaps even save you time?

3. Here are some rather general topics for compositions. Choose two or more that interest you and about which you have a reasonable amount of knowledge. For each, go through the four steps listed above (page 56), writing out each very briefly. When you finish, you will have a short, informal outline for each composition. In class, those who chose the same topics may be interested in comparing outlines. Very different treatments are likely. Those differences reveal the originality that exists in each of you.

Christmas Then and Now
How Rural Life Has Changed
Advantages (or Disadvantages) of Having Brothers and Sisters
My Favorite Holiday
What Becoming Adult Means
What Makes a Book Good?
Fads I Fall For
The Gap between the Generations
Survival
What's Good about Television?
Sport's Finest Hour
I Like Suburbia
Solving the Traffic Problem
The Greatest Need of Our School
Ideas Change the World
Star
Dangers to Small Business
Why Study Mathematics (or Foreign Languages, etc.)?
Whose Values Should Be Taught?
On the Need for Rebels

FOUR BASIC VARIETIES OF WRITING

It has long been customary to divide writing into four
basic classifications, called *expository, narrative, descriptive,* and *argumentative.* It is now generally realized that
these are most likely to be mixed together. Nevertheless
it is useful to know something about the four, if only because they may often strengthen one another. Some students tend to write one type almost exclusively, and as a
result may sometime find themselves faced with the necessity of writing a type which they have not practiced.

The word *expository* means "explanatory." Expository
writing explains something. This book and all your other
textbooks are chiefly expository. The answers you write
in an examination are likely to be expository. If someone
tells you how to make penuche or how to wire a hi-fi set,
he is using exposition.

Narrative is derived from the Latin *narro,* meaning "I
tell [a story]." In narration one tells a story or at least relates a series of events in somewhat chronological order.
The short stories, novels, plays, and epic poems that you
have read are all examples of narration. Popular movies and
the "whodunits" and Westerns on television are also narrative. The first paragraph of the composition on page 49
is narrative at least to the extent that it proceeds chronologically, and narrative bits are included in the composition
starting on page 51.

Descriptive writing reveals the physical appearance of
something or someone. We have seen examples in Chapter 3.

Argumentative writing attempts to make the reader accept a belief or point of view. When it becomes *persuasive,*
it tries to induce the reader to perform a certain action.
Many of the articles in magazines like *Harper's* are at least
partly argumentative. A lawyer's presentation before a

judge or jury is called his argument. Argumentation is discussed further on pages 104–109.

Most of your compositions are likely to be mainly expository, although you sometimes may be encouraged to write narratives about either real or imaginary events. Even in expository writing, however, bits of narration or description may add color and life. Argumentation and exposition often overlap, as for example in an explanation of Frank Lloyd Wright's effect on modern architecture where the author argues that Wright's influence was neither great nor lasting.

EXERCISE FOUR

1. As a class try to think of several additional examples of writing or speaking that would be mainly expository, several that would be mainly narrative, several that would be mainly descriptive, and several that would be mainly argumentative.

2. Read an article (not a short story) in any good magazine you have handy. Is the article mainly expository or mainly argumentative? Try to find in it some narrative or descriptive bits. For what purposes are they introduced? If your teacher requests, be ready to read a narrative or descriptive bit to the class and to explain what it contributes to the article.

THE PLUS-FACTORS: CONTENT

Every teacher knows that a major difference between a superior and a good or average composition is a hard-to-identify "plus-factor" or perhaps several plus-factors. The writer of the good composition does the things we have discussed so far in this chapter: limits the subject, includes essential points but not nonessential ones, and arranges the points in a sensible order; in addition, he is careful with spelling, punctuation, sentence structure, and other mechanics. But the writer of the superior composition goes further. It is the going further that brings the composition to life and makes it worthy of one of the highest grades.

In the rest of this chapter we shall look at three possible plus-factors, which we shall call content, style, and "you." These overlap. We could in fact call all of them "you," for it is always the individuality of your treatment of the topic that results in the plus. It will be clearer, though, if we make the threefold division.

The first ingredient of the content plus-factor we may label *informativeness.* The superior composition carries a cargo of information or ideas that are not already familiar to most persons. Composition 3, on flower names (page 51), is heavily freighted with information; Composition 1, on *in-* words (page 49), has somewhat less; Composition 2 (page 50) says very little that isn't already generally known.

How do you make a composition informative? Parts of the answer have already been suggested. You choose a topic that you know something about, and you limit it to a phase that you can explain in considerable detail. If you try to write on too large a topic—"The Habits of Animals," for example—you are forced by the very size of the topic to be extremely general. But perhaps you have or can readily uncover enough information about one habit—say "Hibernation"—to write a paper that will enlighten your classmates or whoever else reads it. About some subjects you already have so much information that you can treat them adequately if you jot down what you know, throw out or barely mention the items that represent general knowledge, and present the rest in an orderly manner. For some other subjects you may need to supplement your knowledge through reading or conversing.

Informativeness may mean factual information only, but it need not. Thoreau's *Walden* is less crammed with facts than a science textbook is, but it is full of information about Thoreau's thoughts, observations, and ideals. Poe's

"Annabel Lee" is hardly factual at all, but the poem is informative because it reveals clearly the feelings of a sensitive man who has lost his beautiful and beloved wife.

The second ingredient of the content plus-factor is related to the first but is not identical. We may call it *depth.*

Depth in writing and depth in water are both relative. To a small child the water in a bathtub may be deep, but to an oceanographer a vertical half-mile does not constitute great depth, since the Atlantic, the Pacific, and the Indian oceans average much more than that. The fourth-grade child who writes that the elephant is the largest existing land animal, that Indian and African elephants differ in appearance, and that the elephant can grasp objects with its nose (since the trunk is really an enlarged nose) is showing considerable depth for his age. A high school student's paper about elephants would have to convey more knowledge and more insights to be called deep. A zoologist's monograph on elephants would possess depth only if it went more thoroughly into certain phases of the subject than elephantine scholarship had previously done; a psychologist's study of elephants might be considered deep if it revealed formerly unknown information about, for example, how rapidly old elephants can learn new tricks; an economist's research into the comparative economic usefulness of elephants and horses might possess depth if it penetrated further into the subject than other research had.

In other words, writing has depth if it goes beyond what is normal for the group to which the writer belongs. If you write about elephants, your paper will possess this quality if you reveal a greater understanding of elephants than your classmates have. But no one can reasonably expect you to push back the frontiers of pachydermous knowledge until you get a little older.

Sometimes the depth may be attained in part through the use of appropriate quotations, diagrams, tables, and the like. If you read articles on almost any subject in a reputable magazine, you are certain to find that the authors bring in relevant quotations to strengthen whatever case they are making. In addition, if tables, charts, maps, or diagrams will increase the clarity and informativeness, professional writers do not hesitate to include them. Yet many students are unnecessarily reluctant to quote or to illusstrate. A good quotation, with credit of course given to the author, often proves what British Prime Minister Gladstone once said: "Apt quotations carry conviction." Ralph Waldo Emerson declared: "We are as much informed of a writer's genius by what he selects as by what he originates."

Third of the ingredients of the content plus-factor is *development*. The greatest weakness of Composition 2 (page 50) is that the writer has failed to develop his idea. To develop is to unfold. When a road map—of Kentucky, let us say—is unfolded, we see new details of Kentucky's roads and geography with each successive unfolding until finally the whole map of Kentucky lies open before us. The writer of Composition 2 in his four unfoldings (paragraphs) reveals mostly blankness; his completed "map" shows us almost nothing. In contrast the author of Composition 3 (page 51) develops his main idea by telling us first why he is interested in flower names, then by presenting examples of flowers named for persons or mythological characters, after that by giving illustrations of flower names borrowed from other languages, and finally concluding that imaginativeness is characteristic of many names of flowers.

Methods of development will be discussed more fully on pages 100–104. Here we shall say only that extensive use of pertinent details and examples is most frequent, with definition, analysis, comparison and contrast, and logical proof employed less frequently. Both Composition 1 (page 49) and Composition 3 are developed mainly by details and examples.

EXERCISE FIVE

1. Read two articles of about equal length in any good current magazine or magazines. The topics should be some in which you are at least mildly interested. Compare the articles by answering the following questions:

a. Which article presented more information that was new to you?

b. Was all this information factual, or was some of it in the form of unfamiliar concepts or ideas? Try to identify at least one unfamiliar idea in each article. Which writer appears to you to search more deeply beneath the surface?

c. Did either of the writers, or both, use any quotations, tables, diagrams, and the like? For what purposes? Can you find one or more quotations that are especially helpful to the author in making his point?

d. Does each author develop his article in a methodical manner? Does each make greatest use of details, examples, definition, analysis, comparison and contrast, or logical proof?

(For the purpose of this exercise, it will be best if several of you agree to read the same articles and compare your opinions.)

2. Try writing a paragraph twice on the same topic. Make the paragraphs about equally long. Try to make the first paragraph uninformative and shallow, the second informative and relatively deep. The topic may be a question of present interest in your school or an opinion about a current news event.

THE PLUS-FACTORS: STYLE

Very few high school students have, or should have, a fully developed style. Good high school writers, though, are in the process of developing a style. They experiment with words, with arrangement of words, and with sentence structures. They play with short, staccato sentences and long ramblers and judicious mixtures, attempting to find the rhythms that best suit their minds and their tempera-

ments. They try their hands at humor, at serious presentations, at both factual and imaginative descriptions, at narrative bits to enliven exposition. Sometimes, unless the
teacher forbids, they even violate generally accepted principles of sentence structure or punctuation in order to
achieve special effects; such violations seldom succeed, but
on occasion they may be worth trying.

The second plus-factor in a superior composition, then,
may be stylistic experimentation. Like other experiments,
this may fail. Scientists, musicians, and painters often fail
in their experiments, too, but they learn as much from failure as from success.

Your search should be for the style that will best reflect you. "The style is the man himself" is an often-quoted
French saying. If you are basically a serious, straightforward person, your style will probably be direct and rather
unadorned. If you are whimsical, let whimsy gleam through.
If you think in pictures, in comparisons, do not hesitate to
flash an occasionally surprising image or figure of speech.
If you like to play with words, observe how Christopher
Morley, E. E. Cummings, and even those extreme experi-
menters, James Joyce and Gertrude Stein, dallied with words
and combined them and distorted them and attained novel
effects with them.

Novelty or freshness of style, then, is largely a result of
individual expression, daring to be oneself. Several other
features of style may be mentioned briefly. Most of these are
discussed elsewhere in this book:

1. *Precise diction.* A good writer uses words exactly.
Of course he does not confuse words like *accept* and *except*
or *affect* and *effect* or such less easy pairs as *continual* and
continuous. But he goes beyond these rather mechanical dis-
tinctions. For example, he distinguishes *tan* from *beige,*
bluish green from *greenish blue;* he decides whether the
raindrops in a particular shower *pelted* or *plopped* or
splashed or *drove* or did something else; for him some birds

chirp but others *tweet, whistle, shrill, shriek,* or *squawk.*

2. *Concrete, specific words.* Although abstract and general words have a place in writing, a good stylist uses numerous concrete and specific words. Almost never will he write such a sentence as "There are trees on our farm." Instead he will write something like this: "Behind our house seven acres of Jonathan apple trees droop their red-ornamented branches toward the ground."

3. *Transitions.* Skill in using the bridges that join parts of the composition is another mark of good style. The poor stylist either employs too few transitions or else overuses a few such as *then* or *next.* The good stylist, in contrast, has at his command a wide variety of words, phrases, clauses, and sentences that keep reminding the reader of where he has been and where he is going next. These transitions are subordinated, not emphasized; they do their work quietly.

4. *Sentence structure.* The sentence structure should be suitable to the writer, to his purpose, and to his topic. Some writers find it most natural to use short, uncomplicated sentences; others have attained skill in writing clear sentences of considerable length. Sentence structure for narrating an exciting incident is likely to differ from that for a sedate explanation. A topic involving description probably demands more modifying words, phrases, and clauses than does a quick-moving narrative or a succinct argument.

5. *Revision.* When time permits, every composition should be carefully revised. Such revision may involve some reorganization, an addition here, and a deletion there, and of course it necessitates correction of mechanical errors. Moreover, it includes scrutiny of words and sentences to make sure that each statement is presented with maximum clarity and effectiveness.

EXERCISE SIX

1. From any collection of prose available, choose a moderately long paragraph from each of two authors and compare their styles, examining differences in sentence length and structure, in types of words chosen, and in transitions. Suggested authors: Poe, Hemingway, Saroyan, Steinbeck, Swift, Addison, Milton, Dickens, Hardy, Joyce.

2. As a class, try to think of twenty or more adjectives that can be used to describe style. What does each mean?

3. Write a paragraph or two on "The Style I Wish Could Be Mine."

4. Choose one of the following topics, or any other approved by your teacher, and write a paragraph about it twice. Try to use a highly different style in each version. Change the content in any way you wish.

> The Winning Play
> Light in December
> On a City Street
> Smoke
> Construction Job
> And Pastures Green
> Turmoil
> White Paper
> Squirrelly
> Fragment

THE PLUS-FACTORS: "YOU"

As we have said, all the plus-factors must derive from you, but some of them depend especially upon what you are and what you reveal.

Curiosity is one of the characteristics of every notable writer. His mental arteries have not hardened. He is like the four- or five-year-old child, constantly bubbling with

Who? Where? What? When? and especially Why? and How? Like a scientist, he takes nothing for granted, and he is most likely to question what others regard as obvious.

We may call the second characteristic by any of several names: *personality, character,* or *vitality,* perhaps. Whatever the designation, we mean that the writer seems to be someone who would be interesting to know. We sense from his writing that he is mentally alert, that he has wide interests, that he has an unusual way of looking at his world, and that his reactions are not always predictable.

Sensitivity is another quality of the able writer. This means that he has feelings and can express them. He can understand and share another person's sorrow or joy. He is quick to sympathize, to pity, to rejoice. He responds both to beauty and to ugliness.

Related to sensitivity is *identification.* Poet Edith Sitwell refers to a painter who, painting a tree, *became* a tree; she says that Dylan Thomas was a great poet because he too had this power of "becoming a tree." In unmetaphorical language, a writer should be able to identify himself with the thing or person he is writing about. Charles Dickens was especially strong in this respect; he wept as he wrote sad scenes, laughed uproariously at his broad comedy, and in his public readings lived the role of each character as completely as a professional actor could.

Finally, a good writer has *sincerity.* He believes in something, and he writes sincerely about what he believes. Not for him are the emptiness, the pretense, the vapid mouthings of the person who stands for nothing and is nothing. Not for him are words strung together like glass baubles; if a word is only a bauble, he throws it away.

EXERCISE SEVEN

1. Read two or three compositions you have written during the past few months. Try to read each as if you had never seen it before. On the basis of this reading, answer these questions, perhaps for yourself alone:

a. Does the writer of these compositions appear to have a curious, prying mind?

b. What evidence is there that he would be an interesting person to know?

c. What evidences of sensitivity do you see?

d. Is there any evidence that the writer can identify himself with other persons or things?

e. Does the writer always seem sincere? (One teacher, when he suspects insincerity, pompousness, and the like, writes in the margin, "Is that really the way it is, Joe?")

2. Now read an article in any reputable magazine. Answer the same five questions. Be ready to discuss your findings in class.

3. Your teacher may wish to designate topics for one or two compositions you should now write. If not, you may limit one of the topics given on page 66 or choose something suggested by your personal inventory in Chapter 1. Follow as carefully as you can the hints in this chapter, and make sure that at least one plus-factor (content, style, or "you") is apparent.

Letters

KINDS OF LETTERS

Two kinds of letters account for the largest part of the sixty to seventy billion pieces of mail handled annually by the United States Post Office. These are friendly letters (also called personal or social) and business letters.

Both kinds may be subdivided according to their basic purposes. Let's see first what are the occasions for most friendly letters.

1. *News.* Somebody, somewhere, *today,* would like to know what you and your family have been doing, thinking, planning, talking about.

2. *Love.* (Define this one for yourself.)

3. *Thanks.* Someone has given you a present, done you a favor, entertained you. Both courtesy and a warm glow suggest a letter of appreciation. Even someone you don't know and may never meet, such as an author whose book you like, can be inspired and cheered by a note.

4. *Invitations and replies.* Although many informal invitations are today just telephoned, and some formal ones are engraved, on many occasions a written invitation is most suitable. Replies to written or engraved invitations are, of course, written.

5. *Best wishes and congratulations.* A note just before a holiday season or a birthday shows much more personal interest than a printed card does. And if a friend of yours has won a contest or a prize, been admitted to the college of his choice, or done anything else especially noteworthy,

69

a letter will help to show how happy you are in his happiness.

6. *Get well soon.* If a friend is hospitalized or seriously ill at home, nothing will cheer him much more than a personal note.

7. *Apology.* You may have made an unpleasant mistake, lost your temper, broken somebody's valuable candleholder, or the like. A simple letter of apology will make both you and the other person feel better and help to strengthen a friendship.

8. *Sympathy.* The hardest letter to write, one of sympathy, is called for when a friend is bereaved. About all you can say, of course, is that you are thinking of your friend in the time of his sorrow.

Most business letters are written for one of ten purposes.

1. *Orders.* If an order blank is available, use it. Otherwise send a letter to indicate clearly the items wanted, quantity, quality, order number, size, color, price, method of shipment, method of payment, and your name and address.

2. *Inquiries.* Sometimes a letter is the easiest way to get needed information, but if what you need to find out is discoverable in your library, don't bother anyone with a letter.

3. *Replies.* This time someone has asked you for information.

4. *Remittance.* This note accompanies payment.

5. *Acknowledgment.* Companies often send appreciative acknowledgments of orders they have received.

6. *Job-getting.* A good letter may someday help you to get the position you want.

7. *Sales.* Companies do much selling by mail.

8. *Collection.* This, of course, is a request for payment.

9. *Complaint or claim.* Sometimes you may have a

legitimate complaint or a reason for expecting a company to make an adjustment.

10. *Adjustment.* This is the letter the company sends in response to your claim letter.

EXERCISE ONE

1. Think of some typical occasions for sending each of the eighteen varieties of letters, and typical content for a number of them.

2. If you or a member of your family has what seems to be a good illustration of one of the varieties, and if it would be appropriate to share with outsiders, bring it to class for examination and discussion. (Be sure to get permission to bring any letter not addressed to you.)

STATIONERY; FORM

For friendly letters, stationery should be of good quality, with matching or harmonizing envelopes. Increasingly, stationery is used which has the name and address of the sender at the top and on the back of the envelope. Conservative colors, with no decorations or only very inconspicuous ones, are best; women's stationery may be white or any pastel shade, and men's usually white or light gray. Men's sheets and envelopes are generally a little larger than women's. Informal note cards, either fold-over or nonfolding, are also useful. Ink is usually blue or black; watery colors should be avoided. Typing is now considered permissible, but is normally avoided in invitations, replies, notes of sympathy, and other short notes in which a highly personal touch is desirable.

For business letters the usual stationery is 8½ by 11 plain white paper of good quality and about twenty-pound weight. Smaller page sizes may also be used, but may cause the receiver trouble in filing. Envelopes, either small business-size or the larger Number 10, should match or at least harmonize with the sheets. Typing is preferable in business letters, although legible handwriting is acceptable. A carbon copy of any important business letter is essential; in a handwritten letter a carbon is possible if a ball-point pen is used and the sheets are paper-clipped to prevent slipping.

The form of a typical friendly letter is illustrated here:

[heading] Tuesday, January 3

[salutation] Dear Grace,
[body]

_____

_____

[complimentary close] Cordially,
[signature]   Clara Bliss

The heading is usually only the date, although if the writer's address is not printed on the stationery or may be unknown to the recipient, it may be given in the heading or below the signature, and of course on the envelope.

The salutation usually starts with *Dear*. *My dear* is considered much more formal—usually too formal—in the United States. *Darling* or a similar expression may sometimes be appropriate. *Dear friend* is now seldom used, although *Dear friends* is often the salutation in a letter addressed to a whole family. Note the comma after the salutation; a dash is sometimes used but is not standard.

Complimentary closes often used in friendly letters include *Cordially, Cordially yours, Sincerely, Yours sincerely,* with possible variants according to the relationship of sender and receiver. *Yours truly* and its variations are reserved for business letters. A comma follows the close.

If Grace knows only one Clara or if Clara's name is printed on the stationery, the last name need not be used in the signature (assuming that the two persons are on a first-name basis). But if any possibility of confusion exists, inclusion of the last name is imperative. A signature should always be handwritten even though the letter is typed.

The form of a typical business letter (not on a printed letterhead) is this:

```
[heading]        1110 Waldron Drive
                 Cleveland 10, Ohio
                 January 3, 1963
[inside address] The Reed Anchor Company
                 1268 Marlow Street
                 Buffalo 6, New York
[salutation]     Gentlemen:
[body]           ─────────────────────────

                 ─────────────────────────
                 [complimentary close]  Yours truly,
                 [written signature]    James Watts
                 [typed signature]      James Watts
```

The heading gives the exact address to which a reply should be sent, and the correct date. It is usually in block form, as are the other parts of the letter; that is, the second and following lines are not indented extra. Note the punctuation in the example.

The inside address is the name and address of the individual or company which is to receive the letter.

The salutation, followed by a colon, is *Gentlemen* if a company is addressed, *Dear Sir* or *Dear Madam* if an individual is addressed, or *Dear Mr. Gray* or *Dear Miss Gray* if the writer knows the receiver or has had previous correspondence with him or her.

The standard complimentary close is *Yours truly* or *Truly yours* or *Very truly yours,* although increasingly *Yours sincerely* or *Sincerely yours* appears. The close is followed by a comma.

The written signature is a mark of the authenticity of the letter; the typed signature below it perhaps shows the spelling more clearly. If the writer has a title, such as *Business manager,* it may be placed below the typed signature. A woman should indicate in parentheses whether she is *Miss* or *Mrs.* Mrs. Watson signs her name *Patricia*

Armour Watson, with (*Mrs. Charles Watson*) below; if she is divorced, the lower signature is (*Mrs. P. Armour Watson*).

EXERCISE TWO

1. If letters were brought to class for Exercise One, examine them to see what kinds of stationery were used. Also examine the forms employed, and note any variations from the examples on pages 72 and 73.

2. For practice, write three friendly letters and three business letters, drawing lines to represent the body. For the business letters use actual names and addresses.

CONTENTS AND LANGUAGE OF THE FRIENDLY LETTER

We'll confine this section to the newsy friendly letter, since the content and language of the other varieties are pretty obvious.

One of the most famous of letter writers, the eighteenth-century English Lord Chesterfield, wrote this advice to his son:

> Most persons who write ill do so because they aim at writing better than they can, by which means they acquire a formal and unnatural style. Whereas, to write well, we must write easily and naturally. For instance, if you want to write a letter to me, you should consider what you would say if you were with me, and then write in plain terms just as if you were conversing. Take as little trouble as possible. By that means, you will by degrees write perfectly well, with ease.

Not everyone would agree with everything that Lord Chesterfield said, but most persons would agree that the best content of a friendly letter is summarized by his words "what you would say if you were with me." The best language is that used "easily and naturally," "just as if you were conversing."

For a friendly letter *does* represent your half of a conversation. You tell your friend what will interest him, and ask him questions about himself and his doings, just as you would in talking with him.

You adjust what you say to the person you are addressing. Your dear aunt will want to know about little daily incidents in your family: how the puppy is misbehaving, what cute things your little sister said, how completely your father has recovered from his illness, and so on. Your friend in college will want news about your mutual acquaintances, school doings, your own plans for college, and the like; he'll probably even appreciate the opening you afford him to give a little advice based on his recent experiences.

A letter to a person whom you know well doesn't have to be filled with trivia, though. If you and he (or she) have been accustomed to serious discussions, they may be continued in your correspondence. If you *talk* about books, ideas, and your reactions to news events or magazine articles, then *write* about those things. Some of the best authors have been superb letter writers: Jonathan Swift, Horace Walpole, Jane Austen, Percy B. Shelley, Emily Dickinson, H. G. Wells, G. B. Shaw. They have usually written informatively and informally, even playfully at times, but their letters often were meaty as well—full of their thoughts, their interpretations, their hopes and dreams. They were sometimes almost as creative in their letters as in their poems, stories, essays, or plays.

A creative letter assumes a creative reader, or at least an appreciative one. You probably shouldn't waste the meaty letter on the lovely little girl whom you like a great deal but who has only half a brain: she seems to be the meringue type; tell her about the latest dance and just sneak in a philosophical observation or two and find out whether the other half of her brain starts to materialize. Save most of the meat for the meat-eaters. If you've become accustomed to serious discussions with your parents, for instance, they'll enjoy some meaty letters while you're away at camp or college.

The language of any friendly letter should be as appropriate to the receiver as the content is. If you are writing to someone with whom you would talk in slang and breezy sentences, use that kind of language. If you are writing to a minister or a teacher, the language will probably be rather different.

I'm and *you're* and *couldn't* are generally better in friendly letters than uncontracted forms—they're more conversational. Twists of sentences (the kind of thing you stick in between parentheses or dashes, for instance) also reflect the conversational approach.

Be sure to use the receiver's name as often as you would in speech: "And then, Ruth, the most wonderful thing happened!" Don't forget to ask plenty of questions; they help to show your genuine interest in your friend.

Lively observations and colorful comparisons spice up a good letter, and so do bits of conversation: "Little Mike —he's just four now, you know—thought the monkeys at the zoo were more fun than a barrel of people. And he had never seen any kind of trunk except the trunk of a car. We told him the name of the thing on the front of the elephant, and he said, 'It's on the wrong end!' "

EXERCISE THREE

1. For practice, choose three of the short varieties of friendly letters (pages 69–70), excluding the news and love types. Write an example of each. The letters will seem most genuine if they can be based on real situations. You may even want to mail them.

2. Now write two "newsy" letters to actual persons, letters that you will not mind letting the teacher or classmates see.

One of the letters should be filled with interesting trivia suited to the characteristics of the receiver. The other, addressed to someone with whom you have had serious discussions, should concern the kinds of things the two of you like to talk about.

CONTENT AND LANGUAGE OF THE BUSINESS LETTER

Three general principles of effective writing apply to business letters. These are unity, coherence, and emphasis.

Unity means that the letter is about one subject. If you send a letter to a company and order one thing, request an adjustment on a previous order, and ask about the possibility of a summer job with the company, should the mail clerk send the letter first to the order department, the complaint department, or the personnel department? Three short letters, each addressed to the appropriate department, would be preferable.

Coherence means that the parts of the message should be clearly arranged. For example, if you are reporting that part of an order was not received, one logical arrangement would be to give first the fact that this is a request for an adjustment; then the date, serial number, and other pertinent information about the original order; then the information about what is missing; and finally a request for the specific adjustment you hope will be made.

Emphasis involves stressing the most important points. Since the beginning and the end are the positions of greatest emphasis, avoid weak openings such as "I have received your recent letter and shall now reply to it," and avoid weak endings such as the outmoded "Thanking you for your attention to this matter, I remain. . . ." Another principle of emphasis is that the most important point usually deserves the most space.

Six C's are also desirable characteristics: clearness, completeness, correctness, conciseness, courtesy, and character.

Clearness comes partly from coherence, partly from

elimination of irrelevant details, and partly from careful sentence construction. Reading a letter aloud sometimes provides a good test for clearness; asking someone else to read it is another.

Completeness means that all essential information is included. The following letter will require both the company and you to write another: "The sweater you shipped me recently was too small. Please send a larger size."

Correctness means accuracy of statement, accuracy of language, and adherence to standard letter forms. Inaccuracies of statement would involve such things as wrong dates, wrong sizes or colors, or wrong addresses. Inaccuracies of language are faulty word forms, hard-to-understand sentences, misspellings, or mispunctuation. Failure to adhere to standard letter forms means purposeless departure from such a form as that on page 73.

Conciseness requires avoidance of irrelevant ideas and unneeded repetition. One study has shown that 51 letter-writers for one company discovered that they could improve their letters by deleting 3 to 45 per cent of the words.

Courtesy is deeper than the customary *please* and *thank you* which represent politeness. It involves putting yourself into the place of the person receiving the letter. Ask yourself, "If a letter on this subject were sent to me, how should I like to have the subject presented?"

Character, like courtesy, comes from inside you. It shows through almost everything you write. A particularly good test is the way you write a letter of complaint.

Most of what we have so far been saying applies to content, but the comments on coherence, emphasis, clearness, correctness, conciseness, and courtesy apply to language as well. A couple of additional suggestions about language may be useful.

The clipped, formulalike language of the early twentieth century has largely disappeared from modern business letters. Today's businessman does not write, "Yours of the

6th inst. received and contents noted. Said order will be shipped with all due promptness. Same may be expected no later than the 2nd prox. Thanking you for the favor of your patronage, we remain. . . ." He writes instead, "Your order of June 6 can be filled almost immediately, our chief engineer now happily reports. The gear assemblies should reach you by freight no later than July 2. We appreciate your allowing us to serve you in this way."

Note that the language of the business letter is more formal than that of the friendly letter, but not stiff. A few words such as "our chief engineer now happily reports" make the letter seem a human voice and not that of a soulless corporation. Natural ease, then, but not flippancy and slang, is characteristic of the good modern business letter.

EXERCISE FOUR

For practice, write two or more of the letters suggested below, inventing addresses and additional details as needed.

1. An order for some slacks or skirts for yourself

2. An inquiry concerning the admissions policies of a college

3. A note of remittance

4. A request for payment

5. A sales letter, to be sent out in large numbers, intended to persuade men of the community to patronize your father's tailor shop

6. A letter of complaint

7. A letter applying for a job (Supplementary factual information about yourself may be presented on a separate data sheet. In the letter, show that you know something about the company to which you are applying and that you have knowledge and skills of the sort useful in that company. The tone should reflect self-confidence but not boastfulness.)

6

Autobiographies and Biographies

AUTOBIOGRAPHY: LIMITING THE SUBJECT

AN autobiography— that is, an account of your own life— is most likely to be called for on three occasions. One is in high school and college English classes, not because the teacher has an overwhelming or prying curiosity about you, but because he knows that he can teach more effectively if he is familiar with the backgrounds and characteristics of his students. In addition, he is aware that writing on the most personal of subjects—yourself—will help you to "think yourself through," to evaluate yourself, and sometimes to help you in clarifying your goals. A second occasion for an autobiography may arise when you apply for admission to college. College admissions officers may look at various kinds of evidence: high school grades, test scores, letters of recommendation, personal interviews, and samples of your writing. A brief autobiographical sketch may help to reveal to them whether you are the kind of student likely to succeed in their school. Some employers, too, ask for autobiographies—the third occasion. They also try to size up the probable success of each job applicant.

Often you will be told the approximate length of the autobiography—a hundred words, five hundred, a thousand. Obviously the amount you can tell about yourself is limited to some extent by the length. Sometimes a data sheet may accompany the sketch; if so, the data sheet gives the merely factual information, and the sketch can be mainly interpretive.

Even if no word limit is designated, however, the material for your sketch must be restricted. The rare person gifted with total recall must not employ his gift indiscriminately. All the events of your life are not of equal importance. You need to select two or three especially revealing incidents or traits; it is often even better to concentrate upon one, to which essential background information may be related.

Here are four examples of ways in which students have limited their autobiographies:

When Jane was a tiny girl, she began drawing pictures on her little blackboard or anything else handy. After that time art was her central interest; she designed the family's greeting cards, studied art with a private teacher, had paintings displayed in local stores, and won several small prizes. In her letter to a college admissions officer, she rightly concentrated on "Art in My Life," although she was careful to reveal that she did have other interests, too.

Scientist Robert Millikan was Fred's idol. Fred admired not only Millikan's work in physics but also his wide knowledge of art, music, and literature. He centered his autobiography on "The Man Who Has Influenced Me Most."

Anne found in herself a combination of ambition and laziness, a person who tried to crowd forty-eight hours of work into a twenty-four hour day and a person whose favorite dream was of a somnolent Pacific island. In a light vein, under the title "On the Disadvantages of Being Two People," she traced her dichotomy to having had both "serious" ancestors and a great-grandfather who rested from sunup to sundown and then went to bed.

When Clinton was fourteen, his father became severely ill and had to give up his good position. Previously Clinton's life had been easy: his needs, wants, and whims were taken care of unstintingly. "I was spoiled and obnoxious," he said in his autobiography, the central idea of which was shown in its title, "Poverty Is Good for Some People."

The ways of limiting a topic are endless. The advantages of limitation are mainly: 1. the most important points may be stressed; 2. the writer can be specific and hence more interesting; 3. interpretation of facts is made possible, and good interpretation is more significant than bare facts or mere incidents. The fact that you have traveled, let us say around the world, is meaningless in itself; its significance can lie only in what the trip meant to you and what it did to you.

EXERCISE ONE

1. In Chapter 1 you were asked to prepare a personal inventory which might reveal possible subjects for you to write about. Refer to the inventory you prepared, or else reread the items suggested (pages 14–17). Which inventory items might serve you as a focus for an autobiographical sketch?

2. What limitation of subject is suggested by each of these titles? Choose two or three that might apply to you, and summarize the content you could include. 1. Farm Boy 2. One and Only 3. Serious 4. Timid 5. Athletics and I 6. My Grandfather's Name Was Different 7. Light Dawned 8. If I Could Only Be— 9. The Great Reform 10. State of Mind 11. How the Other Half Live 12. Not a Beauty, But— 13. Debut 14. Completely Average 15. The House 16. Greatest Day in the Year 17. So I Made Up My Mind 18. The Twig Is Bent 19. The Hunt 20. Past Imperfect

WRITING THE AUTOBIOGRAPHY

If someone requiring an autobiography—say an employer—specifies length, content, or organization, you of course must meet those specifications. Otherwise you may plan for yourself. It is helpful, though, to be familiar with four general principles.

1. Facts and incidents, as we have seen, are not enough.

The questions to think of constantly are: What makes this fact significant enough to include? What was the effect of this incident on me?

As an example, Lincoln Steffens in his *Autobiography* tells of the influence of the Englishman, Mr. Nixon, who was helping him to get into college. Mr. Nixon told him, "The world is yours. Nothing is done, nothing is known. The greatest poem isn't written, the best railroad isn't built yet, the perfect state hasn't been thought of. Everything remains to be done—right, everything." Steffens tells of the conversations he was permitted to hear between Nixon and a varied group of Nixon's educated friends. "I had never heard conversation before," Steffens says.

While Steffens describes in detail what he learned from Nixon and his friends, he does some interpreting in passing. He says, for instance, "Life filled with meaning, and purpose, and joy." ". . . the truth that even college graduates did not know anything, really. Evidences they had, all the testimony of all the wise men in the historical world on everything, but no decisions. None. I must myself go to college to find out more." Then Steffens concludes with the most important point he wants to make—interpretation again:

But the best thing I got out of it all was objectivity. Those men never mentioned themselves; apparently they never thought of themselves. Their interest was in the world outside of themselves. I caught that. No more play-acting for me. No more dreaming I was Napoleon or a trapper, a knight, a statesman, or the younger son of a lord. It is possible that I was outgrowing this stage of a boy's growth; the very intensity of my life in subjective imagination may have carried me through it, but whether I would have come out clearly impersonal or no by myself, I don't know. All I am sure of is that their conversations, the attitude and the interest of those picked Englishmen, helped and, I think, established in me the realization that the world was more interesting than I was. Not much to see? No, but I have met men since, statesmen, scholars, business men, workers, and poets, who have never made that discovery. It is the scientific attitude, and some scientists have it—not all; and some others, too.

When I went up for my examinations this time in Berkeley I passed, not well in all subjects, but I was admitted to the University, and that fall I entered the University of California with a set of examination questions for the faculty, for the professors, to answer.

2. The organization of the autobiography may be chronological, but need not be. Seldom today do sketches begin as they often did a century ago: "I was born on June 12, 1847, in Harrisburg, Pennsylvania, of poor but honest parents." Information about such things as parentage and place and date of birth, unless there is special reason to emphasize it, may be tucked into a convenient corner.

If the sketch is chronological, the events will center upon the main theme. Jane's autobiography (page 81) was arranged chronologically, beginning with a word portrait of her, at age four, busily drawing pictures on the blackboard, and continuing through the other art-centered incidents. Information about her parents and her schooling was brought in casually.

A variant of chronological organization is the then-and-now type. Clinton's autobiography (page 81) was arranged in this way. Clinton drew a picture of himself as a spoiled youngster of fourteen, showing how he happened to be like that. Then came the turning point, his family's impoverishment. Clinton told of how he had learned to work, to "curb my 'gimmes,' " to share with his brothers and sisters. He concluded with an honest attempt to portray himself as he was at age seventeen, showing that poverty had done much to improve him.

Still another organizational pattern reverses Clinton's. It starts with a current snapshot, a word-picture of what the writer is like today, and then goes back and picks out the significant events that made him that way.

One more of many possible patterns may be mentioned. This is really an interrelated series of portraits: how I appear to my mother (some childhood episodes here), to my father, to one of my teachers, to my best friend, to myself. Skilfully done, this can be effective; unskilfully, ugh!

3. Include pertinent incidents, anecdotes, and conversation. *Pertinent* is the key word here. From the immense amount of detail at your disposal, you need to select what will best reveal you.

For example, Samuel L. Clemens, in his account of his early ambition to work on a riverboat, has a long paragraph about the effect the coming of a steamboat used to have on the inhabitants of the usually sleepy town of Hannibal. He continues with another long paragraph, an anecdote of a Hannibal boy who became an apprentice engineer on a steamboat and who, returning for an occasional brief visit, would swagger about town "in his blackest and greasiest clothes," envied by all the other boys and admired by all the girls. The next paragraphs tell of other boys who got jobs on boats and of Sam's first unsuccessful attempt to become a pilot and come home "in glory." Clemens, that is, brings to life through incidents and anecdotes something that in the hands of a less able writer would have degenerated into the pallor of "When I was a boy I wanted to become a pilot. So did all my friends. At least they all wanted, as I did, to have the glory of a job on a steamboat."

4. Use straightforward language. The pronoun *I* is not a naughty word. Obviously you shouldn't start every sentence with *I* (a conceited actor is reputed to have worn out the *I* key on his typewriter), but neither should you adopt such coy subterfuges as "this shy little blue-eyed boy." Third-person autobiographies are permissible, but usually seem rather faked.

Avoid flowery language in an autobiography—everywhere else, too, but especially in an autobiography. Don't say, "In that transcendent moment when upon the concert stage before me—that white-lighted setting of musical grandeur—appeared the tall, slender, frock-coated figure of the pianist whom from afar I had worshiped, whose every note immortalized in vinyl I had through dint of great persuasion inveigled my parents into purchasing for me—in that moment the highest reaches of ethereal bliss were mine." This is more honest and more specific: "At last I was to hear my pianist idol. He strode purposefully toward the gleaming piano. He was tall and slender, a little older and a little more bald than I had anticipated. He stopped, bowed stiffly, almost grimly, in response to the applause, and as he sat, draped his coat-tails behind the bench. His hands with their long, tapered fingers poised above the keys, and then plunged downward into the impressive opening of Rachmaninoff's 'Prelude in C-Sharp Minor.' The first notes made me forget that he was middle-aged and bald and unsmiling."

EXERCISE TWO

Write an autobiographical sketch of the approximate length suggested by your teacher (perhaps 500–700 words). If you wish, you may make use of work you did for Exercise One (page 82).

BIOGRAPHY: THE SCHOOL REPORT

A teacher sometimes asks a student to prepare a report on a famous author, governmental figure, scientist, or the like. Unnecessarily often, such reports are dull. Factual accuracy and an interesting, moderately creative presentation are quite compatible.

You may get your basic information from the encyclopedia, but your report will be lifeless if you do not supplement that. Try to discover articles or books about the person, and even though you have too little time to read them completely, skim through to find anecdotes or incidents that will reveal the biographee as a human being and not just an abstraction of dates and accomplishments.

One good plan is to cover rapidly the basic biographical details, then report on two or three especially revealing incidents, and finish with comments on the person's accomplishments and lasting significance. The accomplishments, or at least one of them, may be presented somewhat dramatically. A report on Dwight D. Eisenhower, for example, could well include some attention to his activities on D-Day, the beginning of his momentous achievements during the invasion of Nazi-held Europe.

It is useful, too, to select for emphasis whatever is most appropriate for the particular class. Thus a report on Jonathan Swift might stress the circumstances of his writing whatever work of his the class is studying; other information would be included, but somewhat subordinated.

EXERCISE THREE

Choose an author in whom you have become interested, and prepare a biographical sketch appropriate for this class.

BIOGRAPHY: THE PROFILE

Book-length biographies are still of course beyond your scope, but knowledge of their characteristics may be useful in your preparation of the shorter biographical sketch that is sometimes called a profile.

The first type of book-length biography is the tell-almost-everything variety. When Boswell wrote his biography of Samuel Johnson, he filled it with conversation, incidents, and parts of letters. No scrap of information was too small. Lockhart's biography of Sir Walter Scott and Sandburg's life of Lincoln are in the same tradition. They are detailed, three-dimensional portraits, showing the man as he appeared from day to day, doing little things and great ones, expressing petty thoughts and deeply philosophical ones.

Less praiseworthy is the loaded or axe-to-grind biography. Here the biographer selects whatever will help to create the impression he desires. For instance, John Nicolay and John Hay in their life of Lincoln omitted events they thought discreditable; conversely, Edgar Lee Masters, not a Lincoln idolater, stressed what he considered bad in Lincoln's character and conduct.

The psychological interpretation, popularized by Lytton Strachey, Gamaliel Bradford, and Emil Ludwig, attempts an honest portrayal, and relies on principles of psychology for interpretation. It may include imagined thoughts and conversations, which are justified on the ground that this person with this background and these characteristics would undoubtedly have thought and spoken in this way.

All three of these book-length varieties of biography have had their effect on profile writing. A profile is basically a personality or character sketch, usually article-length (say 1,000 to 5,000 words), which does not attempt a systematic biographical treatment. It makes much use of anecdote and conversation and letters. It is frequently written by someone who knows the person well or who at least has interviewed him, although it can be based on reading. The subject of the sketch may be famous, but not necessarily. Both long and short profiles appear often in the *New Yorker* and occasionally in many other magazines.

The tell-almost-everything biography has influenced profile writing by its stress on specific incident and conversation. The axe-to-grind variety has affected it less, although the profile writer usually does adopt a point of view concerning the subject. Writers who know psychology sometimes make use of the techniques of the psychological biography.

No single pattern of organization prevails for the profile. However, the opening usually either shows the subject of the sketch in a typical setting or else portrays him performing a typical action or making a typical remark. Then, through an arranged accumulation of incidents, conversation, and possibly excerpts from letters or speeches, the writer fills in the details of the portrait, bringing in essential biographical details as he goes along. The conclusion may be a summing-up of the person, but is more likely to be a final revealing anecdote.

In the following brief profile of a table-tennis champion, taken from the *New Yorker,* note the opening setting, the extensive use of conversation, the way that biography is worked in, and the unusually abrupt conclusion, which nevertheless serves as a kind of summary. Note also the appropriateness of the style to the subject matter; a high degree of formality would be entirely unfitting in this sketch.

Oasis

At the Riverside Table-Tennis Courts, at Ninety-sixth and Broadway—a basement establishment, with bilious-green walls and ancient wood-and-concrete floors, that is the favorite hangout these days of local table-tennis devotees—some of the most spirited action, we are told, takes place around three o'clock in the morning, when a number of night-shift post-office workers, along with a jazz musician or two and some other nocturnal types, drop in to knock off a few games before going home to bed. We'll have to take that information on trust, since we sleep well, but we can assure you that at ten o'clock one evening recently, when we stopped in for a look around and a chat with the proprietor, things seemed lively enough. All eight of the tables in the place were in use, the players bounding agilely about and bashing the ball back and forth with great vigor. The din was considerable—something like the noise that might be made by a xylophone band warming up in an echo chamber. In a niche near the front of the room we noticed a couple of chess tables, and these, too, were occupied. It was not the most peaceful setting we could think of for chess, but the chess players seemed undisturbed by the racket.

Behind a battered desk near the door we found the owner and manager of the enterprise, a lean, bony-faced man of about thirty named Marty Reisman, who is himself a table-tennis player of formidable ability, being the current United States singles champion. "Did you know that table tennis is probably the most popular competitive sport in the world?" he asked us. "In the world, that is, except for the United States. Japan alone has four hundred thousand registered tournament players. How many does the United States have? Maybe two thousand, at most. I'll bet there are more players in Cambodia than there are here. Incidentally, I met the King of Cambodia once, and I used to give lessons to the late President Magsaysay, of the Philippines. What I mean is I find it strange that the richest, most powerful country in the world should lag in table tennis. When I won the British singles championship, in 1949, there were ten thousand people in the Wembley Stadium to watch the match, but when I won the American championship, last year in Washington, only a handful of spectators showed up." He shrugged. "Ah, well, that's the way it is." Looking about the room, he seemed heartened by what he saw. "Anyway, I do all right in this place," he went on. "I get a dollar forty-eight an hour for each of the table-tennis tables and fifty cents an hour for each chess table. The chess was an afterthought. It doesn't take up much room, and there's not much wear and tear on the equipment. All sorts of people come in here—influential people, uninfluential people. Some of our regulars are former Hungarian Freedom Fighters. Table tennis is a big sport in Hungary. Let's see who's here tonight. At the third table, the fellow on this side is a novelty-toy manufacturer. His opponent is a Chinese waiter. The woman in the green shirt at the next table is a chemical engineer. She's playing with her son. They come in here quite a bit. And the guy in the black shirt at the table next to that—he comes in often, too. He's in Wall Street; that is, he's a messenger down there, delivering sandwiches and coffee."

We asked Mr. Reisman for a brief rundown on his own career, and he said, "I was born on the lower East Side. My father owned a taxicab fleet. As a kid, I was interested in science. I had a microscope and a telescope, and I spent so much time peering into them that my eyes began to go bad. My optometrist suggested it might help my vision if I took up table tennis. I was about twelve then. Well, once I took it up I got completely engrossed in it. Within three or four weeks, I could beat anybody around, and it was already apparent to experts that I would be a great player. Please don't think me immodest, but I am a great player. After all, I won the national junior championship when I was fourteen, and I was nineteen when I won the British championship. By then, I was at the peak of my game. Table tennis started out, about fifty years ago, as a slow, piddling game for old ladies. The Hungarians were the first to bring elegance and style to it. Then the Czechs came along with the concept of the rocklike defense. A point would go on and on until someone made a mistake. In one match, a single point lasted over two hours. After the Czechs, Dick Miles—an American who's been singles champion several times—and I speeded up the game terrifically. We introduced the quick hit—slamming the ball before it reaches the peak of its bounce. Now the Japanese have come along with a new kind of sponge-covered paddle, which has speeded the game up even more. Another thing I brought to the game was humor. When I was young, I liked to clown around. The London *Times* called me 'the Danny Kaye of table tennis.' They take table tennis very seriously over there. The referees wear dark-blue suits. I've been to Europe ten times for competitions or on tours, and I've made three trips around the world. I'm more famous in Hong Kong than I am here in New York."

EXERCISE FOUR

Try writing a profile of either (a) some interesting person whom you know well (perhaps a parent, an older brother or sister, or a friend); (b) a person with whom you can arrange an interview (possibly a teacher, someone in another profession, a businessman, or a person doing a kind of work that especially interests you); or (c) a famous person of the past whom you have come to know well through reading biographies.

7

Articles and Essays

THE OMNIPRESENT ARTICLE

MODERN readers have an insatiable hunger for specific facts, general information, how-to-do-it instructions, and interpretation. As a consequence, newspaper and magazine editors publish a never-ending stream of articles to meet the demand. The articles are on every imaginable subject, from mushroom-shaped clouds to growing mushrooms in your basement, from international problems to infant care, from the behavior of people in mobs to the behavior of army ants. Newspaper editorials and features are special types of articles, which will be treated in Chapter 8.

High school students' papers written for their classes are not normally called articles, but in effect that is what many of them are. A written report or term paper or book review is a kind of article, and so is an English "composition" or "theme," if it is not a fictional narrative. College students are likely to be required to write fairly numerous articles in their various subjects, although the professors probably call them by some other name. Even an undergraduate thesis often may be considered an expanded article.

Why should article-writing be considered creative? We must admit that some articles are only dull rehashes of the commonplace and hence deserving of the adjective in only its most pedestrian sense. But many articles, such as you are likely to find in the better magazines, reflect creative thinking. Their authors have gathered information (often from a variety of sources), meditated on it, and drawn more or less original conclusions. The creativity exists partly, sometimes mainly, in those conclusions. In addition, good articles are written in a creative way, with organization tailored to fit the purposes of the authors and with fresh and appropriate language.

Because of the increased frequency of article-writing in the twentieth century, all kinds of literary styles and an infinite variety of organizational patterns may be observed. Superficially, no two articles are much alike, but, as we shall see, most articles have some elements in common.

EXERCISE ONE

1. As a class, make a count to observe the relative proportion of articles and fiction in current issues of magazines in your school library. Regular columns and mainly pictorial features may be counted as articles. What does your survey seem to reflect about present-day reading tastes?

2. List a number of broad categories into which the articles you find in current magazines seem to fall. Some of the categories, for instance, will be politics, world events, science, personalities, the arts, and helpful hints. Classify the articles you examine. When an article could be put into more than one category, choose the one that seems to be emphasized. Which categories have the largest numbers of articles? What do you think are the reasons?

CHOOSING SUBJECT MATTER

We shall assume, for the purposes of this chapter, that the kind of article you are most likely to write is a result of an assignment in school. If you were writing for a magazine, the techniques would be similar. What we shall attempt to do in the first parts of this chapter is to trace the steps involved in preparing an article, theme, or report requiring a modest amount of reference work. Some articles, of course, entail no material outside the writer's own mind and experience; others may necessitate long and arduous research, not merely in the printed word but also in the spoken, through interviews.

In school you may sometimes simply be assigned a topic for a report or theme. If so, your choice is obviously limited to the point of view you will take toward the topic and the way you will treat it. At other times, though, a teacher will offer a choice of topics or designate a general area within which you will find your own topic.

Let us assume that you are taking a world history course and are now studying the sixteenth century. Your teacher asks each student to choose one event or development of that century and prepare a paper about it for the class. The teacher this time does not offer a list of representative topics, so that the choice is entirely your own.

You jot down a number of subjects or possibilities, including such items as exploration of the New World, the foundations of the Russian Empire, the unification of India under Akbar, the conflicts between Spain and other European countries, the power of the Ottoman Turks, the Reformation, and the continuing spread of Renaissance culture.

In selecting a topic either for a school exercise or for a commercial article, you need to consider these criteria especially:

1. Your own interest. You are likely to do your best work on a subject that engrosses you. Remember, though, that sometimes interest may develop as the amount of your information increases.

2. Availability of information. You may have to discard such a topic as India under Akbar because your library has nothing about it except what is in the encyclopedia.

3. Size of the topic. Inexperienced writers tend to choose topics that are far too large. Any of those jotted down above (concerning the sixteenth century) would have to be considerably reduced to be manageable and really informative.

For an article to be submitted to a popular magazine, one other criterion would also be involved: the possibility of relating the topic to some matter of current interest. Writers call such a relationship a "peg," and are likely to discard a topic whose significance for present-day life cannot be demonstrated. School assignments, however, as well as articles intended for the more scholarly journals, need not necessarily have a peg, although its presence may add to their interest.

As you think about your paper concerning the sixteenth century, you decide that something about Spain would interest you. After mulling over several possible topics, you conclude that the defeat of the Armada would be a good choice. You check your library and notice discussions of the Armada in several history books, as well as a whole volume on the subject, Garrett Mattingly's *The Armada*. The existence of a full-length book on your topic makes you think that the subject may be too large, but you decide that you can probably find some way to limit it further.

EXERCISE TWO

1. Articles and school themes and reports are lumped together in this chapter. Discuss the characteristics that they have, or may have, in common. What differences, if any, are likely to exist?

2. Can you recall any report on which you have not done well because of your lack of interest, the unavailability of material, or the excessive size of the topic? As you look back, would any solution have been possible?

3. What is a "peg"? Find the pegs in two or three articles in current magazines.

GATHERING MATERIAL

The sources of material for articles are personal experience and observation, reading, and one's own thinking. Some articles necessarily rely most heavily upon the first of these, and others most heavily upon reading, but every good article reflects the writer's thinking.

A paper about "Cats I Have Endured," for example, would obviously be based on the writer's personal knowledge of and experience with cats. It might well incorporate the results of his close observation, as does this description, by Charles Darwin, of a cat in an affectionate mood:

> She now stands upright with her back slightly arched, which makes the hair appear rather rough, but it does not bristle; her tail, instead of being extended and lashed from side to side, is held quite stiff and perpendicularly upwards; her ears are erect and pointed; her mouth is closed; and she rubs against her master with a purr instead of a growl.

It would be the writer's thinking about cats, however, that would make the article peculiarly his own. In effect he would be presenting that little segment of his individual philosophy that deals with cats.

In your article on the Spanish Armada, you will have to depend on your reading and your thinking, since it is unlikely that anything in your personal experience would be revealing—unless by chance you know the English Channel or the port of Cadiz or have experienced fire at sea or have been on a sailing vessel caught near a coast in a severe storm.

An encyclopedia provides a good starting place for gathering material, but *only* a starting place. An uncountable number of high school graduates fail in college because they have never learned to use sources other than the encyclopedia. An encyclopedia article is useful in giving broad, general information about a topic, but it does not provide details. Writing based solely on the encyclopedia is only a summary of a summary.

So from your encyclopedia you get general information about European conditions in 1588, Spain's reasons for sending the Armada, British preparations to combat it, the relative sizes of the Spanish and British forces, the results of the battle, and the storm that inflicted further disaster on the Spanish.

The encyclopedia may also suggest to you a specific part of the topic on which you would like to concentrate. Your later reading can thus be more limited than it would otherwise have to be; more important, you will be nearing a topic of workable size.

Let us say that your encyclopedia calls the defeat of the supposedly invincible Armada "one of the world's decisive battles." You wonder exactly what was decided. If the British had lost, what would have been the effect upon later history?

So in the library you see what historians have said about the consequences of the battle. In several books on European history and perhaps in biographies of Howard, Drake, Hawkins, or Frobisher you look up "Armada" in the index and read the accounts with particular attention to the point in which you have become most interested. You take careful notes, sometimes merely summarizing, sometimes copying exactly (in quotation marks) any pertinent sentences or paragraphs you may want to use, along with the author, title, publisher, place and date of publication, and page reference.

As you proceed in this fashion through several sources, you observe that historians are not in agreement concerning the significance of the Spanish defeat. Some say that it marked the beginning of the end of Spanish dominance in the New World, started the decline of Spain as a world power, and resulted in England's becoming the major seafaring nation and a major force in North America; one or two even suggest that the great literary flowering in England in the next couple of decades was inspired by the great victory. But other historians point out that the Armada's defeat did not even end the war with Spain, which dragged on for another fifteen years; that British sea power actually dwindled in the next few years in relation to Spain's;

and that almost two more decades were to pass before England could establish a permanent colony in the New World. Moreover, say these historians, even had the Armada defeated the English fleet and invaded the British Isles, the limited Spanish soldiery could not have completed the conquest.

You ponder. Where, then, lies the truth? That is the question that every serious writer of an article must attempt to answer, because almost invariably more than a single interpretation is possible.

You read more. In Mattingly's *The Armada* you find that this authority on sixteenth-century history believes that the defeat of the Armada was most important as a symbol, a David-over-Goliath triumph, a sign to the rest of the world that Invincible Spain was not invincible, an inspiration to the English. Then in a history of Spain you discover that by 1588 Spain was already beset by troubles both internal and external, its coffers almost empty, its industry and agriculture declining, its taxes exorbitant, its manpower drained by constant war, and many of its people, imitating their nobility, inclined toward indolence.

You ponder some more, and realize that you now have what you need to give your article its individuality. You will attempt to show that history would probably not have been much different had there been no Armada or had it won; the seeds of Spain's decline had already sprouted, and the defeat of the Armada served mainly to call the decline to the world's attention.

In your gathering of material you have done more than assemble facts casually and unthinkingly. You have proceeded methodically, and have reasoned about your findings. As a result you have a significant point to make, a point that will tie together all that you say in your article. Thus your composition will have *unity*, or oneness, a first essential for almost any writing.

Some writing instructors say that for any piece of nonfiction the writer should be able to state a thesis; that is, a single idea which he intends to prove or at least defend in the article. The thesis is a brief sentence, preferably a simple or complex sentence rather than a compound one. The writer who has mastered his material and who therefore knows what he wants to do with it is usually able to write such a thesis. Doing so helps to assure unity and often makes easier the remaining steps in the writing.

EXERCISE THREE

1. Read two or three articles in current magazines. Answer these questions about each:

    a. Did the author apparently rely more on personal experience and observation or on reading?

    b. What evidence of original thinking do you find?

    c. As in Exercise Two, what "pegs" do you find?

    d. What one-sentence summary ("thesis") of the article can you prepare? In other words, what main point was the author trying to make?

2. List in 1, 2, 3 order the steps involved in gathering material for an article based largely on reading.

ORGANIZATION AND DEVELOPMENT

After you have assembled your notes on the Armada, you search for the specific points you will want to include to demonstrate your thesis. Without attempting to arrange them at first, you may have a list like this:

    a. Historians who think the naval engagement decisive

    b. Historians who disagree

    c. Developments in Spain in those years

    d. The Armada's defeat as a symbol

    e. The events of the engagement and the storm

There is no single way in which these parts of your article *must* be arranged. You need to know, though, what the eight major possibilities are, even though these are often combined.

1. *Chronological.* This involves presenting the items in time sequence—perhaps *c e a b d*. For many kinds of articles, such as instructions for making or doing something, explanations of how machines work, explanations of processes, or historical narratives, the chronological arrangement is the most likely.

2. *Spatial.* This requires description of the spatial relationships of something—where the parts are in relation to one another. Your five points about the Armada would not lend themselves to this arrangement, although in the account of the battle, an explanation of the shifting locations of the ships would be useful.

3. *Least to greatest.* This is the order of climax, building up to the most important point. Your point *d* is the "greatest"; hence, following this arrangement, you would build up to *d*.

4. *Greatest to least.* Most newspaper stories are built in this way, starting with the most important facts and then tapering off. For other kinds of articles, though, this arrangement is unsatisfactory because of the diminishing interest.

5. *Inductive.* This involves starting with various related facts and observations, then drawing a conclusion from them. The scientist follows an inductive procedure when he repeats and repeats an experiment and finally decides what the experiment has shown. In our example, an inductive arrangement might begin with internal conditions in Spain at the time of the Armada, then pay particular attention to European public reaction to the defeat, and conclude on the basis of the evidence that the defeat was only a public symbol of Spain's deterioration.

6. *Deductive.* This is the reverse of inductive; it starts with the generalization, the point to be proved, and then adduces the evidence. Following this order, you would begin with *d*, comment briefly on *e*, mention *a* and *b*, and

then emphasize *c*, concluding with a forceful restatement of *d*.

7. *Easy to difficult.* The authors of your grade school arithmetic books followed this system, starting with easy concepts and combinations, building gradually toward those more difficult to understand. This method would probably not be of value for the Armada article, except insofar as the idea of a military defeat as a symbol is hard to grasp.

8. *Comparison or contrast.* If you concentrated on *a* and *b*, the contrasting views of historians, you would be using this type of organization. You could either present all of *a* and then all of *b*, or else present part of *a* and the related part of *b*, another part of *a* and another part of *b*, and so on.

As we have said, writers often combine two or more of these eight kinds of organization; a single article may illustrate several of them. In deciding how you will organize your points about the Armada, you will ask yourself how you can present your main idea most strongly. You will probably decide to build up to *d*, the symbolic meaning of the defeat, because that is the point you want to leave in the reader's mind. You will also probably reason that the actual events of the battle and the storm can be dismissed in a paragraph or so of summary, to remind the reader of what happened, but will deserve little emphasis because your main concern is something else. Perhaps finally you will make up your mind that this variation of the least-to-greatest arrangement will be a good one:

    a. A brief but colorful summary of the defeat of the Armada (Followed by a transition to this effect: What was the significance of this defeat? Was it really the cause of England's replacing Spain as the world's number one power?)

    b. Conflicting views of historians (This combines original points *a* and *b*, presented here by comparison and contrast. Followed by a transition similar to this: To resolve this difference of opinion, we need first to see whether Spain was indeed at the peak of her power in 1588, and secondly what effect the defeat of the Armada had on public opinion in Spain, England, and the rest of Europe.)

c. Conditions in Spain in 1588
d. Public reaction to the Armada's defeat
e. Conclusion: the Armada as a symbol

In developing the separate sections of an article, experienced writers lean especially heavily upon details and examples. Beginners, in contrast, tend to rush from one broad generalization to another. If they were writing about Sequoia National Park, for instance, beginners would be likely to say that the sequoia trees are big and old and impressive, and then dash on to equally uninformative statements about Mt. Whitney and the Kern River Canyon. Professionals, though, would provide enough details about the trees to *show* their size, their age, and their impressiveness. A major difference between mediocre and good writing is this: mediocre writing *tells;* good writing *shows.*

In your paper on the Armada, most of your points will be developed by examples. You will need to give examples of the conflicting views of historians, examples of conditions in Spain, examples of public reaction. Some of the examples will be in summary form; others may be quotations (with credit, of course, to the original writer).

A valuable but less often used method of development is definition. If at any time you use a term that your readers may not understand, or if you use a familiar term in an unfamiliar way, you need to define it. In the Armada article, you will have to show clearly what you mean by *symbol.* If your readers do not grasp that, they will miss your major point.

Analysis is a fourth method of development. This involves breaking a topic into its component parts. Thus in writing about conditions in Spain in 1588, you may comment briefly in turn on Spain's military overcommitments, her poor financial condition, her decline in industry and agriculture, her lack of manpower, the inability of her king to delegate authority, and the attitude of many of her people toward work.

A fifth method of development, which often overlaps and combines with the others, is logical proof. This will be discussed in the next section.

EXERCISE FOUR

1. In two or three current magazine articles (perhaps but not necessarily the same ones you used for Exercise Three) look for the pattern of organization. To do so, jot down, in order, the major points made by the author, and see which of the eight patterns was followed, or what combination of patterns.

2. In the same articles try to find illustrations of development by details, by examples, by definition, and by analysis.

ARGUMENTATION AND PERSUASION

Probably eighty per cent or even more of the articles in today's magazines are intended not merely to inform but also to persuade the reader to accept a belief or a point of view, or to take a certain action. (In your article on the Armada you attempt to persuade the reader that a certain conclusion is correct.) The rare exceptions are usually those that simply explain a process, give instructions, or entertain.

Persuasion is based in part upon presentation of evidence and upon reasoning—which together constitute argumentation—and in part upon a more or less emotional appeal.

Evidence. Evidence may be direct or indirect. Direct evidence comes from your own observation. If, for example, you suspect that a stream is being polluted by a certain factory, and if you go down the stream in a boat and observe waste pouring into the stream just below that factory, and if the waste could not possibly come from any other source, you have direct evidence.

Indirect evidence comes from others. If someone tells you that a factory is polluting a stream, you need to evaluate the source of the information. Was he in a position to observe? Has he any reason to distort the facts? (For example, does he work for a rival company?) Has he a reputation for honesty? Could he have overlooked something significant?

Much evidence comes from printed sources. The questions to be asked here are essentially the same. For example, in your Armada article you would be more likely to believe in the evidence cited by a historian who has specialized in the sixteenth century than in that of one whose major interest is ancient Greece.

Inductive reasoning. From evidence we move toward conclusions. One procedure is to amass all the bits of evidence and try to see what they mean. That was your procedure in the Armada article—gathering the facts and then interpreting them. That is also the procedure of the chemist who mixes three chemicals in various proportions and carefully records each reaction; after a hundred or a thousand experiments he concludes that such and such mixtures bring such and such results.

The tests of inductive reasoning are three: 1. Are there enough instances? For example, if you bite into an apple and find it sour, can you conclude that all apples are sour? 2. Are the instances fair? If you see a classmate pocket a pen belonging to someone else, are you justified in concluding that he is a thief? 3. May coincidence explain the happening? If you wash your father's car and rain begins an hour later, is your father right in saying that it rained because the car was just washed?

Deductive reasoning. Deductive reasoning involves first a generalization, called a major premise: All human beings will die eventually. Then there is a more specific statement showing that someone or something fits into the category named in the generalization: John Doe is a human being. From these two parts comes the conclusion: John Doe will die eventually. The three parts constitute what is called a *syllogism*.

In writing and speaking, a syllogism is seldom expressed in full, and therein lies a danger. Someone says, for instance, "Guido is an Italian, so he must like music." We have here a minor premise and a conclusion, but no major premise. If there were one, it would have to be "All Italians like music." Perhaps *most* Italians do, but we really can't prove anything about Guido's liking for music unless we get more evidence.

Causal relationship. If someone comments, "Helen will fail in that examination because she didn't study last night," he is arguing from cause (lack of study) to probable effect (failure). If he says, "Helen failed in that examination because she didn't study last night," he is reversing the argument, proceeding from effect to its probable cause.

The validity of an argument of causal relationship may be tested with these three questions: 1. Is the cause great enough to produce the effect? For example, is only one night's lack of study sufficient to cause failure? 2. Are there any other possible causes? Could it be that Helen didn't study all semester, that she missed many classes, or that she was ill when she took the examination? 3. Is there a coincidence? Could it be that Helen fails many examinations even when she does study?

Some of the possible flaws in reasoning, or *fallacies* as they are called, have been suggested in the preceding paragraphs. Others are begging the question, ignoring the question, false dilemma, and *non sequitur*.

Begging the question is assuming the truth of what needs to be proved. For instance, if you are antagonistic to a proposal before your Student Council, you beg the question if you merely call the proposal "badly thought out and unworkable." You have to prove that it is. A parent was begging the question when he sent a note to school asking that his son be permitted to read only scientific books and not be allowed to "waste his time" reading fiction or poetry.

Ignoring the question is talking or writing on a related topic instead of the one at issue. For example, if a political candidate discussing the need for greater military preparedness devotes most of a speech to an attack on the present administration, he is ignoring the real question.

The *false dilemma* is a statement that one must choose between this and that, when actually other choices may exist. Thus a school editorial said that students must choose between television and homework. In reality, many students do their homework and also have some time for carefully selected television programs; others are more seriously tempted by other distractions than they are by television.

Non sequitur (Latin for "it does not follow") involves jumping to a conclusion that is not justified by the evidence; it is thus a fallacy of causal relationship. Superstitions often involve *non sequiturs*: "I spilled some salt this morning. That's what made me have such a rough day in school." People sitting in damp night air sometimes got malaria, and hence they once believed that the damp night air caused malaria. The real cause, as science has since shown, was a malaria-bearing mosquito.

Good persuasion makes use of the methods of argumentation we have considered, and avoids the fallacies. But in addition, persuasion attempts to move the reader to a specific act: accept a conclusion, buy a car, watch a program, vacation in Miami Beach, vote for Jones, etc. An article writer may try to move the reader to do any of ten thousand things.

Here are some brief suggestions for effective persuasion:

1. Get the reader into the habit of agreeing with you on small points, and he is more likely to agree also on larger ones.

2. Be modest in your claims; exaggeration, cocksureness, and braggadocio offend.

3. Remember the old saying: Molasses catches more flies than vinegar does.

4. Know the major human motives and relate your persuasive appeal to them when appropriate: the reader's desire for security, desire to be liked and appreciated, desire to help others, desire for a family and for good things for his family.

5. Choose words carefully.

6. Be honest and sincere.

7. End with a strong statement of the case.

Here are techniques of questionable value:

1. Flattery

2. Name calling: attaching bad labels to things you oppose

3. Glittering generality: attaching good labels to things you favor

4. Transfer: associating the thing you favor with the flag, motherhood, and other "good" things in order to transfer some of their prestige

5. Testimonial by an unqualified person: e.g., a movie star's endorsement of something he knows little about

6. False analogy: comparing what you favor or oppose with something not really similar

7. Band wagon: "Everybody's doing it"

8. Card stacking: presenting, honestly or dishonestly, information favoring one's own side of a question, and ignoring or distorting that on the other side

EXERCISE FIVE

1. Read three current magazine articles that do not simply give instructions or explain a process. Answer these questions about each:

    a. Was the writer trying to prove anything? If so, what?

    b. Was he trying to persuade the reader to do anything? If so, what?

    c. Even though the article may have been intended mainly to explain, what techniques of argumentation were used?

(Try to find examples of evidence, inductive and deductive reasoning, and causal relationship.)

d. Do you find any possible fallacies?

e. If the writer is trying to persuade the reader to do something, what techniques other than those of argumentation does he use?

f. Do you find any examples of questionable techniques of persuasion?

2. Be on the watch for fallacies and questionable persuasive techniques in advertising, in speeches (especially political speeches), and in the conversation of your friends and yourself. Bring examples to class for discussion and classification.

BOOK REVIEWS

One type of article, which you may sometimes need to prepare for school or for clubs or other groups, is the book review. Book reviews vary greatly in length. Some may be only "capsules" which do no more than identify the book, author, publisher, date, price, and number of pages, and summarize the main idea and the worth of the book in one or two sentences. At the other extreme are hour-long presentations, often with extensive quotations, which are occasionally given in meetings of women's clubs. Here we shall be concerned with the 300- to 600-word written review such as is required in some school assignments.

A review answers two basic questions: What has the author tried to do? To what extent has he succeeded? That is, the reviewer says something about the *content* and about the *value* of the book.

Your review will normally include most or all of these items, though not necessarily in this order: 1. Title and author 2. Theme 3. Important characters 4. Setting 5. Interesting incidents (not the whole story) 6. Style 7. Your opinion of the book.

Note that items 2–5 concern content, and 6–7 evaluation.

Here are three typical outlines of book reviews:

For fiction or possibly biography:

    I. Setting of the story
    II. The most important characters
    III. The most significant incident
    IV. My opinion of the book

For nonfiction:

    I. The author's purpose
    II. How the author achieved his purpose
    III. The author's qualifications for writing the book
    IV. Importance of the book

For either fiction or nonfiction:

    I. The most impressive phase of the book (theme, plot, character, setting, style, or incident)
        A. A description of this phase
        B. What makes this phase important
    II. Comment on the value of the book to a modern reader

Note that in all these outlines there is only a moderate amount of retelling of the story. The greatest weakness of most student-written book reports, and the reason they are often dull, is that too much time is devoted to plot summary.

In the following book review, written by Margaret Hurley for the *Saturday Review,* observe how a short account of part of the plot is skilfully combined with information about the setting, the chief character, and a brief statement of the reviewer's opinion.

The Hands of Cormac Joyce

Leonard Wibberley's novel *The Hands of Cormac Joyce* (Putnam, $2.95) beatifies the strength and beauty of the simple people who live on one of the rugged islands off the west coast of Ireland, and whose faith in God and in their own hands is their only protection from the stern seas around them. It is a poetic tale of three families of fishermen, the only residents on Inishlacken, and their reactions to a mortally threatening storm rolling in from the ocean. They knew the sea so they knew what was coming. The mackerel weren't biting. Something was wrong: "The young trees were breaking and the old trees were bending and the giants were coming into the land."

The first thing to be done was to get their curraghs (fishing boats) out of the water onto high ground. In doing so, with the assistance of his nine-year-old son Jackie, Cormac Joyce smashed one of the thumbs of his enormous, powerful hands—a major disaster to one whose hands were the tools of his livelihood and his safety. Young Jackie, an endearing, gangly youth, prayed each day to St. Brendan that he would grow to be like his father, with good, strong hands. After all, their strength was the only thing the men of the islands had to offer their wives.

When the Coast Guard cutter came into their harbor to take the women and children—and men, too, if they would—to shelter on the mainland, Jackie insisted upon staying behind with his parents to help moor their meager belongings and defy the storm. He figured that the strength of the whole of himself would possibly offset the loss of his father's incapacitated hand. How the little family met the emergency and reacted to the aftermath of the storm provides a mightily touching sequence.

It is young Jackie, however, who brings the story alive: when he discovers how a miracle—a small one, but a miracle nonetheless—is wrought in the well of St. Brendan; how the sea tastes and how the silvery sprats flash in their abundance along the beach; how his heart beats wildly and his cheeks blush when he is with young Eilis Coneeley. It was inevitable that they will live on the island, too, when they grow up, and never leave. ". . . you could not live on an island only in fair weather, and desert your home and your island to the storm when the weather turned foul. That was not what a man did."

If you love beautifully simple, lilting language describing a singularly moving story about genuine people, you will treasure this little gem of a book.

—Margaret Hurley

EXERCISE SIX

1. Read several book reviews in current issues of the *Saturday Review*, the *Atlantic Monthly*, *Harper's*, or other periodicals. Report to the class on what you find about length, major emphasis, amount of plot summary for fiction books, and patterns of organization.

2. Write a review of a book you have recently read. You may want to include some brief quotations to prove particular points, as Miss Hurley did.

THE PERSONAL ESSAY

The personal essay (also called the familiar essay) is a type of article less frequently published than formerly, although occasional examples are found in some of the better magazines. In school you may have encountered it in the writings of Addison and Steele, Lamb, E. B. White, and others. The decline in popularity of the personal essay is unfortunate, because in the hands of a writer with a lively mind and a whimsical turn of phrase it can be one of the most delightful of literary forms.

The personal essay differs from other articles in three major ways. In the first place, as the name indicates, it is *personal*. That is, it deals with topics the writer knows well from firsthand experience; it takes us inside his mind and emotions, letting us see how he reacts to the things he sees and does; it carries us along into his meditations and his wildest imaginings; it shows us the world—or a bit of world—through his eyes. Second, the personal essay is loosely organized, not carefully planned and balanced as other articles must be. This does not mean that it is incoherent, but rather that it has only the limited coherence that one's mental wanderings are likely to have. It does have a degree of unity, too—that is, it sticks fairly well to a single topic, although side roads often lure the writer on brief detours from which he reluctantly pulls himself back. Often it starts far from the main point, and then, just as one's mind may wander aimlessly for a while until it finds an enticing object for concentration, it spends most of its length on a matter of greatest concern. Third, the style of the personal essay is light. Even if the subject is a serious one, the personal essayist treats it almost breezily. He chats, even gossips; he is good-humored; he is amused and amusing; he is whimsical; he may be satirical or even cynical, but he is not bitter.

The following essay by E. B. White typifies the viewpoint and the style of the personal essayist.

CALCULATING MACHINE
by E. B. White

A publisher in Chicago has sent us a pocket calculating machine by which we may test our writing to see whether it is intelligible. The calculator was developed by General Motors, who, not satisfied with giving the world a Cadillac, now dream of bringing perfect understanding to men. The machine (it is simply a celluloid card with a dial) is called the Reading-Ease Calculator and shows four grades of "reading ease"—Very Easy, Easy, Hard, and Very Hard. You count your words and syllables, set the dial, and an indicator lets you know whether anybody is going to understand what you have written. An instruction book came with it, and after mastering the simple rules we lost no time in running a test on the instruction book itself, to see how *that* writer was doing. The poor fellow! His leading essay, the one on the front cover, tested Very Hard.

Our next step was to study the first phrase on the face of the calculator: "How to test Reading-Ease of written matter." There is, of course, no such thing as reading ease of written matter. There is the ease with which matter can be read, but that is a condition of the reader, not of the matter. Thus the inventors and distributors of this calculator get off to a poor start, with a Very Hard instruction book and a slovenly phrase. Already they have one foot caught in the brier patch of English usage.

Not only did the author of the instruction book score badly on the front cover, but inside the book he used the word "personalize" in an essay on how to improve one's writing. A man who likes the word "personalize" is entitled to his choice, but we wonder whether he should be in the business of giving advice to writers. "Whenever possible," he wrote, "personalize your writing by directing it to the reader." As for us, we would as lief Simonize our grandmother as personalize our writing.

In the same envelope with the calculator, we received another training aid for writers—a booklet called "How to Write Better," by Rudolf Flesch. This, too, we studied, and it quickly demonstrated the broncolike ability of the English language to throw whoever leaps cocksurely into the saddle. The language not only can toss a rider but knows a thousand tricks for tossing him, each more gay than the last. Dr. Flesch stayed in the saddle only a moment or two. Under the heading "Think Before You Write," he wrote, "The main thing to consider is your *purpose* in writing. Why are you sitting down to write?" And echo answered: Because, sir, it is more comfortable than standing up.

Communication by the written word is a subtler (and more beautiful) thing than Dr. Flesch and General Motors imagine. They contend that the "average reader" is capable of reading only what tests Easy, and that the writer should write at or below this level. This is a presumptuous and degrading idea. There is no average reader, and to reach down toward this mythical character is to deny that each of us is on the way up, is ascending. ("Ascending," by the way, is a word Dr. Flesch advises writers to stay away from. Too unusual.)

It is our belief that no writer can improve his work until he discards the dulcet notion that the reader is feeble-minded, for writing is an act of faith, not a trick of grammar. Ascent is at the heart of the matter. A country whose writers are following a calculating machine downstairs is not ascending—if you will pardon the expression—and a writer who questions the capacity of the person at the other end of the line is not a writer at all, merely a schemer. The movies long ago decided that a wider communication could be achieved by a deliberate descent to a lower level, and they walked proudly down until they reached the cellar. Now they are groping for the light switch, hoping to find the way out.

We have studied Dr. Flesch's instructions diligently, but we return for guidance in these matters to an earlier American, who wrote with more patience, more confidence. "I fear chiefly," he wrote, "lest my expression may not be *extra-vagant* enough, may not wander far enough beyond the narrow limits of my daily experience, so as to be adequate to the truth of which I have been convinced. . . . Why level downward to our dullest perception always, and praise that as common sense? The commonest sense is the sense of men asleep, which they express by snoring."

Run that through your calculator! It may come out Hard, it may come out Easy. But it will come out whole, and it will last forever.

EXERCISE SEVEN

1. Page through recent issues of the *Atlantic Monthly, Harper's, Reader's Digest,* or the *New Yorker* (not forgetting "The Talk of the Town" section in the front). See whether you can find an article that could be classed as a personal essay. If so, read it, and be prepared in class to comment on its content, organization, and style.

2. Try your hand at writing a personal essay. If you have no topic in mind, something from the list that follows may start your mind to wandering appropriately.

TOPICS FOR ARTICLES AND ESSAYS

The topics for articles and essays are innumerable. Simply looking around in your schoolroom or your living room at home, you should be able to think of fifty or sixty possible topics, ranging from the manufacture of chalkboards to the yet unrealized potential of television. The following completely random list was compiled by noting some of the topics (not the actual titles) that writers for a few magazines have turned into publishable articles. If you were to write on any of these topics, your treatment of it would probably be completely different from theirs.

1. A tennis champion
2. The British national bird
3. Superstitions about space travel
4. Nobody's a "hayseed" now
5. Should people be required to vote?
6. Blurbs on book jackets
7. Who's a highbrow?
8. Hollywood—a ghost town
9. Radiological warfare
10. Hibernation
11. Writers—always characters?
12. Shortcomings in advertising
13. Results of greater longevity
14. Expense of medical training
15. The decline of privacy
16. Educational TV
17. Japanese movies
18. Tornado warnings
19. Causes of forest fires
20. Booby traps in too much leisure
21. School for diplomats
22. Modern handwriting
23. A summer resort area
24. Beauticians' convention
25. Seven-day diet
26. How many vitamins?
27. Marriage and career girls
28. Cosmetics—which and when
29. New uses for foam rubber
30. Driving schools
31. Cooking with ice
32. Reducing infant mortality
33. How to catch a man

34. Measuring musical IQ
35. Theaters for children
36. Extrasensory perception
37. Why study history?
38. Simplifying the Chinese language
39. Improvements in anesthetics
40. Old cars as museum pieces
41. The electron microscope
42. Fingerprinting
43. American business abroad
44. Small private planes
45. Land-devouring highways
46. Taboos in language
47. St. Louis World's Fair—1904
48. Why women are frustrated
49. Atom-powered trains
50. Unions—too strong?
51. The oddities of English
52. Needed—more fine arts and finer
53. Current superstitions
54. Symbolism in *Hamlet*
55. What we know about the sun
56. Ungeographical frontiers
57. De-salting salt water
58. The greatest string quartet
59. The intellectual today
60. Disc jockeys then and now
61. Glass and architecture
62. Classics are useful, too
63. Canada's attitudes toward the United States
64. The fabulous Finns
65. Changing weather patterns
66. How much informality is desirable?
67. Wasting our heritage
68. Literature on records
69. Toward another ice age

70. How to start a zoo—and why not
71. Significance of TV ratings
72. How high can hi-fi fly?
73. Who's delinquent?
74. Music in a man's life
75. Earthquake
76. Williamsburg
77. Translation by machines
78. Paperback bookstores
79. Needed—more linguists
80. What's happening to opera?
81. Missing persons
82. Modern quacks
83. Are slums necessary?
84. Venice isn't all water
85. The detective story today
86. An age of plenty—for whom?
87. Ancient myths in modern lives
88. New uses for nylon
89. Who writes the cookbooks?
90. Is there an Abominable Snowman?
91. The decline of conversation
92. How to analyze a poem
93. You'd never know the old farm
94. Bird watching—not for sissies
95. The United States mints
96. Origins of surnames
97. The building of a ship
98. Hurrah for tomatoes!
99. Teaching devilish little geniuses
100. Once there was vaudeville

8

Journalistic Writing

GENERAL CHARACTERISTICS OF NEWS STORIES

A NEWS story gives information about an event that has happened or that is scheduled or expected to happen. Three of its major characteristics are thoroughness, accuracy, and impersonality.

Thoroughness. When Bob wrote for the school newspaper a story about a play to be presented by the junior class, he included the name of the play, its author, a little information about the play, the dates of performance, the cast, and the director. But the editor pointed out that Bob had omitted the curtain time, the price of tickets, the places where tickets could be obtained, and the names of important members of the backstage crew. Bob had to make changes in his story because he had not been thorough enough. Readers rely on their newspaper to give them all important facts.

Accuracy. Barbara's assignment was to cover the election of cheerleaders. Barbara obtained the list of candidates from the sponsor and made some hasty notes concerning who had won. After her story appeared in the paper, a correction had to be printed in the next issue, because one student who was named as a winner had actually lost, and another had won. Besides, Barbara had misspelled the name of one cheerleader and had used the wrong middle initial of another. From this sad experience Barbara learned the importance of accuracy.

Impersonality. With the possible exception of sports stories (and certain feature stories, which will be treated

119

separately), news stories are intended to report facts, not to color or interpret them. Therefore a news reporter, except possibly in signed reviews (see page 128), should avoid such statements of judgment as "a splendid performance," "a poor job of casting," "a dull debate," "played the violin beautifully," and "Everyone should plan to be there." The reporter may quote someone else, preferably a person whose judgment is presumably reliable, but in straight news stories he should avoid his own opinions.

EXERCISE ONE

1. Choose a forthcoming event in your school, such as a play, a game, an election, an important meeting, or a concert. List the questions that a story about the event should answer for the sake of thoroughness.

2. From a reliable source or sources, obtain the answers to the questions in Number 1. Double check with your source to be sure the information is correct. (This assignment may be carried out by only a few students, so that the time of activity sponsors or leaders will not be wasted.)

3. Look at several local news stories in a daily paper to see whether the principle of impersonality has been followed. For the same purpose, examine some stories in your school paper.

WHAT IS NEWS?

For a school newspaper, news consists of stories concerning happenings that will interest large numbers of students and other readers. Such news is characterized by appropriateness, timeliness, and importance, and sometimes by unusualness and conflict.

Appropriateness. A newspaper story is appropriate when it is linked closely to the lives of the readers. Assume that a candidate for senator is going to speak at a school assembly. That is probably big news, deserving of a front-page story. However, if the candidate is not speaking at the school, but only somewhere else in the community, and if few students will have a chance to hear him, it would be inappropriate to give the story much space.

Readers enjoy reading about persons they know or know about. "Names make news" is the slogan of countless newspapers. Appropriateness, then, consists in part of presenting information about students, teachers, alumni, and others in the school or known there.

Timeliness. "As stale as yesterday's news" is a comparison frequently heard. Since most school newspapers appear only weekly or less often, their news may sometimes be endangered by staleness. For that reason, school newspapers frequently follow the practice of emphasizing future events —next week's concert, for instance—and including shorter write-ups about past events.

Timeliness also refers to the calendar. Before the Thanksgiving or Christmas holidays, for example, some of the stories should be related to those holidays.

Importance. A story that affects most of the students is more important than one that affects only a few. Thus if the annual staff has arranged for pictures to be taken on certain dates, the story about that should be given considerable prominence, because all students are involved. In contrast, election of officers by the Camera Club is important to only a relatively few persons and should be given less attention.

Importance, of course, is comparative. At times when major news items are scarce, the Camera Club election might have to be given more space.

Few school papers devote space to international, national, or state news. This is probably wise (even though such events are important to students), for student reporters could not get firsthand information about global events and could only summarize what the daily papers report much more completely. However, editorial or other feature articles may and often should show how world events may affect the lives of the student readers.

Unusualness. A news story does not have to be about something unusual, but it often is. You know the old saying "If a dog bites a man, it isn't news, but if a man bites a dog, it is."

Accordingly, routine classwork or routine club meetings are not very newsworthy. But an unusual experiment in the laboratory may make a good story. So may a club's plans for a trip or for a gift to the school, since those events are not commonplace.

Conflict. Most headline stories in daily newspapers pertain to conflicts: war, elections, crimes, and the like. Somewhat less often, important school stories also involve conflicts: athletic contests, competition in music or in speech, bond issues, and so on.

EXERCISE TWO

1. Examine the news stories on the front page of a daily paper. How is each one appropriate for readers in the city in which the paper is published? How timely is each? How important? How unusual? Is a conflict involved in most or all of the stories?

2. Answer the same questions concerning the latest issue of your school paper.

WRITING THE LEAD

The lead (pronounced lēd) is the beginning of a news story. A good lead presents in one or two sentences the most important facts of the story. Actually, if an editor is short of space, he may print only the lead and the story will seem reasonably complete.

Here is an example of a simple lead in a school paper:

Lawrence Wilson and Marlene Kroehler were chosen Monday by Director Miriam Welsh to play the leading roles in the Midvale Senior Class Play on April 2 and 3.

Most leads answer the five *W's* and the *H—who, what, when, where, why,* and *how.* In the example we are told who were chosen, for what they were chosen, when they were chosen, where (Midvale), and how (by the director). In this lead the *why* presumably needs no answer.

Some leads also contain: 1. additional information (e.g., Marlene Kroehler could be identified as an exchange student from Germany), 2. authority (e.g., "Principal J. R. Flagg has announced . . ."), 3. tie-back, relating the story to earlier ones (e.g., a second sentence in the lead might read, "The seniors last week announced that this year's play will be *Our Town*").

One of the *W's* or the *H* is usually given special prominence. In the example above, the *who* is played up. The previous week's story may have emphasized the *what* (the play that was chosen). A *when* lead may, for example, stress a change in date or say something like this:

Five minutes after the last chemistry class had left the room on Tuesday, fire broke out in Midvale's chemistry laboratory. Before it was brought under control, it had destroyed $1,500 worth of chemicals and equipment.

Here is an illustration of a lead stressing *where:*

Franklin High School has been selected as the site of this year's debate preliminaries, to which Midvale will send two teams on February 7.

This lead emphasizes *why:*

The flu epidemic has caused postponement of the debate preliminaries originally scheduled for February 7, Miss Lydia Clancy, speech teacher at Franklin High, has announced.

And this one stresses *how:*

Working only with scrap metal and home-mixed propellants, Mr. Clay Brundage and five of his science seniors have constructed a slender rocket that will be tested May 6.

EXERCISE THREE

1. In your own words, define *lead*. What questions does a lead usually answer? How does a reporter decide which question should be given major emphasis?

2. Examine the leads in several front-page and city-page stories in a daily paper. How clearly does each conform to the principles you have just studied?

3. Choose three or more recent or forthcoming events in your school. Write the lead you would consider appropriate for each. (Remember the importance of accuracy!)

ORGANIZATION OF A NEWS STORY

The diagram that best shows how most news stories are arranged is a triangle, like this:

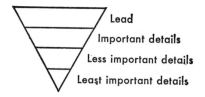

This pattern of organization has become standard for two reasons. First, the reader with little time can get the gist of the story very quickly. The reader with more time or greater interest can read it all and get fairly detailed information. Second, if an editor is cramped for space, he can cut off the story at the end of any paragraph, and his readers will still have the most essential information.

Sometimes the pattern is a little more complicated. Suppose, for example, that a story concerns three decisions made by the Student Council. The triangle would then probably be like this:

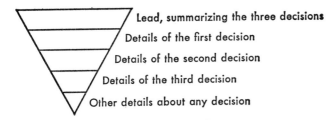

Lead, summarizing the three decisions
Details of the first decision
Details of the second decision
Details of the third decision
Other details about any decision

Now suppose that one decision of the Council is much more important or newsworthy than the other two. Here is the probable organization:

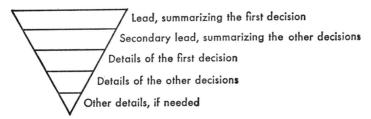

Lead, summarizing the first decision
Secondary lead, summarizing the other decisions
Details of the first decision
Details of the other decisions
Other details, if needed

Still another type of organization is possible in a news story that is partly narrative, such as an account of a game:

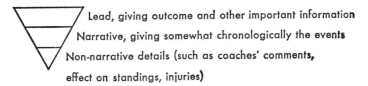

Lead, giving outcome and other important information
Narrative, giving somewhat chronologically the events
Non-narrative details (such as coaches' comments,
effect on standings, injuries)

How much detail to include in a story is sometimes a bothersome question. The answer involves the reporter's good judgment. He needs to decide how to cover the story adequately without descending to the trivial. A reporter must always ask himself, "Will this detail really help the reader to understand? Is it something trivial that can be omitted without harm?" A padded story is as poor as one that omits significant facts.

Paragraphs in news stories are usually short. One reason is that narrow newspaper columns make long paragraphs look even longer than they are—forbiddingly long to some readers. A second reason is that the shorter paragraphs make it easier for the editor to cut off a story wherever he needs to. Third, newspaper writing is concise, and the necessity of short paragraphs forces the reporter to search for a brief method of expression.

Transitions are especially important in newspaper writing. Words or phrases like *later, meanwhile, a year earlier, in contrast,* and *in addition to* help to clarify the relationships of different parts of the story.

EXERCISE FOUR

1. Examine several front-page, city-page, and sports-page stories in a daily newspaper, to see how they are organized. If there are variations from the patterns you have just read about, how do you account for these variations?

2. Pick at random three moderately long stories from a daily paper and find the average number of words in each paragraph. (If possible, members of the class should examine several different newspapers.) Compare the averages you find with those reported by your classmates.

To supplement this exercise, some class members should find the average paragraph length in a few magazine articles (nonfiction, and not condensations) and in nonfiction books. How do you account for the differences?

3. Search two or more news stories for transitions. Be ready to give examples in class and to comment upon the reasons for these transitions.

4. In Exercise Three (page 124) you wrote leads for some stories about school events. Choose one of these, and write the rest of the story. Gather your facts as carefully as if your story were to be printed in the school newspaper.

5. As a class or in small groups discuss the news stories you have prepared. Answer these questions for each: a. How is the story organized? b. Would different organization improve the story? c. Are most of the paragraphs of average news story

length? d. What use has been made of transitions? Would added or more precise transitions have been helpful?

SPECIAL TYPES OF NEWS STORIES AND FEATURES

Sports stories. A sports story differs from other news stories in that it uses fairly established sports jargon and includes more of the reporter's opinions than do others. For example, baseball stories are filled with such expressions as *four-bagger, twin killing, swiped second,* and others equally incomprehensible to an outsider. The sports reporter often expresses his judgment in such terms as *weak-hitting team, fought back valiantly,* and *breezed his sharp-breaking curve past the helpless Tigers.* He usually avoids, however, open criticism of individual players, coaches, or officials, choosing to report their lapses factually. For instance, instead of saying, "Fridger dropped a fly ball that he should have caught," he says, "Fridger was charged with an error when he dropped Manning's high fly to left." Instead of "The umpire called Gray out at the plate, but he was really safe," he says, "The crowd booed as the umpire called Gray out at the plate on a close decision."

Interviews. An interviewer makes an appointment in advance, learns as much as possible about the person to be interviewed, prepares a few key questions, and arrives punctually. During the interview he asks courteous questions in a polite manner, takes adequate notes on the answers, gets permission to quote what has been said, and thanks the interviewee.

The interviewer writes his story while the details are fresh in his mind. He starts with whatever seems most interesting or important, and presents the other facts or ideas in descending order of interest. He makes use of both direct and indirect quotations, and is careful not to distort anything that was said.

Feature stories. Feature stories, often boxed in newspapers, are human interest stories of relatively slight importance. They may concern such trivia as the squirrel that somehow got into the biology classroom, the student who slept not only through class but through the closing bell, interesting vacation plans of faculty and students, and the like. Lightness of touch and a surprise ending or an ending with any unusual twist—like the "punch line" of a joke—often characterize the feature story.

Unlike news stories, features seldom follow the triangular arrangement. The lead is intended not to summarize but to catch the interest. The organization may be chronological or any other that seems effective. A feature usually cannot be cut off before the end, for the ending often reveals the point of the whole story.

Literary features, which appear in some but not all school publications, are poems, essays, or short stories without any special journalistic touches.

News stories usually carry no by-lines, but a feature often does have the author's name.

Reviews. A special kind of feature, also usually signed, is the review of a book, play, movie, or concert. A good review suggests what the book, play, or movie is about, but does not tell much of the story. It may discuss one or more of the chief characters, comment upon the theme or the special significance of the story, or emphasize any qualities that seem especially noteworthy. Directly or indirectly it shows that a book is or is not likely to interest the reader, or that a play or movie is or is not worth seeing.

Comments upon effective performances by the actors in school plays are permissible, but unfavorable criticism of individuals must be either extremely tactful or else be omitted entirely. Both favorable and unfavorable criticisms of professional actors may be made, providing that the reviewer really knows enough about acting that his judgment is valid. A review of a concert, which obviously should be written only by someone rather well informed about music, may be concerned with either the music or the quality of the performance, or both.

Editorials. As a rule editorials are prepared by the editors themselves or by specially designated editorial writers. They tend to fall into five classifications, which may sometimes overlap.

First is the editorial of commendation, which praises a team, a coach, the student body, or someone or something else for noteworthy achievement. Opposed to this is the editorial of criticism, which may, for instance, find fault with a school regulation or students' behavior in the cafeteria. The third type is expository or interpretive; it attempts, for example, to explain a new ruling from the principal's office or the effect of some national event upon students. Fourth, the hortatory, is the editorial which urges the readers to do something: back the team, vote in a school election, stop running in the corridors, and so on. The fifth, rather rare in school papers, is a personal essay intended more for entertainment than for information or inspiration; it may concern, for instance, meditations on falling leaves, the thoughts of a senior about to graduate, or the like.

Editorials follow no single plan of organization, but often begin with background information and then move on to conclusions or recommendations. Since they presumably reflect the policy of the newspaper, they must be carefully thought out and must not be wild-eyed and uninformed.

Columns. Columns in school papers are most often of these kinds: sports, humor, personality, special information, and exchange. All are usually printed with the columnists' by-lines.

The sports column brings in comment that for one reason or another does not fit into regular sports stories. It may, for instance, discuss league standings and how they will change if . . . , interesting facts about athletes and coaches, and information about athletes of earlier years.

The humor column should not consist of clipped he-she jokes, but of humorous observations about goings-on in the school and community, funny original verse, puns, jokes (in good taste) told by students or teachers, and brief humorous essays. The column should be written carefully enough that no one in the school or community could legitimately take offense. Humor which ridicules individuals or groups is especially to be avoided.

The personality column includes bits—serious or humorous but not embarrassing—about students and teachers. It may include, for example, biographical sketches of exchange students or other new students, accounts of interesting hobbies, and travel experiences.

The special information column may be devoted one week to a new development in science, another week to the workings of the Student Council, another to results of a student poll on favorite television programs, and so on. It is intended to provide worthwhile information not readily available to most readers.

The exchange column consists of notes concerning what other schools are doing, the information being derived from the papers received in exchanges with those schools. Unusually good jokes or other feature material may be borrowed. Credit is always given to the paper from which the material is taken.

EXERCISE FIVE

In this exercise, members of the class may choose from the following suggestions the one or ones that most interest them.

1. Arrange to be present at the next athletic event of your school. Take notes as you watch. Write a story about the event, as if for your school paper.

2. Arrange to interview someone whom students in your school would find interesting. Suggestions: a coach, a teacher

with an unusual hobby, a new student from a distant place, a student recently elected to some office. Follow the suggestions on page 127. Write the interview.

3. Write a feature story about a rather trivial but interesting event in a class or at a school function.

4. Write a review of a book you have recently read, or of a play, movie, or concert you recently attended.

5. Write an editorial of any of the five types described on page 129.

6. Pretend that you have been asked to start a regular column for your school newspaper. Choose one of the five varieties described on pages 129–130, and write the first column.

HEADLINES

The reporter does not prepare headlines for his stories; that task is performed by the copy editor when he decides where the story will be placed and how large the head should be.

A good headline summarizes a news story in the form of a statement. MAROON GAME is not a headline; MAROONS TAME BEARCATS is. A headline has a verb, usually stated, sometimes only clearly implied, as in JUNIOR PLAY TRYOUTS TUESDAY. The verb is usually in the present tense: MIDVALERS HEAR GOVERNOR, not MIDVALERS HEARD GOVERNOR. For future events, the infinitive is more often used than the future tense: MIDVALERS TO HEAR GOVERNOR.

Each newspaper has its own headline "schedule," showing the forms and type faces that may be used; two newspapers' schedules may differ considerably because not all printers have the same facilities. The schedule also may give information about how to count headline spaces, since all characters and spaces must be counted and not all letters are the same width.

Among the often used varieties of headlines are these:

Crossline (one centered line)   ————————

Flush (two or more lines, flush at   ————————
    left, irregular at right)   ——————

                                                ———————

Hanging indention (two or more   ————————
    lines, the first flush left, others   ——————
    indented equally, generally   ——————
    fairly even at right)

Pyramid (two or more centered   ————————
    lines, each shorter than the   ——————
    one above)   ————

Step or drop line (two or more lines,   ——————
    about same length, slanting   ——————
    with top line flush left, bot-   ——————
    tom line flush right)

Each line of a head should be reasonably complete in itself. For example, a line should not end with a word like *a* or *to* or *and*.

Here are some examples of poor and good headlines:

Poor	*Better*
MAROONS PLAY	MAROONS BOW
BADLY AGAIN	TO ARABS 31–0

(A story headline should give facts, not opinions.)

| PLAY HAS BEEN | SENIORS PICK |
| CHOSEN BY CLASS | 'RAIN IN JULY' |

(The poor headline here splits the verb, uses a weak passive verb instead of a stronger active one, and gives no specific information.)

| SPEAKER PRAISES A | MAC NAMARA URGES: |
| SHORT BOOKLET | READ 'STUDY HELPS' |

(The poor headline, besides being unspecific, uses the unnecessary word *a*, leaves the first line dangling in midair, and is redundant, since any booklet is short.)

EXERCISE SIX

1. Study the headlines on two of three pages of a daily paper. How many different type faces are used? How many different sizes? How are verbs used? When are verbs only implied? Is any use made of *a, an, the*? Does each headline give the gist of the story? How do headlines differ from leads?

2. If a headline schedule for your school paper is available, study it. What limitations does it place upon headline writers?

3. Write headlines for any news stories you have written for earlier exercises in this chapter.

Section C

WRITING FICTION

9
Characterization

10
Setting and Plot

11
Writing the Short Story

12
Writing the Short Play

Characterization

WHAT CHARACTERIZATION IS

A NEWSPAPER story says, "A forest fire of unknown origin yesterday destroyed five thousand acres of timber in northern Idaho. It was brought under control late last night."

Perhaps that account, with a few added details, makes an adequate newspaper story. It relates an event of some significance, telling briefly what happened, when, and where.

To the fiction writer, though, what happened is less important than the persons to whom it happened. Events— a fire, the sinking of a ship, a sustained drouth—may well have a vital role in fiction, but a reader is always less interested in the events than he is in the people involved.

Suppose that our newspaper story takes this form: "One person is known to have died as the result of a fire that yesterday destroyed five thousand acres of timber in northern Idaho. He was Norton Wells, 24, who lived alone in a cabin in the path of the furious blaze. His body has been recovered."

The reader's interest is increased by this human element. The reader did not know Norton Wells, and the information in the news story is too scanty to cause anyone to care very much about him. Nevertheless, the reader may wonder why a young man lived alone in a cabin in a secluded area, and why he was unable to escape the fire.

The newspaper story did not characterize Norton Wells. It gave only a few facts about him. The fiction writer, though, if he were centering a story on Norton, would have to go much beyond the superficial facts. He would need to let the reader know who Norton was, what kind of person he was, how he became that kind of person, why he lived alone in Idaho, and whether something in his character—rather than mere mischance—contributed to his untimely death. Moreover, the writer would have to make the reader *care* about Norton, not necessarily like him but at least be interested in him, curious about him.

Perhaps the writer is concerned about persons who have never been able to find a satisfying purpose in life. Norton, he decides, is such a person. He is young, vigorous, handsome, intelligent, and rich. Everything has always come easily to him. An only child, he has had every wish and every whim catered to by his parents. Expensive toys as a child, and then bicycles, motorcycles, automobiles, boats, travel—nothing has been denied him. Girls have pursued him for years because of his looks, his quick wit, his wealth. Three college campuses have known his charm and his escapades, and he has failed or been expelled in all three, although a few subjects, notably the biological sciences and philosophy, have fascinated him. But in general he has become bored. The endless pleasures have palled, and being essentially a thoughtful young man, he has begun wondering, "What is life all about? Doesn't it hold anything more vital, more rewarding, more meaningful than parties and enjoyable but empty friendships?"

Norton has decided to spend six months or a year alone to think things through, to find himself. He moves into an isolated cabin in northern Idaho. He lives mainly off the land. He meditates. He happens upon an injured fawn, and attempts to heal it. This renews and increases his interest in animal life, an interest he had once known in college. He systematically captures and tries to treat other injured or diseased animals; in a few months he has several pens and cages full. In serving these creatures he is finding the purpose that had always eluded him: the realization that for him serving is more important than being served. When the fire, caused by lightning, begins raging, he hurries to release his imprisoned animals. Though the effort costs his life, he dies after experiencing the only genuine happiness he has ever known.

The writer who develops such a story adds to our understanding of human nature through its dramatization in the life of one or more persons. He takes us inside his characters, helping us to realize what makes them tick, making us interested in their destinies. This is characterization.

EXERCISE ONE

1. If the forest fire story did not concern Norton Wells, who are several other persons who might have been involved? (For instance, it might be a person who through carelessness started the fire, or one of the firefighters.)

2. Choose one of the persons suggested for Number 1, and tell what information a reader would need concerning him in order to be interested in him and to understand him.

3. Be ready to discuss these questions:

a. In stories or plays you have read, especially famous stories of the sort you have studied in English, do you remember mainly the incidents or some of the people? Give examples.

b. Characterization has been called "the soul of narrative." What do you think this means?

c. Define characterization in your own words.

d. Maren Elwood, in a book called *Characters Make Your Story*, has said, "Unless your characters are real and, therefore, interesting, no sequence of dramatic events, no amount of original and astounding plot will help in the least. Your reader will remain totally unconcerned as to what happens to the puppets in your story. Frankly, he will be bored." To illustrate Elwood's statement, as a class construct an "astounding plot" concerned with space travel. List the incidents that might be included. What would a reader have to know about some of the characters to avoid boredom?

KNOWING YOUR CHARACTERS

Every successful writer knows more about his characters than he puts into his story. Many authors actually write for their own use a biography, a page or several pages long, of each major character, telling about his family, his childhood, the important events of his life before the time of the story. The authors know where and when the character was born, the environment in which he grew up, his education, and his relations with other persons. They know how he thinks, how he talks, and how he will probably react in any situation. Much of this information does not actually appear in the printed story, but if a writer does not have it, the character may not talk as such a person really would, or not react in a consistent way. He will not seem real to the reader because he is not real to the author.

In stories you write for this class, you may or may not have time to write out the biographies of all the major characters you use, but you should at least *think* them out.

No two persons in the world are exactly alike, not even identical twins. You need therefore to decide what qualities each of your characters has that differentiate him from other persons. If he is not distinguished from others, he becomes what authors call a stereotype. A stereotype is the "typical" Italian, the "typical" Negro, the "typical" Baptist or Catholic, the "typical" teen-ager. And there is no such thing! You are not typical, and no one of your classmates or anyone else you have ever known is typical. Stereotypes are to be avoided because they are untrue to life.

EXERCISE TWO

Joe Rogers, seventeen years old, has been promised the use of the family car to take his girl to a major dance at the school. Late in the afternoon Joe's father discovers that he must take the car on an emergency business trip; there is no other transportation available for Mr. Rogers.

Before deciding Joe's reaction, you need to know Joe. Jot down fifteen or twenty significant things about him, his early life, his home life, the closeness of his association with the girl, and anything else pertinent. Then tell what Joe does.

Compare the character traits you have given Joe with the ones given him by several of your classmates. Also compare your solutions. Does each solution grow logically from the imagined background?

THE NINE METHODS OF CHARACTERIZATION

It is possible to reveal a character in nine major ways. Most professional authors use several, or all, of these in a single story.

The nine methods, each of which will be explained and illustrated in the following paragraphs, are: 1. telling about the character, 2. describing him and his surroundings, 3. showing him in action, 4. letting him talk, 5. revealing his thoughts, 6. showing what others say to him, 7. showing what others say about him, 8. showing the reaction of others to him, and 9. showing his reactions to others.

TELLING ABOUT THE CHARACTER

The simplest but generally the least effective way to characterize is simply to tell the reader what a character is like:

Butch Nagel was the most conceited player on the football squad. Because of his size, strength, and speed, he scored many points. Each touchdown made his head swell a little more. He was fairly intelligent, though less so than some of his teammates. Also, under his blustery exterior there lurked a streak of yellow. He was actually rather cowardly. But, like many other cowards, he bullied his fellows.

Experienced writers only occasionally use this method, especially for major characters. In the first place, it is not very convincing. The reader says in effect, "That's what you think of Butch, but what is the evidence?" Second, it is not dramatic. Narration means relating a story, and to relate a story well, events must be dramatized. There is no drama, no action at all, in the paragraph about Butch.

For minor characters, authors sometimes content themselves with a mere telling of whatever should be known. Even then, however, they are likely to mention an incident that reveals the character instead of just using an adjective like "cowardly." If Butch were a minor character, for instance, the author might refer to him as "Butch Nagel, who had been known rather often to stumble and fall just before a big tackler hit him."

EXERCISE THREE

For this exercise and the next eight, you are to choose a character in whom you would be interested and characterize him in various ways. We'll refer to this person as Your Character. Choose someone from a sphere of life that you know fairly well. You may have someone already in mind, but if you have not, maybe one of these will suggest Your Character to you:

a girl (boy) from a rich family
a person who has been told he has a serious, incurable ailment
a spoiled child
a mischievous young brother (sister)
the most popular girl (boy) in school
a person with a lively mind and a dull job
an athlete who hates athletics
the school clown
a would-be explorer
a young singing star
an old man (woman) remembering his (her) days of glory
a boy-crazy (girl-crazy) person
a petty thief
a dedicated teacher nearing retirement

a young person from the slums

an overconfident person

For this exercise, write one or two paragraphs in which you simply tell what kind of person Your Character is. Use no conversation, little if any description, and no incidents.

DESCRIBING THE CHARACTER AND HIS SURROUNDINGS

Butch Nagel stepped out of his red convertible and glowered as usual at the crumpled left fender, but paused to look at his reflection distorted in the gleaming quantities of chrome on the side of the car. He threw back his broad shoulders and then, leaning over as if to examine something, admired his wavy blond hair and rugged face. He stood up again, stretching to his full six two.

He began sauntering toward the outside door leading to the locker room, consciously putting a spring into his step and saying "Hi" casually, sometimes almost regally, to the three or four students whom he met. Once in the locker room, he strutted toward his own locker, largely ignoring the other boys but indignantly shoving a small sophomore out of his way. He opened his locker, where his football practice togs lay in a sodden heap.

Those paragraphs give the reader a rather clear impression of Butch's physical appearance. At the same time they reveal something about his personality. Here the author has not told us that Butch is conceited, but in reading the description we become convinced that he is. Moreover, "his red convertible" suggests that Butch is probably not a poor boy; "the crumpled left fender" hints that he may be a careless driver; "the gleaming quantities of chrome" imply his liking for the gaudy and ostentatious; the "sodden heap" of football togs suggests heedlessness, especially when few people can observe it. His manner of walking, "sauntering" along to be admired, "consciously putting a spring into his step," and then "strutting" among the other players, reveals that he is always acting, trying to impress people.

A few of the details in the two paragraphs are not descriptive, but such details are often mingled with description. The way he speaks (or fails to speak) to his acquaintances and the shoving of the small sophomore tell much about him, though strictly speaking they are nondescriptive.

A skilful writer, one who has observed carefully, can reveal much about a character by describing his facial expression, the way he moves his eyebrows or alters the shape of his mouth or wrinkles his forehead, the way he walks down the street or enters a familiar or unfamiliar place. An able writer may even characterize without ever showing the person at all. He may portray the person's bedroom, for instance, and show much by describing its orderliness or disorder, the furnishings, the decorations, the things fastened to the walls and the way they are fastened.

Description of a character may be static or active. Static description shows him at rest—standing or sitting or sleeping. Active description, like the paragraphs about Butch, shows him doing something. Static description, especially when it is brief, is useful, but active is generally more interesting because of the movement involved.

EXERCISE FOUR

Describe Your Character. Put him into surroundings that will help to reveal him. Let the reader know what he looks like, preferably through active description. Try to give a glimpse of his true character, but do not tell what that character is. A few of your details may be nondescriptive, but most should be descriptive.

SHOWING THE CHARACTER IN ACTION

Butch grabbed the quick handoff from the quarterback and started toward an opening between guard and tackle. As the hole narrowed, he changed his course, veering to the left, trying to cut around end, running more like a halfback than a fullback. But the Tiger end had diagnosed the change of plan and plunged to bring Butch down when he had barely passed the line of scrimmage. A Tiger halfback helped out. Butch fell skilfully, his body between the Tiger end and the nearest official. He flung his knee up into the Tiger's midsection, and his fist somehow found its way to the Tiger's mouth. When the three players were separated, the Tiger end, gasping and bleeding, had to be helped from the field.

This paragraph says indirectly, "Butch was a dirty football player." To those who know football it may suggest something else. Why did Butch change course? A fullback usually tries to go through a hole in the line, even if the hole is narrow, unless there is a much better opening somewhere else. We do not know whether Butch's failure to do so resulted only from bad judgment or from unwillingness to have a massive tackle and guard close in on him.

EXERCISE FIVE

In one or two paragraphs, show Your Character in action. Choose an incident in which he would be likely to appear, and reveal his character by showing what he does and how he does it.

LETTING THE CHARACTER TALK

In the huddle Butch said to the quarterback, "Gimme the ball again. Call Play 23. I'll bust through for a score like I did in the first quarter. And you guys," he pointed to the left tackle and left guard, "take out your men like you're s'posed to. How do you expect me to score points for you if you don't open no holes?"

These few sentences spoken by Butch are very revealing. In the first place, Butch takes over the rightful function of the quarterback and gives instructions. If the quarterback wants to use a different play, valuable time has been lost. Second, when Butch scores he gives himself the credit, but when he fails to gain he blames the other players. Third, he seems to have no respect for "you guys," his teammates. Finally, his rather poor English suggests that he is somewhat slovenly and probably not a good student. He would be expected to use informal language in such a situation, but "bust" and the double negative are below the level of mere informality.

One of the weaknesses of beginning writers is that the conversation of their characters is often not true to life. They tend to put far too polished language into the mouths of persons who would naturally speak with no polish at all. They might have Butch say, for instance, "Give the football to me on this play, James. It appears to me that Play 23 would be a desirable one to employ in these circumstances." The writer who knows Butch is clearly aware that he would not talk like that; probably few other players would either.

A helpful device is to read aloud the remarks your characters make. Note whether they *sound* right, sound like the words and constructions these characters would really use.

EXERCISE SIX

Now let Your Character talk. Imagine a fairly dramatic moment in which he would have something important to say. Someone else may talk, too (in a separate paragraph, of course), but the emphasis should be on what Your Character says and the way he says it. Make his speech reveal as much about him as possible.

REVEALING THE CHARACTER'S THOUGHTS

In the locker room at halftime, Butch sprawled on a bench. The coach had not yet begun to talk to the whole squad, some of whom were talking earnestly among themselves about ways to make better yardage or to stop the Tiger backs. Butch thought, "Only one touchdown so far! What a lousy break! And there's at least them two college scouts in the stands, decidin' whether to offer me a scholarship. I gotta do better the second half. If the other guys 'd do more blocking for me an' make bigger holes, I bet I could score six touchdowns. An' Jim don't call my plays often enough, or else he tries to run me across their big center. That guy's bigger than me! I don't mind a coupla bruises, but I'd sure hate to get my face all messed up. The girls wouldn't fall for me like they do, even if I still was a football hero."

A character's thoughts are usually indicated in quotation marks, like his conversation, although some writers prefer to use italics or not set the thoughts off in any special way. The thoughts may also be summarized, without using the character's own words and therefore without quotation marks.

By taking the reader inside a character's mind, the writer shows us the person as he believes himself to be. If the character is very complex, his thoughts may reveal much about him that does not show in his speech or his actions. (The characters in Eugene O'Neill's play *Strange Interlude,* for example, speak their thoughts, which often contradict what they say to the other characters and which always help to illuminate each character.) If the character is relatively simple, like Butch, the report on his thoughts may merely amplify what is already known about him.

In his thinking, Butch once again blames his teammates for his lack of glorious success. The author, however, also develops further what was only hinted before (that Butch is a bit cowardly) and the suggestion is made that his cowardice is caused by his fear that his face will be "messed up" and that he will then be less attractive to girls. The reference to the scouts in the stands serves to reveal Butch's ambition to win a football scholarship.

EXERCISE SEVEN

Now the thoughts of Your Character are to be presented. In a paragraph or two, show him thinking about something that is very important to him.

SHOWING WHAT OTHERS SAY TO THE CHARACTER

"Butch," the coach said, "you made some good gains the first half, but you also missed some good chances. Watch for those holes that Bill and Ken are making between tackle and guard, and head for them even if they aren't very big. Don't think that you can move your 190 pounds around like a scatback. And your blocking is terrible! I've told all of you, again and again, to take out the men that are coming for the ball carrier. There was one play when you were picking daisies back on the forty when you should have been playing football on the twenty. And remember that defense is as important in this game as offense. Do you know how many tackles you were in on? Exactly one, not counting the times you piled on after the ball carrier was already down. You may be on somebody's All-State team, but you won't be on mine unless you play the game going both ways."

Note that the characterization of Butch being built up is consistent. Although new details are steadily added, the picture of a conceited and perhaps overrated football player continues to show through. The coach's new contribution to the portrait reveals that Butch thinks so much about scoring that he is remiss in helping other ball carriers and in tackling the opponents. The coach also raises in the reader's mind the question of how Butch will react to such blunt criticism.

EXERCISE EIGHT

Write one or more paragraphs in which someone else talks to Your Character. Remember that the person's attitude toward Your Character can be as revealing as what he says.

SHOWING WHAT OTHERS SAY
ABOUT THE CHARACTER

The principal's daughter, Kathy Melchior, sat with her father in the stands. After Butch scored his second touchdown, she screamed and jumped as the other Midvale rooters did, and turned to her father with glowing eyes. "Oh, Dad," she said, "isn't he wonderful! I'm so lucky to have a date with him to-night."

"That was a good play," her father said. "Did you see the block that Jerry made? That was what really freed Butch for the touchdown."

"OK, but it was Butch that scored it."

"Butch will be a better football player and a better man when he learns that cooperation is a two-way street. If—there! Did you see that tackle? That's the best play that Butch has made all day! He saw that Ken couldn't get the Tiger, so he angled through, eluded the blocker, and got him himself. A few more plays like that and I'll have some hope for the boy."

This conversation gives the attitudes of two persons toward Butch. Kathy thinks that Butch is almost perfect, but her father has reservations. However, the father also suggests that Butch is not hopeless—that if he learns the big lesson of cooperativeness, he may yet turn out well.

Notice that the story itself may be moved along by conversation, as it also may with the other devices of characterization. While Mr. Melchior is talking, a play is occurring on the field, and Mr. Melchior's remark shows that Butch may be attempting to overcome his biggest shortcoming.

EXERCISE NINE

Write the conversation of two persons, one or both of whom know Your Character. They may have opposite opinions of him, if you wish.

SHOWING THE REACTIONS OF OTHERS TO THE CHARACTER

Still trailing 14 to 13 with the final two minutes ticking away, the Midvale boys hurried into the huddle. They looked with new respect at Butch, whose furious tackles had kept the Tigers from scoring a third touchdown. Ken slapped him on the back, and Butch grinned. Jerry, though, perhaps remembering how Butch's failures to block during the first half had prevented them from scoring, ignored Butch completely.

"Let's try 23 again," said the quarterback, "and see if we can shake Butch loose."

"Jim," Butch said, and was himself amazed at what he was going to say, "I've noticed that their right end has been moving toward center on our plays when I carry. Let me lateral to Jerry. With his speed he might get around end and go all the way, especially if we block for him."

The players could hardly believe their ears. Imagine Butch suggesting that somebody else carry the ball and perhaps score a touchdown!

As a story advances, the interactions of the characters vary. In the early part of this story, most or all of the other players would have been hostile to Butch, perhaps admiring him for his ability to plunge ahead with the ball but disliking him for his conceit and lack of team play. Now the attitudes have changed somewhat, for he has stopped grandstanding and has been playing hard defensive football. The alteration is not complete, though, because Jerry, at least, still remembers Butch's shortcomings. All are astonished at his offer to give up a chance for personal glory.

The reactions of others to a character are shown in part by what they say, as we have seen. They are also shown in what they *do*—and that is the point of this method of characterization.

EXERCISE TEN

Write a paragraph or two in which you show the reactions of others to Your Character. Although you may use conversation, here you should emphasize the actions of the persons.

SHOWING THE CHARACTER'S REACTIONS TO OTHERS

Never before had the coach or anyone else talked so straight to Butch. He was shocked and angered by the coach's halftime words. "Accusing me of laying down on the job! Who's the big star of this team anyway? Haven't I scored more points than all the other backs put together?" But underneath he knew that the coach was telling the truth. He didn't block the way he should. And he didn't like to tackle. What he liked was the noise the crowd made when he scored a touchdown. But if the coach didn't think he was All-State, would anybody else? Could others see through him as the coach did?

He clenched his fists. If blocking was what the coach wanted, blocking he'd get. If tackling was what he wanted, he'd get tackling. Maybe the girls wouldn't like it so much, but people who knew football would.

Butch Nagel was becoming a man.

All reactions have counterreactions. It is in these reactions and counterreactions that drama lies; it is here that we find conflict, the heart of drama. If Butch had been completely self-centered, he would have reacted differently, but he respected the coach and others who knew football, and therefore he reacted as he did. A complete reformation is always improbable; more than likely Butch would still frequently try to grab more than his share of headlines.

But the changes the coach and the principal hoped for were beginning to occur.

This is the final illustration of the nine methods of characterizing. As was said earlier, the nine may be combined in various ways, with one or two being emphasized in one story, different ones in other stories. These are the tools of characterization which all writers, amateur or professional, need to learn to use with skill.

EXERCISE ELEVEN

Now you will show Your Character's reaction to someone else. Try to select an incident that will require him to make a fundamental decision which will perhaps affect the rest of his life.

ADDITIONAL SUGGESTIONS FOR CHARACTERIZATION

1. *Names.* The name given a character should suggest at least to a slight extent what he is like. This does not mean that the faithful heroine should be named Faith or that the villain should be called Blackie Muggeridge. However, Fauntleroy Lightbody doesn't sound like a good name for a professional wrestler, and Maggie Lostwitz is not especially appealing for a lovely girl. Reasonably common names are generally preferable to very uncommon ones, except when an unusual name appears to fit perfectly.

2. *Selection of character traits.* In a short story it is impossible to develop a character fully, and even a novel cannot and should not include every trait. The narrative writer knows that he must select the traits he wants to emphasize and that the ones he picks should fit together so that the character seems consistent and believable. Experienced authors seldom try to reveal all the complexities and con-

tradictions that exist in real persons; if they were to do so, no clear understanding of the character would emerge. So they simplify by choosing a homogeneous set of traits, the ones that help to show why the character acts as he does in each situation.

3. *Motivation.* Scientists know that everything that happens in a laboratory—or anywhere else—must have an adequate cause. Similarly, every human action must have a cause, or as writers say, must be motivated. Moreover, the motivation must be sufficient to produce the result. In the skeleton of the story about Butch Nagel, in this chapter, the greatest weakness may be that the motivation for Butch's reform is insufficient. Would just the words of the coach drastically alter his style of play and indeed his whole outlook? Possibly, but not assuredly. If the whole story were given, of course, additional causes for Butch's sudden change of heart might be included.

4. *The Chemistry game.* Some authors play a game of solitaire that might be called Chemistry. It involves mentally taking two characters, as a chemist might take two elements or compounds, and bringing them together. What happens—an explosion, a merger, total indifference, or something else? If one of the characters is altered a little—given a little less forbearance or a little more pride, for instance—how is the reaction changed? By playing this game seriously, an author comes to understand his characters better and also sometimes uncovers plot ideas that he might otherwise have missed.

5. *Character growth.* In Shakespeare's *Macbeth* the leading character is at the beginning a respected nobleman and heroic soldier. In the course of the play his character degenerates steadily until he is seeing apparitions, committing senseless murders of women and children, and coming close to insanity. The things that happen in the play all have a dire effect on him. In any long play or novel

the chief characters are gradually altered, for better or worse, by the experiences they undergo. Such changes are generally said to reflect character growth. In a short story or one-act play the extent of character growth is necessarily less, yet the skilful writer even here shows that his chief character is not quite the same at the end as at the beginning.

6. *Background, flat, and rounded characters.* Some characters, usually nameless, are not developed at all. These are usually the taxi drivers, the waiters, or other persons who appear only briefly and then are gone from the story. They are called background characters and correspond to the nameless "extras" in movies. Flat characters are a little more important to the action and are generally given names. They are called flat because they are like two-dimensional portraits, not fully pictured. Like the "walk-on" actors in movies, they say a few words and contribute a little to the action, but there is no reason why the reader should be given much information about them. Rounded characters, however, like the leading roles in motion pictures, are presented three-dimensionally. These are the major figures (or the single major figure) in a story, and are developed in several of the nine ways explained in this chapter.

7. *Characters who live.* If you write enough fiction, you will eventually make this discovery: suddenly, at some point in a story, the characters get out of your control and start acting of their own volition. They talk without your putting the words into their mouths, they make decisions for themselves, and they perform actions without your intervention. The first time this happens to you may be one of the most thrilling moments of your writing career, because you will know that you have indeed created characters with the breath of life in them. You may have to revise what they say and do, because at times they may be too wordy, too exuberant, or too something else, but never-

theless the excitement of the creator will long remain with you, and you are likely to conclude that you write your best when the characters do the writing for you.

EXERCISE TWELVE

1. Think of a name that would be suitable and one that would seem unsuitable for each of these:
> a traffic cop in Boston
> a delicate six-year-old girl
> a big league baseball player
> a pleasant nurse
> a soft-spoken clergyman
> a logger
> a female welder

2. If you were writing an article similar to a "My Most Unforgettable Character" article in the *Reader's Digest,* whom would you choose? What character traits would you include? Why? Which would you omit? Why?

3. Read a short story in a magazine or in a literature textbook. List four or five important actions or decisions of the leading character. Then list his motives for each. Does each act or decision seem to have adequate cause?

4. In the same story choose an episode in which two of the chief characters are brought face to face, preferably in a conflict of some sort. What happens? Now in your imagination change one of the characters somewhat, perhaps making him older, younger, more cautious, more reckless, more intelligent, or less brave. How is the ending of the episode affected? (In this exercise you are playing the Chemistry game.)

5. In a story or play familiar to all the class, analyze the changes that occur in one or more of the chief characters. What are the causes of the character growth?

6. In the same story or play, classify the characters as background, flat, or rounded. How much more fully developed are the rounded characters than the flat ones?

7. If the teacher and class decide to do so, you may now

prepare a fairly long sketch of Your Character, combining several of the methods with which you have previously experimented. The sketch, if you wish, may be in the form of a short story in which Your Character attempts to reach a certain goal but encounters numerous obstacles. Or it may be only a series of incidents that, taken together, reveal his chief qualities.

10

Setting and Plot

THE MEANING AND IMPORTANCE OF SETTING

MOST beginning writers, asked to define *setting*, say that it refers to "the place where the events of a story occur." They are only half right, for setting is as much a matter of time as of place.

For instance, suppose that an author lets us know that the setting of his story is a village in upstate New York. If the time is 1960, that village is very different from the same one in 1760. Not only are the houses different, not only the modes of transportation and other physical things, but also the appearance of the people, their language, their knowledge, their ways of making a living, even their habits of thinking. A lapse of only twenty years, although it will involve less profound changes, nevertheless results in considerable differences. As an example, consider the alterations in Rip Van Winkle's village between the mid-1760's, when Rip went to sleep, and the mid-1780's, when he awoke from his long nap.

Washington Irving begins his most famous story, "Rip Van Winkle," with a paragraph describing the Kaatskill Mountains (now spelled Catskill). Then he continues:

At the foot of these fairy mountains the voyager may have descried the light smoke curling up from a village, whose shingle roofs gleam among the trees, just where the blue tints of the upland melt away into the fresh green of the nearer landscape. It is a little village of great antiquity, having been founded by some of the Dutch colonists in the early times of the province . . . and there were some of the houses of the original settlers

157

standing . . . built of small yellow bricks brought from Holland, having latticed windows and gable fronts, surmounted with weathercocks.

In that same village, and in one of these very houses (which, to tell the precise truth, was sadly timeworn and weather-beaten), there lived many years since, while the country was yet a province of Great Britain, a simple, good-natured fellow by the name of Rip Van Winkle. . . .

[After his long sleep] as he approached the village he met a number of people, but none of whom he knew, which somewhat surprised him, for he had thought himself acquainted with everyone in the country round. Their dress, too, was of a different fashion from that to which he was accustomed. . . .

. . . The very village was altered; it was larger and more populous. There were rows of houses which he had never seen before, and those which had been his familiar haunts had disappeared. Strange names were over the doors—strange faces at the windows—everything was strange. . . .

. . . He found [his own] house gone to decay—the roof fallen in, the windows shattered, and the doors off the hinges. . . .

He now hurried forth and hastened to his old resort, the village inn; but it too was gone. A large rickety building stood in its place, with great gaping windows. . . . Instead of the great tree that used to shelter the quiet little Dutch inn of yore, there now was reared a tall, naked pole, with something on the top that looked like a red nightcap, and from it was fluttering a flag, on which was a singular assemblage of stars and stripes.

The time and place of a story are important because they determine in large part the kinds of persons who may be portrayed and the things that may happen to those persons. If the setting of a story is a large American city of 1900 A.D., the people and the events will probably be very different from those on a farm in the same year, in an Asiatic city in the same year, or in an American city in 1850 or 1950.

To the knowledgeable, every place has its own characteristics. San Francisco and Los Angeles are very different cities; so are Houston and Dallas, or St. Louis and Kansas City. The countryside itself is sufficiently varied that a well-traveled person, parachuted from a plane that has been following a course unknown to him, could fairly easily determine at least his approximate location without asking anyone. Likewise every decade and indeed every year has its own flavor, its own peculiarities, a statement that you can prove for yourself by comparing the chief characteristics of this year with those of last year.

EXERCISE ONE

1. Suppose that a Rip Van Winkle lived in your community one hundred years ago (or less than that if your community is younger). After a long sleep he awoke this morning. What changes does he observe?

2. Now let's try a Rip Van Winkle in reverse. Assume that you were moved backward twenty or fifty years in time, either in your own community or another that you know well. What differences in the place and in the people and their activities would you notice? Why would some of these be important if you were setting a story in the earlier time?

3. Consider any story or stories familiar to most members of the class. How is the setting important? Could the story have taken place, without major alterations, in any other time and place?

TWO TECHNIQUES FOR PRESENTING A SETTING

Earlier writers, much more than modern ones, used long descriptive passages to set the stage for their stories; each time the scene shifted importantly, new descriptions would appear. Thus Charles Dickens began *A Tale of Two Cities* with an overview of France and England in 1775, commenting upon the rulers of the two countries and many events of the year. Laced through the rest of the novel are many other descriptions in one or more paragraphs. Sir Walter Scott began *Ivanhoe* with several pages of description and exposition, letting the reader know where in England the events were to take place, and the historical background of the reign of Richard I.

Readers of a more leisurely era probably enjoyed such descriptions, pausing to reflect upon the details and to envision what they were reading about. Perhaps we hasty ones are missing pleasures that our ancestors knew. Today's readers, in any event, impatiently pass over descriptive passages, rushing along to passages of conversation and action. Consequently, most modern authors have adopted the bits-and-snatches technique for presenting setting.

This means that the background details concerning time and place are generally scattered throughout a story, not offered in a lump or a few lumps. At the beginning a casual reference to Fifth Avenue or the Empire State Building quickly establishes the place as Manhattan; another comment, such as "now that the Korean War had ended," shows the approximate date. Later, with other bits and snatches, the author tells his reader whatever he needs to know about the time and place. He may occasionally employ two or three consecutive sentences for this purpose, but seldom more.

An advantage of the bits-and-snatches technique is that it does not bring the story to a temporary halt. Besides, it allows the author to show the setting as one of the characters would have seen it. The older technique, in contrast, sometimes resulted in a lecture delivered by the author, while the characters waited, almost forgotten, in the wings.

A. B. Guthrie's *The Way West* illustrates how setting may be shown through the eyes of important characters. Here is how that book begins:

The day dawned clear, but it had rained the night before, the sudden squally rain of middle March. Taking a look out the kitchen door, seeing the path leading down to the muddy barnyard and the tracks of his shoepacks splashed in it, Lije Evans was just as well satisfied that things were wet. It gave him an excuse not to work, even if he could be mending harness or fixing tools. Not that he minded work; it was just that he didn't feel like working today.

"Likely I'll go to town, Rebecca," he said, closing the door.

"To talk about Oregon," she said, not quite as if she blamed him.

In approximately one hundred words, Guthrie has accomplished these things:

1. Introduced us to two important characters;

2. Given us some hints of what these characters are like;

3. Shown a rural setting in the United States;

4. Suggested ("mending harness") that the time is probably many years ago;

5. Shown the specific time of year;

6. Suggested that the characters are thinking about going to Oregon.

The bits-and-snatches technique may be a little more difficult than the other, for the writer must be sure that enough details are provided to make the setting clear, and he must space them so that the reader will know what he needs to know at any given moment.

EXERCISE TWO

1. As a class, examine several short stories or parts of novels to observe the ways in which earlier authors and some contemporary ones present settings. Do you find many long descriptive passages? How are the bits and snatches interwoven into some of the narratives?

2. Write a paragraph or two describing an interesting place that you know well. Then rewrite, using the bits-and-snatches

technique. You will need to introduce a couple of characters and some sort of action. Let the reader see the place through the eyes of one of the characters.

THE MEANING AND IMPORTANCE OF PLOT

Let us look first at what plot is not. It is not a factual account of an event: a newspaper story telling about an election or a murder has no plot. It is not a mere incident: a student's composition about a happening on the way to school has no plot. It is not just a series of incidents: a narrative relating the various things you did last Saturday probably has no plot.

In its simplest form a plot is a fictional account, in a series of interrelated episodes, showing a conflict between opposing forces. In its more complicated forms the number of episodes may be large, and several competing or supplementary forces may be involved in the conflict.

The most common plot may be diagramed in this way:

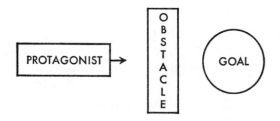

The protagonist (the chief character) has a goal which he hopes to reach. But an obstacle, or a series of obstacles, stands in his way. As he tries to attain the goal, he runs head-on into whatever blocks his path. In a series of episodes he combats the obstacles. He may win some of the battles, or lose some, or lose all, or lose all except the last. The issue is generally in doubt until the end; the reader cannot be sure that the protagonist will win. Although the "happy ending" (generally meaning the protagonist's victory) is the most frequent, sometimes the opposing forces prove too strong, and the protagonist loses.

You have probably heard the expression *weaving a plot.* This implies that, as in a web, all the parts are fastened together, not just in a straight line but in a more or less intricately meshed fashion. This is not a plot:

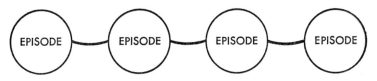

But this is:

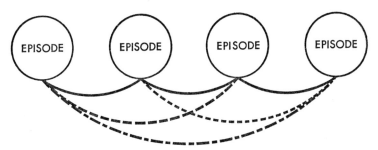

The difference is that in the first diagram, each episode is related only to the previous one; in the second, each is related to all the others. For example, in the familiar boy-meets-girl love story plot, the first episode, involving the meeting, develops characteristics that will be important in all the other episodes. Further, it is likely to suggest some of the obstacles that will have to be surmounted before boy can win girl. The second episode is suggested by the first and grows from it; it may depict the boy's (or girl's) struggle against the first obstacle. The third episode may be a further act in the same struggle, or it may depict a new obstacle emerging from the first or the second episode. These interrelationships are developed and added to in whatever other episodes are necessary, until the culmination is reached.

In a novel the number of episodes may be very large, and some of them may be tied into the plot more loosely than is true in the usual short story. But even in a novel, the loose ends, the lightly connected episodes, are rare.

This careful weaving illustrates a fundamental difference between fiction and real life. Life is full of loose ends. We keep meeting people whom we never see again, and some of the things that happen to us today have no visible connection with anything else in our lives. The fiction writer, however, consciously selects those persons and events that can be woven together into a unified whole. Life is like a creek or river, winding its way across plains and through valleys, making its gentle or sharp turns, backtracking, and meeting with other streams that chance to be moving in the same general direction. A plot, in contrast, is like a series of interlacing canals, planned for a specific purpose.

The plot in fiction is important for three major reasons. The first is that readers are more interested in movement than in still life; a motion picture, for instance, is usually more interesting than a snapshot.

Second, the conflict in a plot parallels or sometimes reflects conflicts that exist in the lives of all of us. Our conflicts differ from one another, but everyone every day encounters forces that prevent him from doing exactly what he wishes. A student, for instance, may be in open or hidden conflict with his parents, his brothers and sisters, or some of his classmates; he may have within himself a conflict of ambitions or a conflict between what he believes to be right and what he believes to be wrong; he may feel conflict with conditions over which he has no control, such as economic forces or the threat of war. A plot gives shape and meaning to conflict, simplifies or clarifies it, turns it into a dramatic action with a solution.

Third, plot is important because it provides a framework that the author uses to present the characters and the theme of his story. The characters or the theme may be much more significant than the series of events, but these interrelated events make it possible to show the characters in action and to make the theme much more exciting than it would be if it were merely stated.

EXERCISE THREE

1. Here is a summary of Jack London's "All Gold Cañon":
First episode: Bill, a prospector, finds a spot likely to hold a gold pocket. He methodically makes tests, and decides that a pocket is probably present. Second episode: Bill carefully digs rows of holes, trying to trace the bits of gold to their origin. He becomes so excited over the rich possibilities that he sometimes forgets to eat, and also neglects to see whether anyone may be spying on him. Third episode: Bill forces himself to look for a possible spy; when he sees a faint hint of smoke, he is so eager to resume digging that he convinces himself it is only haze. Fourth episode: Bill, down in a hole seven feet deep, finds an unbelievably rich deposit of gold. But he senses a presence above him and does not know what to do. A bullet rips through his back. Fifth episode: The intruder, believing Bill dead, leaps into the hole. After a struggle, Bill seizes the gun and kills his unknown assailant. Emerging, he bandages his wound, gathers his gold, buries the other man, and starts back to civilization.
On the basis of this summary, identify the protagonist, his goal, and the three obstacles (one of them in Bill himself) that stand in his way. Then show how the episodes in the story are interwoven, each related to all the others.

2. Now choose another short story and summarize it in the same way, episode by episode. Once more, if possible, identify the protagonist, the goal, and the obstacles, and show how the episodes are interwoven. If the story happens to be one of the rare ones in which striving for a goal is not involved, try to describe the plot in whatever general terms are appropriate.

CONSTRUCTING A PLOT

Where does the idea for a plot originate? Sometimes in a person, an incident, a conflict, a theme, an emotional reaction. Sometimes in an overheard remark ("Jim is so *serious* about bridge"), something observed (a short airplane runway in a mountainous area), a scientific fact (dogs can hear sounds inaudible to people). Actually a plot may come from anywhere or anything. Given a small hint, a writer can elaborate it into a considerable structure. As author Eudora Welty has said, "A story can start with a bird song."

As an illustration, let us think in terms of the protagonist-obstacle-goal plot, which is followed in eighty or ninety per cent of published fiction. The ground rules for this kind of plot are rather simple. First, the protagonist must be an interesting person with whom many readers may identify either themselves or some of their acquaintances. Second, the goal must be a significant one that will provide enough motivation for the great exertions needed and that will arouse the sympathy and good wishes of the reader. (Many editors reject countless stories of what they call the I-want-a-dress variety, explaining that wanting a dress or its equivalent is not a sufficient goal.) Third, the obstacles must be formidable enough that either victory or defeat is possible. Fourth, a victory must be achieved mainly by the protagonist's own efforts, not handed to him by luck or the U.S. Marines; if the protagonist loses, his defeat must be at least partially due to a weakness in himself, a "tragic flaw," as Aristotle called it.

Perhaps the hint that starts our plot construction is a remark we happen to overhear in a crowded school corridor. A girl says, "He wants me to marry him the day after graduation." It occurs to us that many senior girls are debating the relative merits of early marriage and college or a job.

So we take a high school senior named Barbara Elton. She is sure she loves Bob Clifford, who wants to marry her right after their graduation. But her parents, although they have little money, want her to go to college, and she herself would be much interested in learning enough about dietetics to work in a hospital. Barbara's goal, then, is to resolve the conflict between Bob's wishes and her parents' wishes, a conflict heightened by the fact that she herself is inclined in both directions.

Now we must begin to add complications, intensifying the conflict, enlarging the obstacles. Bob, a poor boy, is offered a good enough job in a local factory so that he feels they can afford to rent an apartment as soon as they are married, and his prospects of promotion will be reasonably good. He admits that this will make impossible his hope of becoming a medical technician and working in that capacity with his uncle, but he is eager to sacrifice that hope in order to marry Barbara. Since Barbara had been worried about how they could live without being dependent upon their parents, Bob's job offer makes her more inclined to marry him.

Then Barbara is pulled the other way. Because of tests she has taken earlier, she is offered a scholarship to the University. This makes her parents very happy, but when she tells Bob, he becomes angry because she can even think of accepting. He refuses to talk over the subject rationally, and for the first time Barbara finds herself wondering whether he is really mature enough for marriage.

Barbara and Bob are invited to the wedding of two of their classmates who have not even waited for graduation. Seeing the radiantly happy bride, Barbara decides that marriage must indeed be wonderful, and on the way home that evening, she accepts Bob's proposal.

But when she gets home, her sister Clarice, three years older than Barbara, is there with her husband and her two small children. Clarice married just after high school. She is not unhappy, but Barbara thinks she looks old, and she notes that Clarice's world has narrowed to little more than Sam and the children. "I couldn't stand that," Barbara tells herself. Sam looks harassed and can talk of little except the high cost of living.

Barbara calls Bob's uncle and talks long and confidentially with him. When she meets Bob for their next date, she tells him first about Clarice and Sam. Then she says, "Your uncle is so eager to have you work with him in a few years that he will pay your tuition if you will go to the University. If we're really in love, we can wait at least a couple of years, and we can see each other often at the U. And if we both graduate, we'll be able to work close together after we're married." Half reluctantly but also half happily because of his unexpected chance to go to college, Bob agrees.

The plot we have outlined is not sensational or even unusual. But it provides a satisfactory framework for presenting the two young people and the problem they both face, even though only one of them clearly recognizes that a problem exists. It also offers a dramatization of a theme (early marriage) that increasingly occupies the attention of high school students today. The plot has less action than do the stories that depend heavily upon shootings, wild chases, and the like, but for that very reason it is more realistic than many stories are.

It is generally agreed that the number of plot patterns is limited. No other is nearly so often used as the protagonist-obstacle-goal variety. One variation is the Cinderella story, in which a poor and underprivileged person rises to a position of importance. Another plot shows why the protagonist changes his mind on a matter of importance; for instance, he comes to recognize the good qualities in a person or a group he has despised. Other plots, some of them very slight, you may discover in your reading, especially in quality magazines or volumes of prize stories.

If plotting seems difficult to you, here are three suggestions, each starting with a character:

1. Take a person—real, partly real, or imaginary—who in your opinion would be an interesting one to write about. Decide an important goal that this person might have.

Write down a number of obstacles that might prevent his reaching that goal, probably more obstacles than you would include in a story. Make the obstacles big enough that the person will have real trouble in overcoming them. Invent whatever other characters are necessary to dramatize the events. Decide how the protagonist finally succeeds or why he fails.

2. Once more start with an interesting character. Invent another character, unlike the first in one or more significant ways. Decide upon a conflict that would probably arise when the two characters get together, especially if both want the same thing. Solve the conflict.

3. This time you should put an interesting character into a setting that he finds unappealing or at least unfamiliar; for instance, an idealist in a money-mad society, a happy extroverted youth in the gloom-ridden home of his grandparents, or a criminal in a deeply religious family. Decide how you could dramatize and eventually resolve the conflicts that would result.

EXERCISE FOUR

1. Show that the story about Barbara follows the diagram of the protagonist-obstacle-goal plot on page 162. Show also that its episodes are interwoven in the way diagramed on page 163. Finally, show that it follows the "ground rules" given on page 166.

2. Because plotting causes beginning writers much trouble, here's a chance to practice. Choose several of the following story hints and work out possible plot summaries for them. Use your ingenuity and imagination. Invent any characters or incidents or anything else you need. You may find useful one or more of the three suggestions on this and the preceding page. Each summary should be a page or two in length. Compare your summaries with some of your classmates'.

    a. You should have seen the silly look on Harry's face.

    b. A long row of pay telephones; a rather well-dressed

man, methodically checking the coin-return box of each, and now and then finding a dime

c. A forgotten birthday

d. "The world is too much with us." (Wordsworth)

e. After the shot, there was a pause.

f. I don't really hate my little brother.

g. Every scientist is first of all a doubter.

h. ——————— Both these lines are the same length.

i. Never trust a woman's intuition.

j. Al would be a better player if he had more self-confidence.

k. We'll meet at the swimming pool at twelve.

l. _____ was the most unusual person I've ever known.

m. Daydreamers create for themselves a world more satisfying than the world of reality.

n. Competition is one of man's greatest incentives.

o. Emotions cause changes in pulse rate, blood pressure, breathing rate, brain waves, glandular activity, and digestive activity.

p. I began to wonder whether ghosts really do exist.

q. Each person's greatest need is to feel needed.

r. Ethnocentrism involves a looking down upon persons whose language, religion, and culture differ even slightly from one's own.

s. In that underwater world of unimaginable beauty, who would have supposed . . . ?

t. Sometimes the most handicapped persons are those without any apparent handicaps.

u. The greatest problem faced by some high school students is. . . .

v. How did that town get its name?

w. And in that moment he knew that he was a man.

x. Rugged individualists are lonely souls.

y. There, standing regally at the head of the stairs, was Grandmother!

WRITING AN EPISODE

Each story, as we have seen, is composed of a number of related episodes. An episode is not just an event. For instance, if a small boy steals a pocketknife from a dime-store counter, the act is an event but not an episode. However, if the members of his gang dare him to steal the knife and he fearfully accepts the dare, it is an episode; or if he debates within himself for a while and then takes the knife, it is an episode; or if a clerk sees the boy stealing and either talks with him or reports him, it is an episode. The difference is that an episode, unlike a mere event, is based on some kind of conflict. The series of episodes, then, is really a series of conflicts which contribute to the total conflict that is basic to the plot.

Let us go back to the story of Barbara and Bob (pages 166–168). As summarized, the story would probably consist of five episodes (which a playwright would call scenes). The first would start with Bob's elated telling of the news about his job offer. Since our story emphasizes Barbara, the conflict here is in Barbara, in her reaction to the news. Since she loves Bob, she is happy for him, but she cannot help having misgivings. First she tells him how wonderful the job sounds and how wonderful he is, but then she says, "But Bob, are you *sure* this is what you want? It will mean that you'll probably never be a medical technician, and your Uncle Glenn will be as unhappy as you about that." Further conflict may be unspoken, the conflict within Barbara herself. She wants to go to college and her parents want her to go. But despite her hesitation, she is so happy in Bob's happiness that she is inclined to marry him in June. Marriage wins the first round.

The second episode, in which the conflict is set off by

Barbara's winning a scholarship, is an open disagreement between Barbara and Bob. They quarrel, almost bitterly, and Barbara has serious doubts about the wisdom of marrying Bob. Marriage loses.

The third episode, the friends' wedding, loads the scales in favor of early marriage. Marriage wins. The fourth, showing Barbara's sister, loads the scales the other way. Marriage loses. The final episode brings all the elements of the conflict into focus, and adds a new development, the uncle's offer to pay Bob's tuition. Marriage loses, though maybe not permanently.

Each episodic conflict in a story results in victory, defeat, or no decision. It is possible to go through almost any short story or novel, see how the author has divided it into episodes, note what elements are in conflict in each, and keep a scorecard of the results. A frequent Western story pattern, for example, is bad guys win, bad guys win, bad guys win, good guys win.

The episode that begins the story, especially a short story, should ordinarily be one that occurs as late in time as possible. In the Barbara-Bob story, for instance, a first episode showing them starting to kindergarten together would probably not be appropriate. In fact, some writers would choose to start the story much later than we have suggested on page 171. They might confine themselves to two episodes, containing flashbacks and Barbara's unspoken thoughts as well as the external action. The first episode would be the wedding of the two classmates, with Barbara's confused reactions and her tying that event to her own life; the second would be the scene with Clarice and with Barbara's final decision based on that.

In developing an episode, a writer brings into play many of the things we have been considering in this book. Characterization, of course, is most important; each episode reveals new facets of the important characters. Setting is woven in as appropriate. Each episode makes its contribution to the underlying theme. Diction and imagery are important, as usual.

As an illustration of an episode, let us look at one possible treatment of the Clarice scene in the Barbara-Bob story. The version given here has been cut to its essentials; a professional treatment would put more meat on the bare bones.

When Bob stopped his car in front of her house, Barbara kissed him tenderly. "Oh, Bob, I'm so glad we went to the wedding and that it helped me to make up my mind. I'll try to make you happy, dear."

A little girl toddled out on the lighted front porch. "Oh, that must be Annette," Barbara said. "Clarice's little girl, you know. I haven't seen them for months—not since Billy was born. I'm getting old—an aunt twice now."

"Is that Sam's car?"

"Yes. Yes, it is. Sam was hoping he could get a new one, but I guess he couldn't afford it with the babies and all. . . . I'll have to go in and see them now, dear."

Clarice was holding Billy on her lap in the kitchen. Her cheeks were taut, and Barbara noticed dark half-moons under her eyes. "My goodness," Barbara thought. "She looks almost thirty, and she's only three years older than I am." Though bursting with her own news, she decided to wait and tell her parents when they were alone. She said the appropriate things about how cute Billy was (although he was crying at the top of his six-months-old voice) and about how Annette had grown. Annette was busily tearing apart her grandfather's half-smoked cigar—his only luxury—which she had found in an ashtray.

Clarice rescued the cigar from Annette, or vice versa, and resumed her conversation with her mother and Barbara. For half an hour she recounted Annette's numerous misadventures, Billy's teething troubles, Sam's failure to get a raise, the woes of leaking lavatories and monotonous meatloaf.

In a momentary lull Barbara tried to change the subject.

"Have you read *The Angel of Maywood*—you know, the book that everybody is talking about?" she asked.

"Gracious no!" Clarice exclaimed. "I do well if I find time to read the paper. And we haven't seen a show since before Billy was born. We watch TV, of course, sometimes. Mother, Billy did the cutest thing when we had the TV on last night. He. . . ."

Barbara fled. "I couldn't stand that," she said to herself. "Clarice doesn't seem to mind very much, but I couldn't stand to lose sight of all the rest of the world. This mustn't happen to Bob and me."

She joined her father and Sam in the living room. "Hi, Barb," Sam greeted her, and then went on talking. "Do you know what our grocery bill was last week? Twenty-eight dollars, including milk for the kids. And payments on the furniture and the old car run eighty a month, and the house a hundred and ten. Then there's insurance, and taxes, and gasoline, and doctor bills. I wanted a new suit, and Clarice ought to have some clothes, but there's always clothing and stuff to buy for the kids. The way prices are these days, a man's lucky just to keep his head above water, let alone save anything."

Barbara's father nodded in understanding sympathy, and it occurred to Barbara that she had often heard him talk in the same vein. It had all seemed unreal and unimportant to her before, but now she translated everything she was hearing into terms of Bob and herself. Was this what marriage would be like for them? Would she and Bob become prematurely old, burdened forever with debt, fighting each week the same fight against poverty that her parents and now Sam and Clarice were engaged in? Would it be fair to Bob? Was this the necessary lot of most of mankind? The pursuit of happiness—did that mean just the pursuit of a few dollars to pay the checkout girl at the supermarket?

She excused herself and went to her room to think.

Note that the conflict in this episode is internal, within the protagonist, whereas in others it might be between persons, or between a person and a physical force such as a hurricane or a river. Internal conflict is often less obviously dramatic, but no less real. Here we have Barbara, newly engaged, just come from seeing the happy bride at a wedding, but now seeing the aftermath of another such wedding, a bleak contrast to the dreams of almost every bride. The episode grows naturally from what has preceded it and is related to everything else in the story. It deepens the reader's understanding of Barbara's character, provides hints of her early years, and suggests obliquely the integrity of her family and her own essential seriousness and increasing maturity.

EXERCISE FIVE

1. Choose a short story from a popular magazine. Decide where each episode begins and ends. Answer these questions about each:
   - a. Is there a conflict? Between whom or what?
   - b. How is the conflict portrayed? Through action, conversation, thoughts, or a combination of these?
   - c. Does the conflict result in a victory or no decision?
   - d. How is the episode related to the others?
   - e. What information does it provide about the chief character or characters?

2. In Exercise Four you were asked to write some brief plot summaries. Choose one of the plots and decide upon one episode that should be included. Write that episode.

THE USE OF FLASHBACKS

Suppose that a story you are writing concerns events of the year 1967 and the year 1964, and that to understand what happens in 1967 the reader must know about 1964. Three narrative procedures are possible.

1. *Straight-line narrative.* In the straight-line narrative, everything essential is related in chronological order. Using this plan, you will tell what happened in 1964, make a transition, and then tell what happened in 1967. The advantage of this technique is that it is orderly and unconfusing. The disadvantage, at least sometimes, is that the

story seems to divide into two (or more) distinct parts; it lacks the focus, the singleness of effect, that it might have if it were told entirely from the vantage point of 1967.

2. *Block flashback.* Instead of beginning with 1964, you may start with 1967, introduce your characters and their problem, get the reader interested, hint that there is something in the past that will help in the understanding of the 1967 incidents, and then go back to 1964 and show in a single block (a paragraph or several or many paragraphs) what happened then. The block flashback is no recent invention; such writers as Homer and Milton in their great epics used the trick of beginning *in medias res* (in the middle of things) and then using a block flashback to fill in, and movie makers have used it extensively. Its advantages are that it permits starting the story near the climax, it quickly reveals what problem is to be solved and by whom, it subordinates the background material, and it may help in attaining singleness of effect. Its weakness is that it interrupts the story for a considerable length of time; if the flashback is not handled skilfully, with much interest and even suspense in its own right, the reader may get tired of waiting for the main thread of the story to be resumed.

3. *Scattered flashback.* With the scattered flashback, you will again start with 1967 and get the story off to a good beginning. However, instead of interrupting the story with a block flashback, you will insert very briefly and inconspicuously whatever the reader should know about 1964. A character may say, for instance, "But that's not the way you felt three years ago. At that time you. . . ." Or a character's thoughts may recall quickly a significant event of the past. Or the author may say in his own person, "When they had first moved to Granvilla in 1964, . . ." The point is that the scattered flashback is distributed where needed throughout the story. The technique has the advantages of both the straight-line narrative and the block

flashback; if handled well, it lacks the disadvantages of both. There is a disadvantage, however: the scattered flashback is harder to write than the block. The unskilled writer may forget to include some essentials, or he may drag in the past at awkward times.

EXERCISE SIX

1. A member of the class may report on Edna Ferber's extensive use of block flashbacks in her novel *Ice Palace*, or on the types of flashbacks he has observed in any other novel he has recently read.

2. Each member of the class should examine a different short story, from any source, to discover whether the author has followed a pure straight-line narrative technique or used block or scattered flashbacks. Each should report to the class, cutting the plot summary to just a few sentences, and indicating the technique used. Especially good illustrations of the scattered flashback may be read.

11

Writing the Short Story

SINCE the writing of short stories involves skill in presenting theme, characters, setting, and plot, this chapter pre-
supposes study of Chapters 1, 9, and 10. A review of Chapters 2 and 3 will also be useful.

BACKGROUND

Although it is customary to say that Poe originated the
short story a little over a century ago, its beginnings are
actually lost in the past. The creator of the short story was
the first man or woman who, for whatever purpose, first
narrated a brief series of related fictitious events and took
artistic pride in the telling. The minstrels of long ago often
told or sang what were actually versified short stories. The
Italian Boccaccio's *Decameron*, written over six hundred
years ago, consists of a hundred tales, many of which correspond rather closely to the modern definition of the short
story. If Chaucer, Boccaccio's English contemporary, had
written his *Canterbury Tales* in prose, some of them would
likewise be classed as short stories.

But Edgar Allan Poe, both in his own stories and in his
commentary on the *Tales* of Nathaniel Hawthorne, did
more than anyone else to give specific form to the short
story. His "rules" are now regarded as too narrow, but
their influence is still strong. Here is the heart of Poe's
explanation of what a short story should be and do:

A skilful literary artist has constructed a tale. If wise, he
has not fashioned his thoughts to accommodate his incidents;
178

but having conceived, with deliberate care, a certain unique or single *effect* to be wrought out, he then invents such incidents— he then combines such events as may best aid him in establishing this preconceived effect. If his very initial sentence tend not to the outbringing of this effect, then he has failed in his first step. In the whole composition there should be no word written, of which the tendency, direct or indirect, is not to the one preëstablished design. And by such means, with such care and skill, a picture is at length painted which leaves in the mind of him who contemplates it with a kindred art, a sense of the fullest satisfaction. The idea of the tale has been presented unblemished, because undisturbed; and this is an end unattainable by the novel. Undue brevity is just as exceptionable here as in the poem, but undue length is yet more to be avoided.

Poe's stories were widely imitated almost immediately in America and especially in France, and to a less extent in Great Britain and elsewhere. His theory of construction was less known than his stories. By 1885, however, it had become familiar enough that a then-famous professor, Brander Matthews, ventured to reduce it to this simple formula:

A short story deals with a single character, a single event, a single emotion, or the series of emotions called forth by a single situation.

The uncomplicated tales of Poe, Hawthorne, Bret Harte, and their many imitators began undergoing some changes, though, in the latter part of the nineteenth century and the early twentieth. Under the leadership of such writers as the French Guy de Maupassant, the English Rudyard Kipling, and the American O. Henry, more plot entered. The plot was usually carefully woven, with the loose ends snipped off, but there was more emphasis on action and variety than in the Poe story, even though some unity of effect usually remained. O. Henry in particular liked to build his plots toward a "surprise ending" that yet seemed real and inevitable.

From about 1910 to about 1940 the popular short stories, such as appeared in the widely circulated magazines,
tended to stress plot, as indeed they still do. But the more
artistic ones of this period had little plot and much characterization. Many of them were in effect psychological studies, showing a character during an especially significant
moment or moments of his life. Some highly experimental
stories were comparable to abstract paintings, with a design and an impact that could be perceived only with the
most careful scrutiny.

Today's short stories refuse to fit into any formula. Many
magazines, it is true, print nothing but action stories
based on the protagonist-(physical) obstacle-goal pattern described in Chapter 10. The more literary magazines have
been tending toward blends of plot, theme, setting, and
characterization, with the emphasis most often still on character, but less so than in the often plotless psychological
studies of some years ago.

Just before World War II William Saroyan put into
words what many of the artistic short story writers have
been attempting to do since that time:

Think of America, I told myself this morning. The whole
thing. The cities, all the houses, all the people, the coming and
going, the coming of children, the going of them, the coming
and going of men and death, and life, the movement, the talk,
the sound of machinery, the oratory, think of the pain in
America and the fear and the deep inward longing of all things
alive in America. Remember the great machines, wheels turning,
smoke and fire, the mines and the men working them, the
noise, the confusion. Remember the newspapers and the moving
picture theatres and everything that is a part of this life. Let this
be your purpose: to suggest this great country.

Then turn to the specific. Go out to some single person and
dwell with him, within him, lovingly, seeking to understand
the miracle of his being, and utter the truth of his existence and
reveal the splendor of the mere fact of his being alive, and
say it in great prose, simply, show that he is of the time, of the

machines and the fire and smoke, the newspapers and the noise. Go with him to his secret and speak of it gently, showing that it is the secret of man. Do not deceive. Do not make up lies for the sake of pleasing anyone. No one need be killed in your story. Simply relate what is the great event of all history, of all time, the humble, artless truth of mere being. There is no greater theme: No one need be violent to help you with your art. There *is* violence. Mention it of course when it is time to mention it. Mention the war. Mention all ugliness, all waste. Do even this lovingly. But emphasize the glorious truth of mere being. It is the major theme. You do not have to create a triumphant climax. The man you write of need not perform some heroic or monstrous deed in order to make your prose great. Let him do what he has always done, day in and day out, continuing to live. Let him walk and talk and think and sleep and dream and awaken and walk again and talk again and move and be alive. It is enough. There is nothing else to write about. You have never seen a short story in life. The events of life have never fallen into the form of the short story or the form of the poem, or into any other form. Your own consciousness is the only form you need. Your own awareness is the only action you need. Speak of this man, recognize his existence. Speak of man.

EXERCISE ONE

1. Reread carefully the quotation from Poe (page 178). Discuss the meaning of each sentence, restating it in different words and providing any illustrations that occur to you.

2. From your recollection of any story by Poe, or from rereading one or more, try to decide what single effect he tried to create in each story.

3. Recall Poe's insistence that the opening sentence of a story is of great importance. Some later writers (though by no means all) have interpreted this to mean that if the story is mainly a character study, the opening should show something significant about the character; if it is a story developing a theme, the opening should suggest the theme; and so on. Here

are the openings of three such stories. What do you suppose
the author of each stressed in the story?

a. There is a belief that woman's beauty is a power which
captures man unfailingly. And certain it is that beauty is a net
for ensnaring his eyes. But there are other invisible qualities
which catch and hold a man's heart. One of these is gallantry
in women.   (Lois S. Montross, "A Day in New York")

b. It wasn't about anything, something about making
punch, and then we started fighting and I slipped and he had
me down kneeling on my chest and choking me with both hands
like he was trying to kill me and all the time I was trying to get
the knife out of my pocket to cut him loose.

(Ernest Hemingway, "After the Storm")

c. "You ought to change your clothes, Pa."

"What you in such a hurry to get my clothes changed
for?"

"Well, you want to be ready when George comes in,
don't you?"

"Aw, he won't get in today. How can he get the car
through all this snow?"

"He will, too. Didn't they invite us out there?"

(Ruth Suckow, "Golden Wedding")

4. Reread the two paragraphs by Saroyan (page 180). Compare them with this statement by the nineteenth-century Russian writer Anton Chekhov: "Why write about a man getting
into a submarine and going to the North Pole to reconcile himself to the world, while his beloved at that moment throws herself with a hysterical shriek from the belfry? All this is untrue
and does not happen in real life. One must write about simple
things: how Peter Semionovich married Marie Ivanovna. That
is all."

5. Saroyan has been called a sentimentalist. Which sentences
in the two quoted paragraphs suggest that he may be sentimental or anyhow optimistic? How might a pessimistic writer
have expressed Saroyan's basic ideas?

6. You will soon begin the writing of a short story. What
have you learned so far in this chapter that can be helpful?

THE FLEXIBILITY OF THE MODERN STORY

Robert Louis Stevenson once told his biographer, Graham Balfour:

"There are, so far as I know, three ways, and three ways only, of writing a story. You may take a plot and fit characters to it, or you may take a character and choose incidents and situations to develop it, or lastly . . . you may take a certain atmosphere and get action and persons to express it and realize it. I'll give you an example— 'The Merry Men.' There I began with the feeling of one of those islands on the west coast of Scotland, and I gradually developed the story to express the sentiment with which the coast affected me."

Stevenson might have mentioned a fourth way of writing a story, starting with a theme (an idea to be dramatized) and finding the persons, setting, and plot to illustrate it. He perhaps omitted theme on the ground that a story of any of the other three types would necessarily have a basic theme.

Modern short story writers generally agree with Stevenson's classification, though some do add theme as a fourth and distinct starting place. They agree also with the major part of Poe's dictum—that a short story should have singleness of purpose and singleness of effect. But some of them have been able to demonstrate that these limitations may be observed in stories that are somewhat longer and more complicated than Poe believed. They sometimes introduce turns and convolutions of plot that would have distressed him. Some of the most dexterous of them weave plot, character, setting, and theme into a unified whole, instead of choosing one for special emphasis as Stevenson believed necessary.

In other words, modern writers are showing the short story to be a highly flexible literary form. They accept certain rules, as baseball players do, but within the framework of those rules infinite variety is possible, just as no two baseball games are exactly alike.

The analogy with baseball soon breaks, though, for the persons who appear in short stories are much more varied than are those likely to be found on the diamond, and many more things may happen to them, in a much greater assortment of places, and with more varied significance.

Another analogy might be between the short story writer and a movie photographer who was permitted to go wherever he wished, capturing on sound film the record of the troubles, joys, and passions of mankind. The photographer can picture events, catch fleeting facial expressions, and observe and perpetuate love, hate, kindness, cruelty, victory, defeat, the deflation of the pompous, and the elevation of the meek. Through judicious cutting and rearranging and splicing the photographer can recount a compelling tale.

This analogy breaks, too, though, for the photographer necessarily deals with externals, with the picturable. He can only suggest the internal, the thoughts and emotions that make each person what he is. The writer, however, can go deep inside to the wellsprings of the individual, can account for every act and for every other external symbol.

We have noted in Chapter 10 that most stories follow the same protagonist-obstacle-goal plot. Even within that apparently rigid pattern, though, there is so much variety in persons, in obstacles, and in goals that most readers are not aware of the basic similarity.

Artists in the short story form, even though they may often follow the protagonist-obstacle-goal plan, know of limitless possibilities both within and outside that framework. They know, for instance, that they can do such things as these:

1. Show a character in a time of high emotional stress, revealing him through his reactions to it;

2. Show the influence of an environment upon a person; conversely, "characterize" a place through a look at its inhabitants;

3. Reveal in dramatic form any personal belief or theory of the author;

4. Show a character's growth in his understanding of himself or others;

5. Portray the too-late moment when a person realizes that he has dreamed the wrong dream, lived the wrong life;

6. Show an "epiphany," as James Joyce called it, a moment of revelation that signals a major change in a character;

7. Show a rebellion against the customary;

8. Reveal the drama in the commonplace.

EXERCISE TWO

1. "You may take a plot and fit characters to it," said Stevenson. Here is the skeleton of a simple plot: A boy (or girl) lies about his father's occupation because of shame. The lie is discovered, first by those who were told it, then by the father. The boy (or girl) attains a degree of maturity because of the incident.

Discuss how characters could be fitted into this plot, what they should (or might) be like, what their motives would be, which character would be stressed and why, what their various reactions would be, how the incident would help to mature the boy or girl.

2. "You may take a character and choose incidents and situations to develop it," according to Stevenson. Here is a suggestion for a character: A student has earned a reputation as the class clown. He is actually rather introverted, serious, studious.

What "incidents and situations" might develop this character in a somewhat dramatic fashion?

3. "You may take a certain atmosphere and get actions and persons to express it and realize it," Stevenson said. Here are two suggestions of such an atmosphere: (a) A tenement house in a large city, with crumbling plaster, dilapidated furniture, rats scurrying insolently about, an alley for the children's playground; (b) A run-down farm, without electricity, with poor soil and undernourished livestock.

Choose either (a) or (b) and "get actions and persons to express it and realize it."

4. At this time you should begin the planning and writing of a short story of your own. You may already have an idea for one. If not, the suggestions of Stevenson (page 183), of Saroyan (page 180), or of Poe (page 178) may help, or perhaps one of those listed on page 185 or a hint in one of the exercises in Chapter 1 or 10. If you wish, you may use the familiar protagonist-obstacle-goal plot, but do not feel obligated to do so.

A LOOK AT TWO STORIES

It may be helpful to you in your writing of a story to examine independently the structure of several stories of the protagonist-obstacle-goal variety that you are likely to find in almost any popular magazine that carries fiction. For comparison and contrast, you may also want to look at some "quality" fiction in such a magazine as *Harper's* or the *Atlantic Monthly*. It may be revealing too to note the structure of some stories in cheap Westerns, love magazines, or the more sensational variety of science fiction; you are likely to find that these stories contain more action, more episodes, and shallower characterization than the others.

The first of two stories we shall now examine is by MacKinlay Kantor, author of such best-selling books as *The Voice of Bugle Ann* and *Andersonville,* and a winner of the Pulitzer Prize for fiction. "That Greek Dog" was first published in the *Saturday Evening Post* in 1941.

That Greek Dog

by MacKinlay Kantor

In those first years after the first World War, Bill Barbilis could still get into his uniform; he was ornate and handsome when he wore it. Bill's left sleeve, reading down from the shoulder, had patches and patterns of color to catch any eye. At the top there was an arc—bent stripes of scarlet, yellow and purple; next came a single red chevron with the apex pointing up; and at the cuff were three gold chevrons pointing the other way.

On his right cuff was another gold chevron, only slightly corroded. And we must not forget those triple chevrons on an olive-drab field which grew halfway up the sleeve.

People militarily sophisticated, there in Mahaska Falls, could recognize immediately that Mr. Basilio Barbilis had been a sergeant, that he had served with the Forty-second Division, that he had been once wounded, that he had sojourned overseas for at least eighteen months, and that he had been discharged with honor.

His khaki blouse, however, was worn only on days of patriotic importance. The coat he donned at other times was white —white, that is, until cherry sirup and caramel speckled it. Mr. Barbilis was owner, manager, and staff of the Sugar Bowl.

He had a soda fountain with the most glittering spigots in town. He had a bank of candy cases, a machine for toasting sandwiches, ten small tables complete with steel-backed chairs, and a ceiling festooned with leaves of gilt and bronze paper.

Beginning in 1920, he had also a peculiar dog. Bill's living quarters were in the rear of the Sugar Bowl, and the dog came bleating and shivering to the Barbilis door one March night. The dog was no larger than a quart of ice cream and, Bill said, just as cold.

My medical office and apartment were directly over the Sugar Bowl. I made the foundling's acquaintance the next day, when I stopped in for a cup of chocolate. Bill had the dog bedded in a candy carton behind the fountain; he was heating milk when I came in, and wouldn't fix my chocolate until his new pet was fed.

Bill swore that it was a puppy. I wasn't so certain. It looked something like a mud turtle wearing furs.

"I think he is hunting dog," said Bill, with pride. "He was cold last night, but not so cold now. Look, I make him nice warm bed. I got my old pajamas for him to lie on."

He waited upon the sniffling little beast with more tender consideration than ever he showed to any customer. Some people say that Greeks are mercenary. I don't know. That puppy wasn't paying board.

The dog grew up, burly and quizzical. Bill named him Duboko. It sounded like that; I don't know how to spell the name correctly, nor did anyone else in Mahaska Falls.

The word, Bill said, was slang. It meant "tough" or "hard-boiled." This animal had the face of a clown and the body of a hyena. Growing up, his downy coat changed to wire and bristles. Duboko resembled a fat Hamburg steak with onions which had been left too long on the griddle.

At an early age Duboko began to manifest a violent interest in community assemblage of any kind or color. This trait may have been fostered by his master, who was proud to be a Moose, an Odd Fellow, a Woodman, and an upstanding member of the Mahaska Falls Commercial League.

When we needed the services of a bugler in our newly formed American Legion post and no bona fide bugler would volunteer, Bill Barbilis agreed to purchase the best brass instrument available and to practice in the bleak and cindery space behind his store. Since my office was upstairs, I found no great satisfaction in Bill's musical enterprise. It happened that Duboko also lent his voice in support; a Greek chorus, so to speak, complete with strophe and antistrophe.

Nevertheless, I could register no complaint, since with other members of the Legion I had voted to retain Bill as our bugler. I could not even kick Duboko downstairs with my one good leg when I discovered him in my reception room lunching off my mail.

Indeed, most people found it hard to punish Duboko. He had the ingratiating, hopeful confidence of an immigrant just off the boat and assured that he had found the Promised Land. He boasted beady eyes, lubberly crooked paws, an immense mouth formed of black rubber, and pearly and enormous fangs which he was fond of exhibiting in a kind of senseless leer. He smelled, too. This characteristic I called sharply to the attention of his master, with the result that Duboko was laundered weekly in Bill's uncertain little bathtub, the process being marked by vocal lament which might have arisen from the gloomiest passage of the Antigone.

Mahaska Falls soon became aware of the creature, in a general municipal sense, and learned that it had him to reckon with. Duboko attended every gathering at which six or more people were in congregation. No fire, picnic, memorial service, Rotary conclave or public chicken-pie supper went ungraced by his presence.

If, as sometimes happened on a crowded Saturday night, a pedestrian was brushed by a car, Duboko was on the scene with a speed that put the insurance-company representatives to shame. If there was a lodge meeting which he did not visit and from which he was not noisily ejected, I never heard of it. At Commercial League dinners he lay pensive with his head beneath the chair of Bill Barbilis. But, suffering fewer inhibitions than his master, he also visited funerals, and even the marriage of Miss Glaydys Stumpf.

Old Charles P. Stumpf owned the sieve factory. He was the richest man in town; the nuptials of his daughter exuded an especial aura of social magnificence. It is a matter of historical record that Duboko sampled the creamed chicken before any of the guests did; he was banished only after the striped and rented trousers of two ushers had undergone renting in quite another sense of the word. Grieved, Duboko forswore the Stumpfs after that; he refused to attend a reception for the bride and bridegroom when they returned from the Wisconsin Dells two weeks later.

There was one other place in town where Duboko was decidedly *persona non grata*. This was a business house, a rival establishment of the Sugar Bowl, owned and operated by Earl and John Klugge. The All-American Kandy Kitchen, they called it.

The Brothers Klugge held forth at a corner location a block distant from the Sugar Bowl. Here lounged and tittered ill-favored representatives of the town's citizenry; dice rattled on a soiled mat at the cigar counter; it was whispered that refreshment other than soda could be purchased by the chosen.

The business career of Earl and John Klugge did not flourish, no matter what inducement they offered their customers. Loudly they declared that their failure to enrich themselves was due solely to the presence in our community of a Greek—a black-haired, dark-skinned Mediterranean who thought nothing of resorting to the most unfair business practices, such as serving good fudge sundaes, for instance, to anyone who would buy them.

One fine afternoon people along the main street were troubled at observing Duboko limp rapidly westward, fairly wreathed in howls. Bill called me down to examine the dog. Duboko was only bruised, although at first I feared that his ribs were smashed on one side. Possibly someone had thrown a heavy chair at him. Bill journeyed to the Clive Street corner with fire in his eye. But no one could be found who would admit to seeing an attack on Duboko; no one would even say for a certainty that Duboko had issued from the doorway of the All-American Kandy Kitchen although circumstantial evidence seemed to suggest it.

Friends dissuaded Bill Barbilis from invading the precinct of his enemies, and at length he was placated by a pleasant fiction about a kicking horse in the market square.

We all observed, however, that Duboko did not call at the Kandy Kitchen again, not even on rare nights when the dice rattled loudly and when the whoops and catcalls of customers caused girls to pass by, like pretty Levites, on the other side.

There might have been a different tale to tell if this assault had come later, when Duboko was fully grown. His frame stretched and extended steadily for a year; it became almost as mighty as the earnest Americanism of his master. He was never vicious. He was never known to bite a child. But frequently his defensive attitude was that of a mother cat who fancies her kitten in danger; Duboko's hypothetical kitten was his right to be present when good fellows—or bad—got together.

Pool halls knew him; so did the Epworth League. At football games an extra linesman was appointed for the sole purpose of discouraging Duboko's athletic ardor. Through some occult sense, he could become aware of an approaching festivity before even the vanguard assembled. Musicians of our brass band never lugged their instruments to the old bandstand in Courthouse Park without finding Duboko there before them, lounging in an attitude of expectancy. It was Wednesday night, it was eight o'clock, it was July; the veriest dullard might know at what hour and place the band would begin its attack on the Light Cavalry Overture.

Duboko's taste in music was catholic and extensive. He made a fortuitous appearance at a spring musicale, presented by the high-school orchestra and glee clubs, before an audience which sat in the righteous hush of people grimly determined to serve the arts, if only for a night.

The boys' glee club was rendering selections from Carmen— in English, of course—and dramatically they announced the appearance of the bull. The line goes, "Now the beast enters, wild and enraged," or something like that; Duboko chose this moment to lope grandly down the center aisle on castanetting toenails. He sprang to the platform. . . . Mahaska Falls wiped away more tears than did Mérimée's heroine.

In his adult stage, Duboko weighed forty pounds. His color suggested peanut brittle drenched with chocolate; I have heard people swear that his ears were four feet long, but that is an exaggeration. Often those ears hung like limp brown drawers dangling from a clothesline; again they were braced rigidly atop his skull.

Mastiff he was, and also German shepherd, with a noticeable influence of English bull, bloodhound, and great Dane. Far and wide he was known as "that Greek dog," and not alone because he operated out of the Sugar Bowl and under the aegis of Bill Barbilis. Duboko looked like a Greek.

He had Greek eyes, Greek eyebrows, and a grinning Greek mouth. Old Mayor Wingate proclaimed in his cups that, in fact, he had heard Duboko bark in Greek; he was willing to demonstrate, if anyone would only catch Duboko by sprinkling a little Attic salt on his tail.

That Greek dog seldom slept at night; he preferred to accompany the town's watchman on his rounds, or to sit in the window of the Sugar Bowl along with cardboard ladies who brandished aloft their cardboard sodas. Sometimes, when I had been called out in the middle of the night and came back from seeing a patient, I would stop and peer through the window and exchange a few signals with Duboko.

"Yes," he seemed to say, "I'm here. Bill forgot and locked me in. I don't mind, unless, of course, there's a fire. See you at Legion meeting tomorrow night, if not at the County Medical Association luncheon tomorrow noon."

At this time there was a new arrival in the Sugar Bowl household—Bill's own father, recruited all the way from Greece, now that Bill's mother was dead.

Spiros Barbilis was slight, silver-headed, round-shouldered, with drooping mustachios which always seemed oozing with black dye. Bill put up another cot in the back room and bought another chiffonier from the second-hand store. He and Duboko escorted the old man up and down Main Street throughout the better part of one forenoon.

"I want you to meet friend of mine," Bill said. "He is my father, but he don't speak no English. I want him to meet all my good friends here in Mahaska Falls, because he will live here always."

Old Mr. Barbilis grew deft at helping Bill with the Sugar Bowl. He carried trays and managed tables, grinning inveterately, wearing an apron stiff with starch. But he failed to learn much English except "hello" and "good-by" and a few cuss words; I think that he was lonely for the land he had left, which certainly Bill was not.

One night—it was two o'clock in the morning—I came back to climb my stairs, stepping carefully from my car to the icy sidewalk in front of the Sugar Bowl. I moved gingerly, because I had left one foot in the Toul sector when a dressing station was shelled; I did not like icy sidewalks.

This night I put my face close to the show window to greet Duboko, to meet those sly and mournful eyes which, on a bitter night, would certainly be waiting there instead of shining in a drifted alley where the watchman prowled.

Two pairs of solemn eyes confronted me when I looked in. Old Mr. Barbilis sat there, too—in his nightclothes, but blanketed with an overcoat—he and Duboko, wrapped together among the jars of colored candy and the tinted cardboard girls. They stared out, aloof and dignified in the darkness, musing on a thousand lives that slept nearby. I enjoy imagining that they both loved the street, even in its midnight desertion, though doubtless Duboko loved it the more.

In 1923 we were treated to a mystifying phenomenon. There had never been a riot in Mahaska Falls, nor any conflict between racial and religious groups. Actually we had no racial or religious groups; we were all Americans, or thought we were. But, suddenly and amazingly, fiery crosses flared in the darkness of our pasture lands.

I was invited to attend a meeting and did so eagerly, wondering if I might explore this outlandish nonsense in a single evening. When my car stopped at a cornfield gate and ghostly figures came to admit me, I heard voice after voice whispering bashfully, "Hello, doc," "Evening, doc. Glad you came." I was shocked at recognizing the voices. I had known the fathers and grandfathers of these youths—hard-working farmers they were, who found a long-sought freedom on the American prairies, and never fumed about the presence of the hard-working Catholics, Jews, and black men who were also members of that pioneer community.

There was one public meeting in the town itself. They never tried to hold another; there was too much objection; the voice of Bill Barbilis rang beneath the stars.

A speaker with a pimply face stood illuminated by the flare of gasoline torches on a makeshift rostrum, and dramatically he spread a dollar bill between his hands. "Here," he cried, "is the flag of the Jews!"

Bill Barbilis spoke sharply from the crowd: "Be careful, mister. There is United States seal on that bill."

In discomfiture, the speaker put away his bank note. He ignored Bill as long as he could. He set his own private eagles to screaming, and he talked of battles won, and he wept for the mothers of American boys who lay in France. He said that patriotic 100-per-cent Americans must honor and protect those mothers.

Bill Barbilis climbed to the fender of a car. "Sure," he agreed clearly, "we got to take care of those mothers! Also, other mothers we got to take care of—Catholic mothers, Greek mothers, Jew mothers. We got the mothers of Company C, One Hundred Sixty-eighth Infantry. We got to take care of them. How about Jimmy Clancy? He was Catholic. He got killed in the Lorraine sector. Hyman Levinsky, he got killed the same day. Mr. Speaker, you don't know him because you do not come from Mahaska Falls. We had Buzz Griffin, colored boy used to shine shoes. He go to Chicago and enlist, and he is wounded in the Ninety-second Division!"

It was asking too much for any public speaker to contend against opposition of that sort; and the crowd thought so, too, and Duboko made a joyful noise. The out-of-town organizers withdrew. Fiery crosses blazed less frequently, and the flash of white robes frightened fewer cattle week by week.

Seeds had been sown, however, and now a kind of poison ivy grew within our midnight. Bill Barbilis and Duboko came up to my office one morning, the latter looking annoyed, the former holding a soiled sheet of paper in his hand. "Look what I got, doc."

The message was printed crudely in red ink:

We don't want you here any more. This town is only for 100 per cent law-abiding white Americans. Get out of town! Anti-Greek League.

It had been shoved under the front door of the Sugar Bowl sometime during the previous night.

"Bill," I told him, "don't worry about it. You know the source, probably; at least you can guess."

"Nobody is going to run me out of town," said Bill. "This is my town, and I am American citizen, and I am bugler in American Legion. I bring my old father here from Greece to be American, too, and now he has first papers." His voice trembled slightly.

"Here. Throw it in the wastepaper basket and forget about it."

There was sweat on his forehead. He wiped his face, and then he was able to laugh. "Doc, I guess you are right. Doc, I guess I am a fool."

He threw the paper away and squared his shoulders and went downstairs. I rescued a rubber glove from Duboko and threw Duboko into the hall, where he licked disinfectant from his jaws and leered at me through the screen.

A second threatening letter was shoved under Bill's door, but after that old Mr. Spiros Barbilis and Duboko did sentry duty, and pedestrians could see them entrenched behind the window. So the third warning came by mail; it told Bill that he was being given twenty-four hours to get out of town for good.

I was a little perturbed when I found Bill loading an Army .45 behind his soda fountain.

"They come around here," he said, "and I blow hell out of them."

He laughed when he said it, but I didn't like the brightness of his eyes, nor the steady, thrice-assured activity of his big clean fingers.

On Friday morning Bill came up to my office again; his face was distressed. But my fears, so far as the Anti-Greeks were concerned, were groundless.

"Do you die," he asked, "when you catch a crisis of pneumonia?"

It was one of his numerous cousins, in Sioux Falls. There had been a long-distance telephone call; the cousin was very ill, and the family wanted Bill to come. Bill left promptly in his battered, rakish roadster.

Late that night I was awakened by a clatter of cream cans under my window. I glanced at the illuminated dial of my watch, and lay wondering why the milkman had appeared some two hours before his habit. I was about to drop off to sleep when sounds of a scuffle in the alley and a roar from Duboko in the Barbilis quarters took me to the window in one leap.

There were four white figures down there in the alley yard; they dragged a fifth man—nightshirted, gagged, struggling—along with them. I yelled, and pawed around for my glasses, spurred to action by the reverberating hysterics of Duboko. I got the glasses on just before those men dragged old Mr. Barbilis into their car. The car's license plates were plastered thick with mud; at once I knew what had happened.

It was customary for the milkman to clank his bottles and

cans on approaching the rear door of the Sugar Bowl; Bill or his
father would get out of bed and fetch the milk to the refrig-
erator, for there were numerous cream-hungry cats along the
alley. It was a clinking summons of this sort which had lured
the lonely Mr. Barbilis from his bed.

He had gone out sleepily, probably wondering, as I had
wondered, why the milkman had come so early. The sound of
milk bottles lulled Duboko for a moment.

Then the muffled agony of that struggle, when the visitors
clapped a pillow over the old man's face, had been enough to
set Duboko bellowing.

But he was shut in; all that he could do was to threaten and
curse and hurl himself against the screen. I grabbed for my
foot—not the one that God gave me, but the one bought by
Uncle Sam—and of course I kicked it under the bed far out of
reach.

My car was parked at the opposite end of the building, out
in front. I paused only to tear the telephone receiver from its
hook and cry to a surprised Central that she must turn on the
red light which summoned the night watchman; that someone
was kidnaping old Mr. Barbilis.

The kidnaper's car roared eastward down the alley while I
was bawling to the operator. And then another sound—the
wrench of a heavy body sundering the metal screening. There
was only empty silence as I stumbled down the stairway in my
pajamas, bouncing on one foot and holding to the stair rails.

I fell into my car and turned on the headlights. The eastern
block before me stretched deserted in the pale glow of single
bulbs on each electric-light post. But as my car rushed into
that deserted block, a small brown shape sped bulletlike across
the next intersection. It was Duboko.

I swung right at the corner, and Duboko was not far ahead
of me now. Down the dark, empty tunnel of Clive Street the red
taillight of another car diminished rapidly. It hitched away to
the left; that would mean that Mr. Barbilis was being carried
along the road that crossed the city dump.

Slowing down, I howled at Duboko when I came abreast of
him. It seemed that he was a Barbilis, an Americanized Greek,

like them, and that he must be outraged at this occurrence, and eager to effect a rescue.

But he only slobbered up at me, and labored along on his four driving legs, with spume flying behind. I stepped on the gas again and almost struck the dog, for he would not turn out of the road. I skidded through heavy dust on the dump lane, with filmier dust still billowing back from the kidnapers' car.

For their purpose, the selection of the dump had a strategic excuse as well as a symbolic one. At the nearest boundary of the area there was a big steel gate and barbed-wire fence; you had to get out and open that gate to go through. But if you wished to vanish into the region of river timber and country roads beyond, you could drive across wasteland without opening the gate again. I suppose that the kidnapers guessed who their pursuer was; they knew of my physical incapacity. They had shut the gate carefully behind them, and I could not go through it without getting out of my car.

But I could see them in the glare of my headlights—four white figures, sheeted and hooded.

Already they had tied Spiros Barbilis to the middle of a fence panel. They had straps, and a whip, and everything else they needed. One man was tying the feet of old Spiros to restrain his kicks; two stood ready to proceed with the flogging; and the fourth blank, hideous, white-hooded creature moved toward the gate to restrain me from interfering. That was the situation when Duboko arrived.

I ponder now the various wickednesses Duboko committed throughout his notorious career. Then for comfort I turn to the words of a Greek—him who preached the most famous funeral oration chanted among the ancients—the words of a man who was Greek in his blood and his pride, and yet who might have honored Duboko eagerly when the dog came seeking, as it were, a kind of sentimental Attican naturalization.

"For even when life's previous record showed faults and failures," said Pericles, with the voice of Thucydides, to the citizens of the fifth century, "it is just to weigh the last brave hour of devotion against them all."

Though it was not an hour by any means. No more than ten

minutes had elapsed since old Mr. Barbilis was dragged from his back yard. The militant action of Duboko, now beginning, did not occupy more than a few minutes more, at the most. It makes me wonder how long men fought at Marathon, since Pheidippides died before he could tell.

And not even a heavy screen might long contain Duboko; it it is no wonder that a barbed-wire fence was as reeds before his charge.

He struck the first white figure somewhere above the knees. There was a snarl and a shriek, and then Duboko was springing toward the next man.

I didn't see what happened then. I was getting out of the car and hopping toward the gate. My bare foot came down on broken glass, and that halted me for a moment. The noise of the encounter, too, seemed to build an actual, visible barrier before my eyes.

Our little world was one turmoil of flapping, torn white robes—a whirling insanity of sheets and flesh and outcry, with Duboko revolving at the hub. One of the men dodged out of the melee and stumbled back, brandishing a club which he had snatched from the rubble close at hand. I threw a bottle, and I like to think that that discouraged him; I remember how he pranced and swore.

Mr. Barbilis managed to get the swathing off his head and the gag out of his mouth. His frail voice sang minor encouragement, and he struggled to unfasten his strapped hands from the fence.

The conflict was moving now—moving toward the kidnapers' car. First one man staggered away, fleeing; then another who limped badly. It was an unequal struggle at best. No four members of the Anti-Greek League, however young and brawny, could justly be matched against a four-footed warrior who used his jaws as the original Lacedaemonians must have used their daggers, and who fought with the right on his side, which Lacedaemonians did not always do.

Four of the combatants were scrambling into their car; the fifth was still afoot and reluctant to abandon the contest. By that time I had been able to get through the gate, and both Mr. Barbilis and I pleaded with Duboko to give up a war he had won. But this he would not do; he challenged still, and tried to fight the car; and so, as they drove away, they ran him down.

It was ten A.M. before Bill Barbilis returned from Sioux Falls. I had ample opportunity to impound Bill's .45 automatic before he came.

His father broke the news to him. I found Bill sobbing with his head on the fountain. I tried to soothe him, in English, and so did Spiros Barbilis, in Greek; but the trouble was that Duboko could no longer speak his own brand of language from the little bier where he rested.

Then Bill went wild, hunting for his pistol and not being able to find it; all the time, his father eagerly and shrilly informed Bill of the identifications he had made when his assailants' gowns were ripped away. Of course, too, there was the evidence of bites and abrasions.

Earl Klugge was limping as he moved about his All-American Kandy Kitchen, and John Klugge smelled of arnica and iodine. A day or two passed before the identity of the other kidnapers leaked out. They were hangers-on at the All-American; they didn't hang on there any longer.

I should have enjoyed seeing what took place, down there at the Clive Street corner. I was only halfway down the block when Bill threw Earl and John Klugge through their own plate-glass window.

A little crowd of men gathered, with our Mayor Wingate among them. There was no talk of damages or of punitive measures to be meted out to Bill Barbilis. I don't know just what train the Klugge brothers left on. But their restaurant was locked by noon, and the windows boarded up.

A military funeral and interment took place that afternoon behind the Sugar Bowl. There was no flag, though I think Bill would have liked to display one. But the crowd of mourners would have done credit to Athens in the age when her dead heroes were burned; all the time that Bill was blowing Taps on his bugle, I had a queer feeling that the ghosts of Pericles and Thucydides were somewhere around.

EXERCISE THREE

Read "That Greek Dog" carefully at least twice. Then answer the following questions.

1. Plot

a. Find the beginning and end of each of these parts of the story: the introduction of Bill, the introduction of Duboko, the characterization of Duboko, the introduction of the Brothers Klugge, further characterization of Duboko, the arrival of Spiros Barbilis, the beginning of intolerance in Mahaska Falls, the threats against Bill, the kidnaping, the fight against the kidnapers, the aftermath. Why is this order followed? Which of the items named are actually episodes, and which are mainly expository or descriptive?

b. Draw a simple diagram like this:

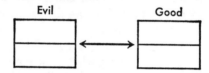

In the top half of the first square list the chief persons who represent the evil force in the story. In the top half of the second square list the chief characters who represent the good force. In the bottom half of each square indicate what the evil force and the good force are; that is, what the characters you have listed above stand for or are fighting for.

c. Attempt also, by dividing the story into its major episodes, to draw a diagram representing the plot. See page 163 for an example.

d. Show that this story presents a slightly modified version of the protagonist-obstacle-goal plot. Who are the two protagonists? What is the obstacle? What is the goal? How do the protagonists attain their goal?

2. Characterization

a. Why does Kantor in the first four paragraphs pay so much attention to Bill's military background? Where is this important in the story?

b. A first-person narrator (the "I" in the story) sometimes plays a major part, sometimes a minor one. Which is it in this story? Does Kantor give us as much information about the narrator as he does about Bill and Duboko? Why or why not?

c. Read the numerous parts of the story that characterize Duboko. Which of the nine methods of characterization in Chapter 9 does Kantor use? Point out bits of humor in the characterization. What do the humorous touches contribute to our attitude toward the dog?

d. Where and how are the representatives of evil characterized? Why is this characterization less thorough than that of Bill and Duboko?

e. Is Bill a completely "good" person? What human weaknesses does Kantor depict in him? Would the story be better if there were no such weaknesses?

3. Setting
a. What is the setting (time and place)?
b. How is the setting depicted? Why is little description necessary in this story?

4. Theme
a. The theme of this story is related to the lower half of the drawing you prepared for question 1b. Try to state the theme in as few words as possible.
b. How does Kantor present this theme clearly without ever stating it directly? Would the story be stronger or weaker if the theme were directly stated?

5. Read once more the quotations from Poe, Saroyan, and Stevenson (pages 178, 180, and 183). To what extent does Kantor conform to the recommendations of each?

The second of our stories first appeared in *Seventeen.* Most of the readers of that magazine are girls and young women. As you read, decide why this story is especially appropriate for that readership but also how it is broadened to make it general in appeal. Note too the plot, the characterization, and the glimpses of setting, and try to decide what the theme of this fairly subtle story is. The paragraphs have been numbered for your convenience in answering the questions in Exercise Four.

WHO IS THE BEAUTY? WHO ARE THE BEASTS?

by Jeannette Miller

1   I had been home only two hours, but I could have packed up right then and there and headed back to school, long before spring vacation was over. What an insane birdcage that house was!

2   I have a great deal of respect for my parents and all that, but honestly it was like coming back to the House of the Dead. My parents and my older brother Ben . . . well, as I said, they're all right, but they're just not overly aware of things. I mean, they never want to talk about books or world affairs or anything that's really essential. All they do is putter around in the garden or sit on the front veranda drinking ice water and talking about all the fine places they're planning to visit, which, of course, they never will, just sitting around all the time. "Taking life's ease," they call it.

3   I couldn't think that they knew what life was about.

4   I had just finished my first semester at Stanford and had done pretty well. I was somewhat self-impressed, to say the least, and had become grim-as-grime about the whole business: had my hair cut off almost completely to resemble Gertrude Stein or a pious, young, Saint Theresa-type nun (I don't remember now which it was), wore the same shabby dress every day, wouldn't go out, wouldn't stop studying before three in the morning, wouldn't stop for meals more than twice a day . . . as I said before, I was pretty self-impressed.

5   Well, anyway, I didn't even get through that first meal without my family's getting on my back. In the first place, my brother was home. He is a chemist in Berkeley, but as far as being aware of what's going on, he just isn't; all he ever does is read Thoreau and ride around the hills on his Vespa. The first thing he said when we sat down for dinner, even before hello, was "Lord, Joanie, you do look like a D.P.! What happened, did they lock you up in old Hoover T and

throw away the key? Gee, kid, if I had known I would have sent a CARE package!"

6   Needless to say, my brother pictures himself as a big wit, and to make matters worse my parents think so too. They sat there grinning like a couple of Cheshires thinking, no doubt, how great it was to have such wholesome, brilliant children.

7   "For your information," I said coldly and smiled my new, sour, Gertrude Stein smile, "I got all A's except for history and, besides that, my lit professor said that I was exceptionally perceptive *and sensitive* and would probably be a distinguished literary figure someday, which is more than anyone ever said about you."

8   Ben didn't even look up; he started cutting his steak up and talking with his mouth half full. "Bully for you, girl, bully for you, but don't act so saintly about it. You're ruining my appetite."

9   My mother interrupted pleasantly (she always interrupts pleasantly because of this big thing she has about peaceful dinnertime conversation and not aggravating my father's ulcers), "You know that story about the swallows you sent last month? I copied it down and sent it over with a cake to Mr. Simioni for his birthday. He was really touched and brought over some chrysanthemums. He said that it was the best present he'd ever received since he came to the United States and that you must be a very fine girl. I could barely understand him with his accent but he had tears in his eyes; he really did. What a dear old man!"

10   My mother's Florence Nightingale sentimentality absolutely made me want to gag. She's always getting so ridiculously upset over little dead birds and stray cats and things like that.

11   "Mr. Simioni?" I said it too loud and my father frowned a little. "You mean the Chamberlins' gardener? Oh, come off it, Mom. 'Dear old man' nothing! He's a seedy little wino and you know it. He was probably so stoned when he came over that he didn't even know what he was talking about. If you *must* pass around my story, stop playing humanitarian and at least give it to someone who will dig it, huh?"

12   My mother looked at me and said in that cool, formal tone she has when she's leading up to something shocking: "I realize, Joan, that it's not of great importance to you, or to Stanford, or to the general scheme of things, but it so happens that Mr. Simioni is dying. He has leukemia; Helen Chamberlin told me, and seedy old man or not, I'll bring him cookies or your stories or whatever I please without your criticism, thank you."

13   I put my fork down and scowled at my brother, who wasn't paying the least bit of attention. "Oh, for Pete's sake . . . there's a lot more worthwhile suffering being done in the world than by winos and dear little birds—"

14   My father kept wiping his mouth with his napkin. "For goodness' sake, Joan, calm down. We know you're tired out and all, but just put away this world-reformer business until after dinner, will you, please?"

15   "I will not calm down. Here I come home for one silly week and can we have a civilized conversation about anything that really matters? Oh, no, we have to sit around bawling over some grimy old man. Very intellectual, I must say."

16   No one said anything. You can't even argue on a rational level with those people. They just sit there fiddling with the silver.

17   Finally my mother glanced up at my father and let out a long breath as if she were very bored or tired—when she looks at him like that, I can never tell if she's mad or sorry or what. And then, looking back down at the chocolate soufflé that Clara had just brought in, she said, "Your father and I are very glad that you're doing so well at school." She stopped and stared out the window at the garden. "You should be very proud of yourself." And then she excused herself and went upstairs without even touching the dessert.

18   So you can see what I mean about my family. I hoped I would be more intellectually alert than that when I was older.

19   As I said in the beginning, I would have packed up and gone back to college that night. But since the dorms were locked up, I had to stick it out.

20 The next morning, I locked myself up in my room and started *The Brothers Karamazov*. I decided that I might as well make the best of it and try to get one report out of the way before the next semester. But then at about ten o'clock Ben started banging on the door.

21 "Hey, Joanie, do you want to walk in to town with me? I have to get some stuff for my scooter."

22 "No, I don't want to walk in to town. I've got *work* to do," I said.

23 "Oh, for Pete's sake, girl, you're getting so glued to that cross of yours, you'll never be able to get down. Even Spinoza went out once in a while. Do it for your precious brain's oxygen supply if nothing else."

24 "All right, all right, if you must be so boorish as not to realize when someone wants to be left alone."

25 It had rained the night before and the trees along the road were almost ready to bloom, their tight little bundles of leaves quite light against the wet, black bark. It was still cloudy and the ground was muddy in places, but there was a fine, washed smell in the air. We walked along the Chamberlins' high iron fence. Ben was whistling and kicking pebbles along the path and not being sarcastic for a change. For the first time I was glad I had come home and glad to be away from books a while (although I wouldn't have admitted it for anything).

26 We were just passing the end of the Chamberlins' yard when I heard a voice calling softly, almost in a whisper. "Miss-a Martin, Miss-a Martin."

27 I turned around and there was the gardener, Mr. Simioni, standing stoop-shouldered in his dirty overcoat, looking like a discarded, lumpy scarecrow with his face, dark and wrinkled like old bark, pressed between the bars of the fence. His gray hair was blown across his forehead like a piece of dried moss and his eyes were watering a little.

28 He beckoned through the bars. "Miss-a Martin. I want to show you something, please." He spoke softly and smiled apologetically and I could see how yellow his teeth were. What did he want anyway? He might have been a maniac for all I knew. I was glad I wasn't alone and started turning

back so Ben would know enough to walk on and ignore him.

29   But my brother grabbed my elbow and smiled at the old
man and said, "Good morning, sir, how are you?" He's such
a fanatic about being polite even if it's a big bother and
bound to get you involved and all.

30   The old gardener put both hands through the fence and
gestured with them as he spoke. They were long, lean hands.
The fingernails were grimy but the skin was smooth and
clean-looking and the contrast they made with his lumpy,
stooped body made me think for a moment of the hands in
the pictures of the *Pietà* statue which was in my Western
City book, but I caught myself: Don't get corny, I thought.

31   "I like to show you something," the gardener repeated to
Ben, slowly and with a heavy accent. "A minute, it take you
only a minute."

32   I started to say no, but Ben hit my arm sharply. "Of
course, Mr. Simioni, we'd like very much to see what you
have."

33   He opened the gate and we followed him back along the
dark path leading to the cabin where he stayed. He hurried ahead of us, turning to smile and beckon as if to hurry
us along too. The gravel path was still puddled and I could
feel the water oozing into my shoes. Ben tapped my shoulder
and pointed to a rosebush with one early bloom, deep scarlet
and fully opened; I hadn't noticed it. Mr. Simioni held the
door open for us. We went in.

34   The building was little more than a shack, and it was so
dark inside that I couldn't see anything at first. When my
eyes grew accustomed to the dimness, I saw the contents of
the room: a bed in the corner with the sheets and blankets
pulled up neatly, an old lamp, about five orange crates with
jars of pussy willows on top and books, so old that the titles
were worn away, lined up tightly inside. That was all, except
for a large, canvas-covered hulk which took up about half
the space in the small room. The sun had just come out and
was shining through the window in a shaft of light which illuminated the paint-stained canvas.

Mr. Simioni went to the huge form and carefully removed the cloth, folded it and laid it on the bed. The fine-grained wood of an organ shone softly there in the sunlight. It looked very old and was carved over and over with leaves and faces and heavy scrolls. By the light of the sunstream which poured through the open window, the organ looked like an altar-piece from a great cathedral.

36   Without looking at us or speaking, the old man sat down in front of the instrument. He rested his thin, brown hands on the keys for a moment and then slowly his fingers began to move over them. They moved like ten strong dancers and the music came not from the organ, it seemed, but from the sunstream. As Mr. Simioni played, I thought of the early-blown rose in the garden and of something else.

37   I cannot remember *what* I was thinking, I only remember a small hurting inside as if a bird were there trying to stretch his wings each time the melody came out over the top of the music. I shivered because the music seemed deep and cool, like pools hidden far back in a forest, with the melody floating up like a balloon released suddenly at a summer fair. But also I shivered because the old man played his organ in the sunlight, while I listened in the dark.

38   The music ended slowly and it was silent in the room.

39   "You like?" Mr. Simioni said hesitantly.

40   "Oh . . . oh, how . . ." I mumbled hopelessly, like an idiot, hypnotized, entranced.

41   "You surprised, eh? A dirty old man cannot want to write music, to love organ, you think?"

42   He pushed a strand of hair back from his forehead, shyly, and touched the carvings of the organ gently, as if he might injure them if he pressed too hard. Looking at the carving intently he said, as if to the instrument, "If my music good enough to . . . how do you say? . . . to dedicate, first I dedicate it to my father and to my son in Greece. My father die long time, but before, in our country, he made for me this organ. For me!" He pointed to himself like a child who has received a gift so fine that he cannot believe it is for him. "For me, who could not reach even the keys. And books—Homer, Sophocles, Virgil—so much, he gave. It took too long

to read them enough." He sighed. "After my father and son in Athens, I dedicate it to you if it good enough," Mr. Simioni said.

43   He let his hands fall from the organ into his lap and looked up at me. He smiled apologetically. "You wonder that I bother you to come to listen? I never play it before for anyone."

44   "Oh, no, no, Mr. Simioni, you mustn't . . ." Again I couldn't think of the right thing to say.

45   "Before, was no melody. Hard for old man like me to find melody. But your story for my birthday . . . that a nice girl like you wants to write about swallows for old man . . . you give me the melody for my birthday, eh? Like that—it came so quick!" He made a sudden gesture as if he really had caught a swallow in his hand.

46   Mr. Simioni stood up and leaned against the side of the organ. Suddenly I remembered that he was an old man, old and very tired.

47   "If only time, time to make, to compose a better music— good enough for my son, for you, but there is no more . . ."

48   "Oh, thank you, thank you for letting us listen." I realized how polite, how empty the words sounded.

49   But the old man did not even seem to hear; he stood looking out the window into the garden. The sunlight had disappeared and the carved faces of the organ seemed to frown hopelessly. It was just then, for the first time since we had been in the cabin, that I noticed the heavy wine smell of the old man's breath and I wondered why I hadn't noticed it before.

50   Ben, who had been standing next to the door, went to the old man and put his hand on his shoulder. "Mr. Simioni . . . Mr. Simioni . . ." He did not say anything more but leaned down and swiftly, awkwardly, kissed the side of the old man's face.

51   He stood there a moment longer, looking into the gardener's face and then, dropping his hand from his shoulder, he turned and ran from the cabin.

52   The old man looked surprised then, as if he, too, had just

realized something for the first time. "My son . . . I see him not again . . ."

53   I could not speak. I tried to smile but I couldn't even do that right. Mr. Simioni was not looking at me but stared through the open door into the garden; I ran outside as fast as I could and started back down the path after Ben. This time I noticed a beetle—black and shiny—crawling across the rose that Ben had pointed to before.

54   When I caught up with my brother, I grabbed his sleeve and blurted out before I could stop myself, "Mom and you and Father didn't know about that at all, did you? Mr. Simioni said he hadn't played it for anyone else. I mean you would have told me before, wouldn't you?"

55   Ben kept walking rapidly and didn't even turn to speak. "I don't have to say what I could say, do I?"

56   "Oh, Ben, I'm so—"

57   And then my voice got stuck and all I could do was start running across the road and up the walk to our house. I didn't turn back when I heard Ben shouting behind me, "Hurry up, girl! I'll wait for you at the corner."

EXERCISE FOUR

Read "Who Is the Beauty? Who Are the Beasts?" several times. Then attempt to answer the following questions.

1. Plot

a. The story is told in this way: MAJOR EPISODE—transitional episode—MAJOR EPISODE—concluding episode. Where does each episode begin and end?

b. The story presents two conflicts, one external and one internal. What are they? Which is the more important? How are the two solved simultaneously?

c. Plot, as we have learned, often results from character. To what extent is that true here?

d. The most frequent plot, you will recall, is that of protagonist-obstacle-goal. Who is the protagonist in this story? What does she think her goal is? What do you think her real goal is? What obstacles stand in the way of her supposed goal?

What obstacle stands in the way of her real goal? Why is she satisfied at the end even though she has not reached her supposed goal?

2. Characterization

   a. What do we learn about Joan in paragraphs 1–4? Why do we like or dislike her? Her family?

   b. What details do we learn about Joan in paragraphs 5–8? What do we learn about her brother, Ben?

   c. Study paragraphs 9–18. Referring to the nine methods of characterization explained in Chapter 9, show which ones the author has employed in these paragraphs. Note especially the skill with which Miss Miller reveals certain important things about each of five persons, while the story continues to move ahead.

   d. How does paragraph 20 confirm our previous impressions of Joan? Answer the same question for paragraphs 32 and 33.

   e. Mr. Simioni is characterized in paragraphs 9, 11, 12, and 26–53. How does the portrait "grow"? That is, how does the author keep adding to and rounding out the portrait? Are any previously unused methods of characterization (among the nine you know about) employed in any of these paragraphs?

   f. At what point in the story do we realize that Joan's attitude toward Mr. Simioni is changing? Why is this change central to the story? How does the author make it convincing?

   g. How is the last paragraph of the story significant? Show that Ben's last words are in harmony with the picture of him that the author has built up. Show also that it foreshadows the considerate kind of person that Joan is likely to become.

   h. Turn back for a moment to paragraph 18. In light of the whole story, why is this worded "I hoped I would . . ." rather than "I hope I will . . ."? What does this simple illustration reveal about an author's carefulness with details?

3. Setting

   a. Why is the season spring?

   b. How does the description in paragraphs 34 and 35 contribute to an understanding of Mr. Simioni?

   c. Why is setting less important in this story than in many

others? Could it just as easily have been placed, for example, in New York or in another decade?

4. Theme

What do you believe the author's purpose is in this story? Try to summarize the author's theme in a single sentence. (As with your statement of the theme of "That Greek Dog," remember that this is not the same as summarizing the events; rather, you should be interested in getting at what the events illustrate.)

SYMBOLS IN STORIES

A short story (and a novel also) may be read as simply an account of events or an interpretation of character. That is the way that perhaps the majority of readers do read, and it is likely that some stories *should* be read only in that way, for fiction writers frequently tell a story for story's sake rather than for deeper significance.

Huckleberry Finn, then, may be read as only a story of an exciting and often amusing trip down the Mississippi. *Moby Dick* may be read as merely an account of the adventure-filled and fatal pursuit of a giant white whale. But these two books are like icebergs, with most of their body beneath the surface. *Huckleberry Finn* reflects, in part, a nation's struggle with its conscience concerning the rightness or wrongness of slavery; Huck's indecision about helping to free a slave symbolizes the nation's indecision, and the slave is of course a symbol of all slaves, of slavery itself. In *Moby Dick* both Captain Ahab and the whale symbolize evil; Ahab's evil is probably the greater, for in effect he considers himself a god who can eliminate a force created by God.

A symbol in a story may be defined first as some specific person or thing that represents something larger *outside* the story. In "That Greek Dog" the major symbol is Bill, who represents all those persons, sometimes called "hyphenated Americans," whose families have not been long in the United States and who without reason are persecuted in some places or on some occasions. Even beyond that, Bill represents any minority group. And since every one of us is a member of several minority groups, Bill becomes a symbol of any of us who fight against forces that would deprive us of any of our constitutional rights.

The symbols in "Who Is the Beauty? Who Are the Beasts?" are somewhat more subtle. Joan represents any young person who rebels against what he or she considers the narrowness or shallowness or other shortcomings of his family. Part of growing up is striking out on one's own and acquiring new ideas. It is a painful process, for one still loves his family but would like to remake them after one's newfound image. The family does not want to be remade; often, in fact, it may be superior in some ways to the young person's idea of what it should be. Joan perhaps reminds us of Mark Twain's remark that when he left home at fifteen he was convinced that his father was stupid and ignorant, but when he returned at twenty-one he was surprised to discover how much his father had learned in a few years.

Smaller symbols, with their significance *inside* the story, are also discernible in "Who Is the Beauty?" The mother, for example, in her feeling for "little dead birds and stray cats" and for Mr. Simioni represents the compassion that Joan is in danger of losing. The reader likes the mother, and he realizes that if Joan continues the way she is going, she will be a great contrast to her mother—hard, brittle, with few endearing qualities.

In paragraph 30 is a symbol that may be easily overlooked. Noting the contrast between Mr. Simioni's clean, smooth skin and his lumpy, stooped body, Joan thinks for a moment of a religious statue that he resembles. Even though she dismisses the thought as "corny," it is significant that it enters her mind. It reveals that she is not actually so hard and unsentimental as she believes herself to be. It thus prepares the way for her later change of heart.

The symbolism of the rose in paragraphs 33, 36, and 53 may be open to question. Perhaps it stands for Joan herself, and the black beetle may represent the blackness that was preying on her, endangering her. The music described in paragraph 37 suggests the beauty that may exist where we least expect it; the revelation in paragraph 42 that Mr. Simioni knows Homer, Sophocles, and Virgil varies that suggestion.

The key to the whole story of "Who Is the Beauty?" is the symbol in the last sentence of paragraph 37: "But also I shivered because the old man played his organ in the sunlight, while I listened in the dark." Mr. Simioni, old and gnarled and wine-sodden though he was, was better off than Joan in her self-imposed darkness.

In your own writing, at least for a while, you should be more concerned with telling a story well and with portraying characters effectively than with symbols. Sometimes symbolism will appear unbidden, and you of course need not try to cast it out. But the ability to handle it well, to think through its many implications and ramifications, to make it consistent, is an ability that can come only after much experience.

EXERCISE FIVE

1. What additional symbols, of either the outside or the inside variety, do you find in "Who Is the Beauty?" and "That Greek Dog"?

2. After the members of the class have completed their stories, if the teacher wishes, the class may be divided into groups of four or five students. Each group will read and discuss the stories written by its members, pointing out both strengths and weaknesses in plot, setting, characterization, and theme,

and noting any use of symbols that may possibly have occurred.
One story from each group may be chosen for presentation to
the whole class. The story chosen need not necessarily be the
one considered best by the group, but rather one that offers
the most interesting points for discussion of technique.

12

Writing the Short Play

THE first three parts of this chapter concern the writing of various kinds of playlets for class or assembly use—relatively simple and unliterary manuscripts. The last part presents some suggestions for the much more difficult one-act play with at least modest literary pretensions.

PURPOSES OF ORIGINAL SCHOOL PLAYLETS

The purposes of playlets written by students for performance in school may vary widely. The following examples reflect a number of those purposes:

1. A dramatized book review. E.g., a dialogue between two students, one who dislikes the book and one who likes it; or a scene or scenes from the book, rewritten as conversation, possibly with a narrator.

2. A dramatization of a short story. E.g., de Maupassant's "The Necklace" or Irving's "Rip Van Winkle."

3. A dramatization of a historical event. E.g., the signing of the Declaration of Independence, or a meeting of Lincoln's Cabinet.

4. A dramatization of a great moment in science or invention. E.g., the time when it became evident that the Salk vaccine would probably be successful, or the first telephone message, or the first flight of the Wright brothers.

5. A dramatization of a sociological problem. E.g., a criminal who has served his time but has difficulty in finding employment, or a dope peddler who is brought to trial.

6. A dramatized version of a problem of many young people. E.g., "My parents don't trust me," or "Shall I go steady?" or "Should I take a part-time job?" or "How can I build self-confidence?"

7. Dramatization of "the advantages of. . . ." E.g., the advantages of a college education, or the advantages of using good English.

8. A dramatized tribute. E.g., a tribute to a coach, a team, a teacher, an exchange student from overseas, the senior class.

9. "Your First Days in Springdale H.S." I.e., a dramatization designed to acquaint incoming students with customs and regulations of your school.

10. A radio or television playlet which interprets some phase of school life or dramatizes what certain classes have been studying.

To this representative list you can no doubt add many items. The single underlying reason for all such playlets is to present information, possibly tinged with a little emotion, in more dramatic form than that of a lecture.

EXERCISE ONE

1. Do you know of any original playlets recently presented anywhere in your school? If so, what were they about, and why were they prepared?

2. Try to think of several subjects for plays that might be appropriate for one of your classes or for an assembly program in your school.

PLANNING THE SCHOOL PLAYLET

The first step in planning a school playlet is deciding upon its specific purpose. This should be simple enough to be summarized in a brief sentence. Without a definite purpose the playlet is likely to be wandering and vague.

As an illustration, let us assume that the Dramatics Club of which you are a member has become interested in preparing a play, "Your First Days in Springdale H.S.," and that school officials have approved the project subject to seeing the manuscript of the play. Members of the club would present the play, during the late spring, in the school or schools from which most entering students come to your school. Given this background, you can rather easily decide that the purpose of the play is this: To acquaint next year's entering students with important customs and regulations of Springdale H.S.

The second step is determining the basic content of the playlet. Not yet will you be concerned with characters or a story. In our illustration, you will need to decide which customs and regulations are important enough to include. You try to remember what things you wondered about before you entered your school. Perhaps you also have a chance to ask some future students what kinds of information they think should be included. You make a list of the items to be covered, and group them under such headings as choice of subjects, orientation week, corridor and cafeteria regulations, and extracurricular activities.

The third and fourth steps are not completely separable. These involve deciding the story line and the characters.

The story line in a playlet intended to inform is usually very slight. It is hardly a plot as plot has been described in Chapter 10. If you were dramatizing a historical or scientific event, your story line might be ready-made. For your "First Days" playlet, however, you are faced with the problem of dramatizing something that is not basically a narrative. You think first, perhaps, of having a new student ask a number of questions of a senior, but you reject that because it would be only a dialogue rather than a play. Then you think of following a bewildered new student through his first days, but you rule that out because too many scenes and too many people would be required.

Still without a story line, you try a different tack. What characters might be involved? You recall one student who entered school when you did—a smart-alecky boy who thought he knew all the answers and who had to learn the right answers the hard way. Another student, in contrast, was so shy that he (or should this one be a girl?) made bad blunders because he hesitated to ask questions. A glimmering of an idea begins to appear. Perhaps these two students can represent the entering class. They can talk with some upperclassmen, and gradually the smart-aleck can be led to see that it may be wise for him to subdue his smart-aleckism, and the shy girl (yes, let's make this one a girl) can be encouraged to see the need for asking questions.

You thus have the basis for a sufficient story line, as well as your key characters. Where should the action take place? This is your fifth decision, and is relatively easy. Setting is normally not very important in such playlets. They are usually presented without scenery and with a minimum of stage "props" (furniture or other properties). You decide that a student hangout a week before school opens would be an appropriate setting. You can have a fairly large table and some chairs and some soft drinks; no other furnishings or props will be needed.

You decide that the two new students and the president of the Student Council will be present at the table throughout the playlet. Other upperclassmen will wander by and stop briefly: perhaps an athlete, an activity leader, the best friend of the president. Possibly a teacher or a guidance counselor can also be impersonated if it seems desirable. The total number of characters should be kept small, seldom more than six or eight.

You have now advanced far enough to begin the writing of a scenario, which will be discussed in the next section.

EXERCISE TWO

On page 216 reread Numbers 6, 7, and 8. Choose one of the illustrative topics suggested, or a similar one, that you think you would like to dramatize. Then do the following:

1. Determine the purpose of the playlet. State it in one simple or complex sentence.

2. Decide the basic content (not story or characters). List the items to be included.

3 and 4. Decide the story line and the characters. Write a paragraph in which you summarize what will happen to whom.

5. Determine the setting and the simple props. Describe them in a couple of sentences.

WRITING THE SCHOOL PLAYLET

Someone has said that a play is not written, it is rewritten. Perhaps no other form of writing undergoes so many changes before it is completed. Broadway plays, for instance, are generally revised again and again before they reach Broadway, and small revisions are often made even then.

Professionals frequently follow this procedure after they have gone through the steps described in the previous section. They first write a *scenario* about a page long. This summarizes the action and conversation of the play. Then they decide whether the incidents are in the best order, whether any characters may be deleted, whether additional characters or scenes are needed, and so on. They rewrite the scenario in somewhat expanded form, including some bits of conversation and more details of the action. This enlarged scenario begins to catch some of the individual traits of the characters. Still other drafts of the scenario may follow, or the writing of the actual play may begin.

In writing your playlet, you will find a draft or two of

a scenario very helpful and timesaving. After you start on the playlet itself, try to keep these principles in mind:

1. Make every word count. Any sentence or word that does not forward the action, provide essential information, or serve to characterize should be deleted. Remember the basic purpose of your playlet, and eliminate any scene or speech that does not contribute to it.

2. Avoid long speeches. They are hard to memorize, and unless they are dramatic, they tend to become preachy and dull. Read speeches aloud to *hear* whether they seem natural.

3. Keep characters consistent, but permit gradual growth. In "First Days," for instance, the smart aleck should be consistently smart alecky, although near the end something may show that he is becoming a bit subdued.

4. Use the techniques of characterization explained in Chapter 9, pages 141–152. The only one of these that does not apply to drama is the first.

5. End on a climactic note, trying to leave the audience with the feeling that the purpose has been achieved.

As to the mechanics of setting up the script, there are no set rules. The essentials are illustrated here:

YOUR FIRST DAYS IN SPRINGDALE H.S.

by _____ _____

Cast, in order of appearance:
  DON MALCOLM, an incoming student
  LESLIE WALTERS, president of the Student Council
  (etc.)
  Place: The Rendezvous
  Time: This year, a week before school starts

[*The opening curtain shows a table in The Rendezvous, a favorite meeting place for Springdale H.S. students. LESLIE, DON, and SHARON are at the table, which also has two unoccupied chairs. LESLIE, center, is calm, self-possessed, a na-*

tural leader. DON, at Leslie's left, is freckled, lively, with an engaging but rather arrogant grin. SHARON, at Leslie's right, is pretty, but her often downcast eyes suggest shyness. Soft drinks are on the table. Other students, wandering by and stopping from time to time, bring their own refreshments. If available, a record suggesting the hum of offstage conversation may be played at low volume throughout.]

DON: I bet we'll stir up some excitement when *we* get into high school. We'll be running it in six months. Oh, of course, Leslie, we'll still let you have the *title* of president of the Student Council.

LESLIE: [*after a moment of looking at him quietly, and speaking without obvious sarcasm*] That's nice of you, Don. I wish that when I first came I had known as much about Springdale High School as you say you do.

SHARON: I wish I knew *anything* about it. Frankly, I'm scared to death, with school almost ready to start.

Note that the characters are usually listed in order of appearance, with their names in capital letters, followed by a brief identification. Stage directions are generally underlined (italicized in print) and enclosed in brackets. Names of characters are again in capitals, as they are before speeches in the play itself. The script is set up with the speeches sufficiently indented that the names of the characters are clearly visible. A colon is the usual mark after the speaker's name, although a dash, a centered period, or simply a space may be used. Note how the stage direction after Leslie's name is indicated.

Aside from the mechanics, note that the stage directions give only the most essential information about the setting and the characters. Chatty stage directions such as you sometimes find in modern plays, like those of J. M. Barrie and G. B. Shaw, are especially written for readers' editions, not for actors'.

Observe also that the first three speeches get the play

well under way. The theme—getting accustomed to a new school—is suggested. The audience learns that Don and Sharon are incoming students and that Leslie is president of the Student Council. Leslie and Don are identified by name for the audience, and Sharon probably will be in the next speech. In addition, all three of the speakers reveal something significant about themselves.

EXERCISE THREE

Write a scenario of the playlet you planned in Exercise Two (page 219). Then write the opening page or two of the playlet. If the teacher and class wish, each student may go ahead and complete his playlet. Alternatively, a few of the best ideas may be selected, with students in small groups working out detailed scenarios and complete playlets based on some of these ideas. Ideally, some of the playlets should be presented before the class and possibly before other groups in the school.

THE "LITERARY" ONE-ACT PLAY

A literary one-act play, like a short story, leaves a single unified impression. It normally employs only a few characters, and focuses upon a single theme or action, with emphasis upon one particular person. The school playlet *can* be literary, but generally is not, since its basic purpose is usually the utilitarian one of conveying information. The literary play, in contrast, is less concerned with information than with mood, atmosphere, revelation of character, and general literary effectiveness.

Many famous playwrights have tried their hands with this form: Eugene O'Neill, Anton Chekhov, J. M. Barrie, Noel Coward, Maurice Maeterlinck, A. A. Milne, G. B. Shaw, and Thornton Wilder, among others. Irish playwrights Lord Dunsany and Lady Gregory are known best because of their use of this medium. A study of the techniques of any of these authors will be valuable to you.

The literary one-act play is difficult to write—perhaps except for poetry the most difficult genre to write *well*. The need for compactness, for quick but sharp characterization, and for rapid development of the story is one of the reasons for the difficulty. Another is the fact that the stage imposes physical limitations unknown to any other literary medium. Action must be confined to the few square feet of floor space, not the limitless expanse permitted by short stories, novels, or motion pictures. The time limitation is no less severe: the dramatist is always portraying what *is*, unlike the novelist who may spend much of his time showing what *was*. The story can be moved ahead only by conversation and by the small amount of physical action possible to depict upon the stage. Description is impossible except for a few descriptive words spoken by a character or a few hints from the stage setting. The play must have dramatic interest and the almost indefinable quality of "actability." Perhaps because of these many difficulties, some authors highly successful in other genres were ineffective as dramatists: Cervantes, Milton, Samuel Johnson, Thackeray, and Henry James, as well as many others.

Most high school students should not try to write a literary play. The suggestions that follow are intended for the guidance of the occasional student who may want to experiment with such a demanding form. As dramatist Channing Pollock once said, ". . . playwrights must be born *and* made."

A playwright's background. Firsthand knowledge of the theater is essential. Among twentieth-century playwrights who earlier were actors are Eugene O'Neill, George M. Cohan, Rachel Crothers, Clifford Odets, and Noel Coward. For writers without much acting ability, backstage work may be a satisfactory substitute.

Many journalists have found that newspaper background has given them valuable knowledge of people, a sense of the dramatic, and skill with words. J. M. Barrie, G. B.

Shaw, Lillian Hellman, Channing Pollock, Ben Hecht, Edna Ferber, Marc Connelly, A. A. Milne, and Robert E. Sherwood are just a few of the recent playwrights with journalistic experience.

Seeing plays and studying plays—dozens and scores of them—are obviously useful. Channing Pollock recommended that young playwrights recall occasionally a play seen or read months before, and that they try to write the scenario for the half-remembered play and then compare that scenario with the way the original author constructed the play. Observation of audience reaction, trying to decide why people respond (or fail to respond) as they do to each part of a play, is also invaluable.

The essence of drama. Ferdinand Brunetière, an influential French critic, said in 1894: "The theater in general is only the place for the development of the human will, attacking the obstacles presented to it by destiny, chance, or circumstances. . . . Drama is one of us thrown living upon the stage, where he struggles against fate, against social law, against one of his fellow human beings, against himself, or if necessary against the interests, the prejudices, the folly, or the malevolence of those who surround him."

There is the essence of drama—some believable kind of struggle carried on before the eyes of an audience for whom we have knocked out one of the four walls of a room. George Pierce Baker of Harvard and Yale, America's greatest teacher of playwriting, said that an emotional response must be aroused by this struggle, or the play fails. And an emotional response is possible only if the audience can be brought to *care* about what happens. The people of the play, then, or at least some of them, must be people in whom we are led to become deeply interested. The author holds us in suspense, wondering whether these new but already thoroughly familiar friends of ours will win or lose something of great importance to them.

Characters. Tragedy is a higher type of drama than

melodrama, not because it ends "unhappily," but because it focuses upon character whereas melodrama stresses situations and events. Comedy is a higher type than farce for the same reason. The audience seldom cares very deeply about what happens to the people in melodramas and farces; it does not come to believe that they really *are* people.

In modern plays the chief characters are highly individualized, not types or abstractions such as you find in *Everyman* ("Good Deeds," "Fellowship," "Beauty," etc.) In the "First Days" playlet discussed on pages 217–222, the characters would almost inevitably be types because of the nature of the play, but the literary playwright attempts the hard task of making each important character a unique person who yet possesses some elements of universality. The minor figures, or "dummies" as dramatist John Van Druten has called them, are purposely not made memorable or even very distinctive.

Shakespeare and his contemporaries made use of soliloquies and "asides" by which a character could reveal his thoughts to the audience. Today's dramatists try to be more realistic, arguing that people don't really talk to themselves or to an audience. Modern writers, therefore, scorn soliloquies and asides, making use only of such techniques of characterization as are discussed in Chapter 9.

Peculiarities of the one-act form. Rachel Field's "The Londonderry Air," a once very popular one-act play, may be used to illustrate typical characteristics of the form.

Playing time: about thirty minutes (range usually twenty to forty)

Time represented: about eight hours (often only the same as the playing time; seldom more than a day)

Settings: only one

Number of scenes: two (one is more frequent)

Number of characters: four (range usually two to eight)

Beginning of action: as near the climax as possible

Plot: An unhappily engaged girl succumbs to the lovely music and the romantic charms of a peddler, after giving her doltish fiancé a final chance to compete. (Most one-act plots are similarly uncomplicated.)

Theme: The impulse toward beauty and affection may be stronger than desire for security. (Gotthold Lessing, eighteenth-century German playwright and critic, said, "Purposeful creation is that which distinguishes genius from the petty artists who create only to create." American playwright Robert E. Sherwood said that the best dramatists show man reaching toward Heaven.)

Miscellaneous hints.

1. In a play of more than one scene, each scene should present part of the basic conflict, with its outcome—victory, defeat, or no decision.

2. Remember that each time an important character enters or leaves the stage, the "balance of power" shifts, and the interrelationships of the characters are different.

3. Each character must have a legitimate reason for each entrance or exit.

4. When a character has left the stage to perform some specific task, allow enough time for him to do it before bringing him back.

5. A character's actions must be consistent with the way he has been portrayed, but not so obvious that the audience can always predict what he will do next.

6. George Bernard Shaw said, "My dialogue and characters are absolutely inextricable, each being the essence of the other."

7. Let the audience in on some secrets. (Coleridge said that expectation is more dramatic than surprise.) But maintain suspense by giving no clear hint as to the eventual outcome or the way it will be achieved.

8. Humor is often desirable, but avoid a joke or any other humor that does not grow naturally from the play itself.

9. Avoid the *deus ex machina,* an outside force (rich uncle, U.S. Cavalry, etc.) that arrives unexpectedly at the end to straighten everything out.

10. Eugene O'Neill once said, "The only ones who can successfully break the rules are the people who know them."

EXERCISE FOUR

Summarize in your own words the reasons why a "literary" play—one-act or other—is difficult to write.

Section D

WRITING POETRY

13
How Poetry Expresses You

14
How to Express Poetry

How Poetry Expresses You

WHY DOES ANYONE WRITE POETRY?

PERHAPS many students feel like Bill, who had been asked to write a poem and who, in final desperation, turned in this parody:

Sorry, Kilmer

> I think that I shall never see
> A poet lousier than me,
> A poet that sits around all day
> Before he thinks of something to say.
> If poems were made by fools like me,
> Not a single poem would there be.
>
> (Bill Foley)

[All student-written poems in these chapters were published originally in issues of the *Illinois English Bulletin,* and are included here by permission of the Illinois Association of Teachers of English.]

Probably Bill had a number of misconceptions about poetry. He may have thought of a poem as something that must rhyme, that must deal with lilies or daffodils or knights or pangs of unrequited love, and that must be filled with impossible-to-understand upside-down sentences and words like *thee* and *o'er.* Maybe he believed that a poet is a person who waits for something called "inspiration" to descend upon him and guide his pen effortlessly.

Let's try to correct those misconceptions first. A poem *may* rhyme, but it doesn't have to. Rhyme is only one of the many tools a poet may use to create the impression he desires. We'll look at several of them later.

As to subject matter, anything that a person feels strongly about may be appropriate. Modern poets have written about such varied subjects as an injured hawk, a crowd at a ball game, and the quiet of a museum.

Sometimes a poem *is* hard to understand, because the poet may have a complicated emotion or series of emotional reactions to express, or because poetry tends to be highly compressed, or because he has found it necessary to use words or allusions that are not widely familiar, or because he has decided to use some common words with meanings other than their usual ones. But difficulty is not an essential quality of poetry; that is, the poet does not set out deliberately to make it hard to understand. Often, in fact, as in the poetry of Robert Frost or some of that of William Wordsworth, it is deceptively simple.

As to the language and the "upside-down sentences," most modern poets generally try to avoid unnaturalness. Unless good reason exists, they do not use *thou* and *eftsoons* and other outworn words. They *do* try to find the precise word, regardless of age or source, that best fits the purpose of the poem and that is most in harmony with the other words in the poem. Their sentences are compact, but only occasionally unusual in word order.

The final misconception, that a poem results from inspiration and that something beyond the poet's control really does the writing, has an interesting history. The ancient Greeks and Romans believed in "Muses," supernatural beings, not quite goddesses, who were supposed to help writers, dancers, and other artists while they were creating. Writers quite understandably encouraged this superstition, because having a pretty and brilliant Muse as an assistant set them a notch higher than other mortals who were not equally favored—something like having a good-looking and brainy secretary to do most of their work for them. So they played up their indebtedness, making it a point in their poetry to beg the appropriate Muse for help and thanking her when she complied. Later poets (but not many modern ones) continued the tradition. The superstition about Muses certainly contributed much to the widespread but now generally discredited belief in inspiration. Most of today's poets cheerfully admit that they experiment, think, write and rewrite, revise, and polish, and that although at some times the writing is much easier than at others, they seldom find that a whole poem flows effortlessly from the pen.

Bill and others like him need to think of a poem as an honest attempt to express effectively a thought, belief, feeling, or impression. Although poets and critics have argued endlessly over a completely acceptable definition of poetry, the following sentence is worth considering: "A poem is a form of expression in which an unusual number of the resources of language are concentrated into a patterned, organic unit of significant experience." [1]

In that definition all the parts are important, but especially the last two words: "significant experience." The poet attempts to find words to convey to others an experience that seems meaningful to him. "Experience" may be broadly defined. It can be a glimpse of a person, a reaction to a newspaper story, the sound of a siren late at night, a passing mood, or almost anything else. And it can be "significant" without being deeply serious. As Professor Gilbert Highet has said, ". . . many of the most famous poets of the past and the present have written both serious and light verse. . . . [Good writers of light verse], just like the writers of serious verse, are interested in exploring the resources of language and of poetic technique; and sometimes they use skills which their serious contemporaries neglect." [2]

Why does anyone write poetry? Not to make money

[1] [M. L. Rosenthal and A. J. M. Smith, *Exploring Poetry*, The Macmillan Company, 1955, p. 89.]
[2] [Gilbert Highet, *The Powers of Poetry*, Oxford University Press, 1960, pp. 213–214.]

—at least not today in the United States, where no more than a half dozen men and women earn a good living from poetry alone. Not for glory. Modern poets in the United States are mistakenly regarded as too "different," too "impractical," to be much admired; this was not always true here, and is not today in some European and many Latin-American countries, where poets may be national heroes and are often elected to high political offices.

The best reasons for writing poetry are to get something off one's chest and to have the pleasure of creating something that is as artistic as one's ability permits. The act of getting something off the chest, in other words the relating of a significant experience, something that moved him, angered him, or consoled him perhaps, enables the writer to think intensely about the experience, reach a conclusion, and express that conclusion vigorously. The pleasure of creating a poem is similar to the pleasure caused by any other creative act. The hot-rodder who builds a lively car out of a miscellany of parts gets about the same kind of pleasure, and so do the composer of a sonata, the builder of a boat, the engineer or architect who designs a bridge or building, and the painter or the sculptor. And the pleasure is not necessarily proportionate to size or importance; the student who makes an attractive pair of book ends in the school shop and the student who writes two good lines of poetry may both enjoy richly the pleasure of creation. "Making little poems," Robert Frost once said, "encourages a man to see that there is shapeliness in the world."

EXERCISE ONE

1. Have you held any of the misconceptions about poetry discussed on pages 231–233? If so, how do you account for your beliefs? To what extent may they be true conceptions?

2. Re-examine the suggested definition of a poem: "A poem is a form of expression in which an unusual number of the

resources of language are concentrated into a patterned, organic unit of significant experience." Discuss and try to illustrate what is meant by "an unusual number of the resources of language," "concentrated," "a patterned, organic unit," and "significant experience."

3. Members of a high school class once suggested these rather picturesque definitions of poetry. Try to decide what each means, and what may be true or false in each definition.

a. Poetry is like either compasses or girls. Most of the time it runs you in circles.

b. Poetry is an expression of one's longings: a small boy wanting to fly, an old man wanting his youth.

c. Poetry is as dark as the darkest shroud and as bright as the brightest star. It is like a bridge linking reality and dreamland.

d. Poetry is the beauty, the ugliness, and the explanation of life itself.

4. Using a comparison, try to formulate your own definition of poetry.

WHERE DOES A POEM START?

Nancy saw a blind beggar fiddling on a street. As she watched, another beggar sidled up to him and slipped out some of the coins that passersby had given him. Nancy was moved by the experience. She wished impossibly good things for the old man. At home she thought of him again, and tried to find words for what she had seen. This was the result:

A Man Who Fiddled

Once, on a corner in Quebec City, there was a man who fiddled,
And into his open case people would drop small coins,
Or hurry by, and look the other way or mention the weather to
    their companions
And well out of earshot, would say,
"I feel so sorry for that poor old man; he makes me cry—
But I look so silly putting money in his case."

They did not need to wait till they had passed.
He could not hear or see.
And on that corner in Quebec, younger beggars than he would
    steal his few coins as he fiddled,
With a scratched, unvarnished fiddle and a loose, unrosined
    bow,
His wild, tumultuous melodies.
There was always something too wistful in those screeching
    sounds, too savage and too longing,
Too melancholy and, somehow, too beautiful.

I would see him now on some celestial cloud, playing that same
    sweet, wild, lonely melody
For children who could not sleep, or men who feared,
And I would see him now with his case full of roses, thrown
    there by grateful angels
Who saw how he lulled this world of sleepless children and
    fearing men.
I would see his dull eyes shining and his sad lips smiling, as he
    fiddled his lullaby.

But they say he is still there, on a corner in Quebec, fiddling,
While people drop small coins, or pass him by,
And younger beggars than he steal his coins.
Someday, I pray that he will play music to quiet my waking
    children's voices, and my own fearing heart.

                                                    (Nancy Lipe)

Tom's poem got its start in his reading about the beat-
niks, groups of young, somewhat eccentric, and would-be
artistic men and women of the late 1950's and early 1960's.
He later saw a few of them and was depressed rather than
impressed. He tried a poem to show his scorn, and found
that Whitman-like verse could express it best:

The New Individual

I speak of the birth of the new individual, who out of
    morass of nineteen forties War and conforming
    Suburbia rises.

Man one in himself, and the hell with it all, the money
and strife and sameness and false pretty, and
all of it false with nothing really there.
Man called Beat, no longer Bohemian and ahead of it all,
only no one knows.
Man drinking red wine in Frisco, smoking pot in Denver,
mocking time at CCNY and living it all right now.
Man living anywhere, sleeping anywhere, going where it
swings and then going someplace else where it
swings and then going someplace else where it
swings.
Man mad to live, mad to love, mad to go and be with it, in.
I speak of the birth of the new individual, narcotic,
neurotic, poetic, alcoholic, maladjusted, and
you name it.
The new individual intellectual who can't think, much less
see through opium haze and crude rantings of
Kerouac equally degenerate.
The new individual, real swinging and real living and also
real filthy.
And, God, what have we done to deserve him?

(Tom Klug)

Caroline wondered to herself, "How is it that some people get so much done? I never have enough time for anything." In four quick-moving, lightweight lines she expressed what many of us have thought but perhaps never
said so catchily:

A Mystery

It's always a puzzle for me to see
The amazing amount of work
That minds sublime can get done in time
And minds like my mind shirk.

(Caroline Wild)

The real origin of Duncan's poem may have been a personal incident, but the poem grew from combined emotions
of bitterness and resignation:

Two

Two!
Two pebbles lying together upon the white sand,
The sand, each grain of which came from such as these.
Washed up by the tide
And time,
They touch for but a moment,
And then someone, upon passing,
Chances upon the two, lying there.

When we see how, with gentle fingers disguised in the blood of
        friendship,
One is taken away,
Our dry voices cry out in meager protest
And
Are swallowed by the echoing wind,
Drowned by the rushing of the sea,
And lost in the mocking voices of eternity.

Two!
Two pebbles lying separately
On different shores, on separate seas,
Yet washed by the same tide
And time—
Yes, time is inescapable as the furies of the souls of men.

Two pebbles lying upon the sands,
Two, two that touched for but a moment,
And then were broken apart.
Though it was for but a moment, these had eternity.
They have still what none can take away,
Neither time
Nor tide
Nor the sea
Nor the selfishness of man.

(Duncan Bradley)

So we observe that from something or someone seen, from something read, from a commonplace thought, from an emotion or combination of emotions, from almost anything, a poem may get its start. A poem is "a thought-felt thing," Robert Frost declared. Given an initial impulse, the poet thinks about it, analyzes how he feels or how someone else might feel. He starts searching for the words, the comparisons, the pictures; and sometimes a word, a comparison, or a picture stimulates new thoughts, new feelings. Literature, poet John Ciardi has said, is not about ideas, but about "the experience of ideas." A poem reflects the final development of such experience. It grows like a child; it does not spring full-bodied "like Venus from the dawn-encircled sea." Henry Rago, editor of *Poetry* magazine, has said, "A poet doesn't quite know what his poem knows until the poem is done."

EXERCISE TWO

1. For each of the four poems quoted on pages 235–238, select details to show that it is "a thought-felt thing."

2. From another book select one or two poems that you enjoy. Show that they too are thought-felt things, and make your best guess as to what may have started each author to writing on the subject.

3. What have you seen, heard, read, thought about, or felt today or within the past few days that might be the subject of a poem?

CONCRETENESS, EXACTNESS, AND INTENSITY

In his book *The Nature of Poetry* Donald Stauffer chooses seven adjectives to describe what he considers the chief characteristics of poetry. One of them, *significant,* we have already touched upon. Three of the others are *concrete, exact,* and *intense.*

First, let us consider concreteness. The young Shakespeare knew its importance. In fact, he wrote about it in
one of his early plays, *A Midsummer-Night's Dream.* He
said that a poet's imagination "bodies forth the forms of
things unknown," and explained half-humorously what he
meant:

> Such tricks hath strong imagination
> That if it would but apprehend some joy,
> It comprehends some bringer of that joy;
> Or in the night, imagining some fear,
> How easy is a bush supposed a bear!

In other words, the poet seldom writes directly about such
abstractions as joy or fear; instead, he writes about concrete, specific persons or things which represent the abstraction.

Here is how a ninth-grade girl made concrete what she
felt about a peaceful mood:

Moods

Peace is a puppy saturated in sleep,
His tummy comfortably filled with warm milk.
The accustomed odors of oatmeal and shredded newspaper
Linger in his stubborn wooly hair.
Peace is the length of time a pup's eager, sensitive body is at
rest.
Peace is the full moon riding like a luminous spider on a web
of clouds,
A militia of cattails gracefully drilling to the rhythm of a
zephyr,
The ease of a bird's wing slicing a summer sky,
A contented heart.

(Mary K. Tingley)

In later stanzas of "Moods," Mary continued the comparison with dogs, saying, in part, "Torment is the emerging of a homeless mongrel / Out of the thickets of night,"

"Joy is a pup's frantic exertion at play. / . . . Wittily his pink tongue lolls between mischievous teeth," "Loneliness is an old dog drowsing to the hissing of a fire. / . . . A greying paw twitches in reverie."

Concreteness is often achieved through such comparisons. Robert Frost once told John Ciardi that a man is doing well "when he thinks of something in connection with something else that no one ever put with it before." This "two-ness," the sensing that two unlike things belong together, Frost found essential to his own writing of poetry; so, probably, do most other poets, though few of them have expressed it so simply.

Here are more examples of this kind of two-ness, this imagery, this concreteness, from student poems. David saw that the early sun "fires the dingy panes of the Clybourn tenements." Describing another dawn in another place, Jane said, "Slowly brightening into a pale glow, / The timberline is bathed / In a shimmer of clouds." Betty, regretting her tendency to forget things, declared, "Remembering is like a water-filled colander." Ella found that "The cold north wind is a blaring trumpet" but "The warm south breeze is a strumming guitar."

It is possible, of course, to be concrete without using figures of speech. Mike builds to his generalization mainly through a series of details:

Canadian November

The first snow lies cold and grey upon the ground,
A patchwork quilt, still untransformed to the noble white of
    winter, the king.
An awed silence lies upon the forest, broken now by creaking
    trees. . . .
Here a squirrel chatters angrily at a marauder fox,
Stalking quietly through the woods, hoping to surprise an un-
    wary grouse.
Elsewhere the bear growls uneasily, and searches for a den,

Deep enough to hold back the icy reach of winter.
A tenseness, felt by all, is in the air.
Canadian November is uneasy;
A restless pause in the everlasting race of life.

(Mike Chamberlin)

Exactness is partly a matter of honesty. What a poet says should be either literally or figuratively true, insofar as a writer can present truth and a reader interpret it. We sometimes suspect that even admittedly great poets are inexact and hence insincere at times. Keats wrote "I stood tiptoe upon a little hill," and Shelley, "I shrieked, and clasped my hands in ecstasy." Well, maybe they did stand tiptoe and shriek respectively, but it seems a bit doubtful; such apparent exaggerations have helped to give poets a bad name. Students have made the same mistakes, claiming that the scent of a honeysuckle makes them faint with joy, or that "I wish I were a cricket, / So I could chirr all night," or that icicles are "tiny silver bells tinkling in the cold," or that the forest cries "It's Spring!"

Exactness results from choice of words, choice of images, choice of rhythms. Jacqui chose carefully in her portrait of a little boy:

A Deserted Road

A small boy walks down a dark deserted road.
Giant trees watch him from their haughty height.
A bitter wind bends the yielding grass.
Icy stars pierce the black.
A night-bird calls through the darkness.
The incompassionate universe surrounds
One boy—
　　Cold,
　　　　Afraid,
　　　　　　Alone.

(Jacqui Strunk)

To be exact, a writer must know, must have observed. James unquestionably isn't a city boy who just guesses what cows are like:

Wisconsin Barn

The red barn
In the middle of the farm
Its haymow filled with sweating hay.

Cattle below,
Two rows of black and white,
Stare straight ahead at whitewashed walls,
Swish black rope tails,
And move loose cuds
To the rhythm of the milking machine.

At one far end
Two wobbly knock-kneed calves
Bellow for their mothers.
Two cows move restlessly
From side to side.

Into the churn
The farmer pours the golden layer
From last night's milk
And churns the cream for the dairy show.

(James Long)

Intensity comes most often from selection of details, only infrequently from piling them up. In this familiar poem by William Wordsworth, from the group he wrote about a girl named Lucy, observe especially its compactness and the restrained intenseness of the outcry at the end. Wordsworth could have written much more description of Lucy and could have examined his heartache more minutely, but he compressed into twelve lines all that really needed saying:

She dwelt among the untrodden ways
  Beside the springs of Dove,
A maid whom there were none to praise
  And very few to love.

A violet by a mossy stone
  Half hidden from the eye!
—Fair as a star, when only one
  Is shining in the sky.

She lived unknown, and few could know
  When Lucy ceased to be;
But she is in her grave, and, oh,
  The difference to me!

Rus knew this virtue, but when she learned it still better, she might have concentrated this poem still more and increased its effectiveness:

Apology

i.

A purple teddy bear sprawls on the bed,
And I at my window watch a gray man
Striding up a cold street, swinging a lunch bucket,
Huffing and puffing clouds of life into the sullen air,
And a barren poplar, each branch swaying in delicate
    counterpoint to the others
    and the wind,
And the stony silver sky.
Behind a noncommittal window
In the sad drab house next to mine,
An old crone lurks and spies on life.

ii.

The purple teddy bear and I
Are figmentary things
Not of this world of reason;

Not of this world of snarling large and logically
    brown bears (hibernating now);
Not of this world of lurking age
And gray men swinging life
Up the cold streets at dawn
In lunch buckets.

iii.

We are the soft and shapeless
Inhabitants of a similarly
Soft and shapeless world of maybe
Somehow wandered by mistake
Into the rigid universe
    of
    Now.

                   (Rus Wilday)

Intensity through economy is characteristic of the Japanese verse form called the *hokku*, which restricts the writer to seventeen syllables in lines of five, seven, and five syllables (like a Japanese flower arrangement, Gilbert Highet has said). Here is one imitation by an American boy:

Silence

The music has stopped.
Oh, bird of the wind! Send one
Fluted Remembrance.

                  (Lonny Lunde)

Ancient Hebrew poetry featured repetition. The first line or clause was often followed by another with the same idea expressed differently. The two lines, each compact in itself, reinforced each other. Intensity is well illustrated in Barbara's modern imitation:

A Candle Burns

A match is lit,
A union.

Flame sputters, then begins,
The birth.

It gains momentum,
Growth.

Now brightly it burns,
Youth.

Then steady, intense,
To span time.

It flickers, now bright, now dim;
The wick grows short.

Suddenly, only pools of tallow and a charred string;
Death.

(Barbara Chandler)

Intensity may come also from contrast. In the famous drunken porter scene in *Macbeth*, which comes immediately after the murder of Duncan, the absurd humor intensifies the horror of the preceding scene. In *Othello*, perhaps the best-remembered line is "Put out the light, and then put out the light," spoken by Othello just before he kills his beautiful and innocent young wife. The line gains most of its effect from the contrasted meanings of *light*: the first light is a candle, the second, Desdemona's life; the second *light* carries at least two more meanings, since Desdemona was the light of Othello's life, but he now believes her to be "light," i.e., unfaithful.

A student effectively uses two simpler bits of contrast in this cinquain:

Spring

Gray grass
With dabs of green,

A drab brown road edged by
Young windswept trees that swirl with song
In spring.

(George Niemola)

Perhaps by now your head is swimming. "Significant experience, concreteness, exactness, intensity, and still more stuff to come. How can I remember all these things when I try to write a few lines of poetry? Won't I be like the centipede who couldn't crawl when he tried to figure out which leg to move first?" That's a legitimate question. The answer, of course, is that you don't think of all the characteristics of poetry at the same time. You choose the subject, the thought-feeling, and you say what you have to say as well as you can. *Then* you ask yourself, "Is it concrete enough? Exact enough? Intense enough? Is there a better way to say this or this or this? Is this really the way things are and this thing is? Do all the parts fit together?" And you ask yourself other questions about rhythm and rhyme and so on, to be discussed in the next chapter. And you make the changes that the answers to your own questions demand.

EXERCISE THREE

Here are a number of statements in ordinary prose. Choose several that refer to things you know well, and try to say each of them concretely, exactly, intensely.

The north wind was blowing sleet against my face.
In the office, five secretaries were typing.
Two small children were playing and laughing.
The school corridor was filled with students going to their next classes.
Again my answer was wrong.
Several pictures are on my dresser.
Children ask many questions.
Music from the jukebox made us want to dance.
Our players looked small in comparison.
The trained porpoise leaped high to grab the fish.
For the first time I knew what loneliness is.

For the first time I knew what loveliness is.
As I sat there quietly, deep in the woods, small noises and
movements became apparent.
The shallow stream flows over a rocky bottom.
Death had come.
Then I knew about God.
Warren was a worthless old man, the town drunk.
The houses look alike.
I sometimes wonder whether a life simpler than ours might
not be preferable.
Words have their individual characteristics.

SYMBOLS

It is a mistake to assume that every poem means something different from what it says on the surface, and poets
have sometimes objected to the far-fetched interpretations
made by some readers. Yet often a poem, or something in a
poem, does suggest more than the literal meaning.

In the poem "Two" (page 238) Duncan obviously intends the pebbles to represent two human beings, forced
to separate from each other by some unintentionally cruel
persons. The pebbles, then, are *symbols* of people. In "A
Candle Burns" (page 245) the lighting and burning of the
candle symbolize human life. In "Apology" (page 244)
the purple teddy bear, so unlike the "large and logically
brown bears," symbolizes what the narrator thinks is her
out-of-touch life. In "Silence" (page 245) "bird of the
wind" and "Fluted Remembrance" are subject to several
possible interpretations.

This doubleness of meaning is related to the "two-ness"
to which Frost referred (page 241). The poem casts a
shadow, so that in effect there are two poems in one, and
often the shadow, once we have seen it, looms larger and
more important than the immediately obvious body.

In Elaine's cinquain, rain is probably more than drops
of water:

Rain

The soft
Rain fell upon
Me standing there and I
Was glad I was alive and could
Get wet.

(Elaine Siden)

Rain perhaps symbolizes the many things in our surroundings—often apparently unpleasant, as rain sometimes is—
that make our lives worth living.

There is little suggestion of symbolism in Monica's
poem until we reach the end:

Hard Journey to Tomorrow

I ride the bus of the Hard Women,
The women returning from counter and desk,
The women of the strained eyes and taut faces,
The Hard Women.
Next to me, the zebra-coated brunette of the
Flashing earrings,
Phony smile, and
Glinting snake eyes
Gossips dryly on the stupidity of employers.
A student, book-laden and with softing beard,
Enters, to stand an aisle-bound victim in a cloister of
Scornful glances,
Hated at once for saying nothing and for
Daring to intrude on
Them.
He stares, red-eared, at the ceiling.
The gross one of the red-tinted hair
Sneers
At the man, one of the many, one of the sex
That never flattered her, or respected her,
Or married her.

Sophistication, the angry-cheeked young secretary,
Stares
Coldly at him, evaluating and rejecting.
Young, pretty, she has lots of time to
Pick the lucky catch
Or become one of
The Hard Women.
And I ride that bus of the Hard Women
To get home.
And I watch them and the young student,
And I hear their gossip
And taste their frustration,
The while my lips thinning,
My face pinching,
And my heart lapsing bitter
    and Hard.

(Monica Pannwitt)

The last lines show, obviously enough, the narrator's fear
that she will become one of the Hard Women, and looking
back at the title, we now realize its significance. But we
can go a step further. What has happened to the Hard
Women and what may happen to the narrator may also
befall anyone else, female or male. The Women and the
narrator, then, are universal symbols.

In the definition of a poem that we have been using
(page 233) we have paid particular attention to the words
"significant experience." One way a poet makes an experience significant is to make it a symbol of many experiences,
of even a universal experience, as Monica did in her poem.

EXERCISE FOUR

1. Here is a list of items. Discuss what each might be made
to symbolize in a poem:

mink coat   brilliant trumpet solo in a jazz
American flag   combo
light in a laboratory at midnight   photograph on a doctor's desk

deserted locker room	shanty
child learning to read	rosebud
flashbulb	new highway
first frost	jet streak
fresh sheet of paper	crust
grain of sand	a larger television set
the smallest particle of matter	fence
	foothills

2. Now for the reverse of what you have just done. Here are some general statements. What specific symbol or symbols might be useful in a poetic presentation of each? (The symbol, of course, may be a person, a thing, or an incident.)

Time goes faster every year.
Some fathers love their children more than other fathers do.
Competition is an effective incentive.
Intolerance is learned, not inherited.
Nature is wasteful.
Flaws exist in even the most beautiful things.
Love of country and respect for the rest of mankind are not incompatible.
To err is human.
The invention of movable type has had profound effects.
"When a modifiable connection between a stimulus and a response is made and is followed or accompanied by a satisfying state of affairs, that connection's strength is increased. When made and accompanied by an annoying state of affairs, its strength is decreased." (Psychologist E. L. Thorndike's Law of Effect, pertaining to how we learn)

14

How to Express Poetry

SOUND AND RHYTHM

In the definition of a poem on page 233, we learned that "an unusual number of the resources of language are concentrated." Among those resources are sound and rhythm.

The most obvious use of sound effects in poetry is in rhyme. Rhyme can and should be much more than decoration. Once more we have here an illustration of Frost's "two-ness": the rhyming words pair up like Noah's animals. Rhyme satisfies a universal longing for continuity: what was before will be again. It helps, also, to build stanzaic patterns and thus again builds an awareness of repetition. The final rhyme of a stanza ties up the package with a little bow. Rhyme may help, too, in revealing the mood of a stanza or a poem; light combinations are breezy, unexpected ones may be humorous or satiric, and heavy ones are somber.

You probably already know, without studying, these two "rules" of rhyme:

1. Sounds, not letters, determine rhyme. The vowel sound and the concluding consonant sound must be the same, but the consonant sound preceding the vowel sound must be different. Thus *bit* and *pit* rhyme, but *bite* and *bight* do not; neither do *sight* and *cite*, nor *sit* and *sip*. *Grown* and *tone* rhyme, despite the different spellings. *Father* and *rather* do not rhyme in general American pronunciation, despite the similarity of spelling.

2. Only stressed (accented) syllables carry the rhyme, but if unstressed syllables follow, they must be the same

as in the word to be rhymed with. Thus *slightly* and *tightly* rhyme, but *slightly* and *tighter* do not.

Most rhymes come at the ends of lines, and hence are called end-rhymes. When, as in Poe's "The Raven," some rhymes come within the line, those rhymes are called internal.

When final stressed syllables rhyme (as in *large* and *barge* or *depend* and *amend*), the rhyme is said to be masculine. Rhymes like *slightly* and *tightly,* in which the stressed syllable is followed by an unstressed, are called feminine. Triple rhymes, as in *tenderly* and *slenderly,* appear occasionally, and for humorous effect writers like Ogden Nash may use quadruple or even quintuple rhyme.

The English language is not rich in rhymes, as Italian, for example, is. John Ciardi has pointed out that only about a half dozen rhymes for *life* are possible, but that hundreds exist for the Italian equivalent, *vita.* The paucity of rhyme words in English explains the first two of these five *don'ts* about rhyme:

1. As an amateur, don't attempt stanza forms in which the same rhyming sound is needed several times.

2. Don't let rhymes determine content.

3. Don't have rhyming words too far apart.

4. Don't, as a rule, have similar rhyming sounds very close together. Poor: *train, trait, main, strait.* Satisfactory: *train, slow, main, low.*

5. Don't rely so heavily on rhyme that rhyme alone distinguishes your verse from prose.

The rhyme scheme of a stanza may be described in abbreviated form by letting *a* represent the first end word and everything that rhymes with it, *b* the second, and so on. Thus a stanza ending in the words *plays, walk, prays, talk* would be described as *abab.* If the end words were *plays, walk, hurry, talk,* the rhyme scheme would be *abcb.*

Experienced poets often make use of near-rhyme, e.g., words like *saint* and *wait* or *quill* and *spell,* but the beginner should proceed cautiously here because his near-rhyme may be interpreted as a near-miss.

Experienced poets also gain some of their effects from what is called assonance, a similarity of vowel sounds. Assonance may be either identical vowel sounds with different consonant sounds, as in *cat* and *pan,* or merely similar vowel sounds with different consonants, as in *boot, rode,* and *tall,* or *meet, send,* and *him,* or *quell* and *quill.* The beginner need not know the rather complicated rules governing assonance; he can usually trust his ear to tell him whether the words close to one another sound right.

Alliteration, the use of the same consonant sounds close together, is illustrated in the tongue twister about Peter Piper or in Tennyson's "The *m*oan of doves in i*mm*e*m*orial el*m*s,/And *m*ur*m*uring of innu*m*erable bees." Modern poets use it only infrequently, and only for specifically planned sound effects.

Rhythm is one of the other "resources of language" especially needed in poetry. Some definers, in fact, claim that the presence of rhythm chiefly distinguishes verse from prose, although much prose has rhythm of its own (Hemingway's is a good example). Rhythm in poetry may be most simply defined as a fairly steady recurring pattern of stressed and unstressed syllables.

Rhythm shows two-ness also. In nature it is revealed in the inrushing waves and their slow subsidence, in the ebb and flow of the tide, in the alternation of summer and winter, in the waxing and waning of the moon, in the growth of green leaves and their brown falling, in a thousand other things. In English poetry it usually shows in an unstressed syllable followed by a stressed one (marked ⌣ and '):

$$\text{Bĕsíde thĕ spŕings ŏf Dóve.}$$

The unstressed-stressed pattern occurs in countless English words and phrases, such as:

ăló̆ne   ămŏng   rĕdéem   dĕcláre

ŏf cóurse   wĭth cáre   tŏ líve   rĕmémbĕr mé

This commonest of English rhythms—unstressed-stressed —is called an iambic foot. Whole books have been written about the rhythms, the meters, of English poetry, but Robert Frost put the essence of the matter into four short sentences:

In English the meter is either strict iambic or loose iambic. If it is strict there is only one light syllable between stresses. If it is loose, the meter may have two light syllables between stresses. Then, of course, if it is strictly loose with two light syllables between every two stresses, that is anapestic.[1]

The reason for loose iambics is that an unvarying buh-boom buh-boom buh-boom rhythm would become monotonous. So poets maintain the basic rhythm but depart from it enough to avoid monotony, Sometimes, as Frost suggested, they put two or even three light syllables between stresses; or they may now and then put two or even three stressed syllables together; or they may start a line with a stressed rather than an unstressed syllable. Here is an example from Shakespeare's *Macbeth*, in which Lady Macbeth is counseling her husband:

Yŏur fáce, mў tháne, ĭs ăs ă bóok whĕre mén

Mӑy réad stránge mátterš. Tŏ bĕgúile thĕ tíme,

Lóok lĭke thĕ tíme; bĕar wélcŏme ĭn yŏur éye,

Yŏur hánd, yŏur tóngue: lóok lĭke thĕ ínnŏcĕnt flówĕr,

Bŭt bĕ thĕ sérpĕnt únder't.

Basically a Shakespeare line is ⌣′ ⌣′ ⌣′ ⌣′ ⌣′ (five iambic feet). But in line 1 of the illustration, a natural

---

[1] [John Ciardi, "Robert Frost: Master Conversationalist at Work," *Saturday Review*, March 21, 1959, p. 18.]

reading puts no stress on *as*, so that line really consists of three strict iambic feet and one loose one. Line 2 starts with a strict iambic, then has two stressed syllables, then a loose iambic, and finally a strict iambic. Line 3 begins with a stressed syllable. Both it and line 4 contain other variations similar to those found in lines 1 and 2, and line 4 ends with an unstressed syllable.

An anapestic foot, to which Frost referred, is ⌣ ⌣ ′, as in the opening of a poem by Byron:

> The Assyrian came down like the wolf on the fold.

Your teacher may want you to know these other feet, too, though it is simplest to consider these, as Frost does, as variations of the iambic or the anapestic:

trochaic	′ ⌣	wánder
spondaic	′ ′	wíde héarths
dactylic	′ ⌣ ⌣	gréedily
amphibrachic	⌣ ′ ⌣	compélling

There are about a dozen others, but they are seldom found except, once again, as variants of iambic and anapestic.

Lines of verse may be described in terms of the number of feet in each. These are useful names to know:

monometer (one foot): The híll

dimeter (two feet): Upón | the híll

trimeter (three feet): And stóod | upón | the híll

tetrameter (four feet): Then wént | and stóod | upón | the híll

pentameter (five feet): Then wént | and stóod | upón | the lít|tle

                          híll

hexameter (six feet): She sighed, | then wént | and stóod | upón|

                       the lít|tle híll

heptameter (seven feet): Shĕ síghed, | thĕn wĕnt | ănd stóod |

upŏn | thĕ lít|tlĕ híll | ănd wépt.

It is possible to be much more technical than we have been in describing the sounds and rhythms of poetry, and anyone who wants poetry to be more than an avocation must learn much more of the technicalities. But you now have enough basic information to use in the creation of good verse.

EXERCISE ONE

1. Without consulting a dictionary of rhymes, think of as many rhyming words as you can for each of these: *ash, eel, ice, coal, tender.*

2. No reasonable rhyme exists for *orange.* Try to think of several other words of which this is true.

3. In any collection of poetry you have handy, copy the end-rhymes of several poems, like this: *friends, joy, ends, destroy.* Indicate the rhyme scheme of each stanza. Does every line end in a rhyming word? Do you find any apparent exceptions to the rules of rhyme on page 252? Do you find any near-rhymes? If possible, also find some internal rhymes in one or two poems.

4. In the same poems you read for Number 3, try to discover the metrical pattern. Do so by reading lines aloud, noting which syllables are stressed, which unstressed. Attempt to describe the lines as iambic pentameter, anapestic tetrameter, and so on. Have the authors followed a pattern without any variation? What kinds of variations do you find?

5. Most of the student-written poems quoted in Chapter 13 have no rhyme, and some have little rhythm or only a very irregular rhythm. Which seem to you to be most regular in rhythm? Which are least rhythmic? Would the latter be better poems if the rhythms were more definite, or have they enough other poetic qualities to atone for the lack of rhythm?

6. As an experiment in rhythm, copy and complete the following lines with *buh* (unstressed) and *boom* (stressed), continuing the rhythm that starts each line:

    a. The stream below ⎯⎯ ⎯⎯ ⎯⎯ ⎯⎯ ⎯⎯ ⎯⎯

    b. From the brow of the cliff ⎯⎯ ⎯⎯ ⎯⎯ ⎯⎯ ⎯⎯ ⎯⎯

Now replace the buh-booms with words that make sense, and add another line in the same rhythm.

7. Choose one of the symbols you discussed in Exercise Four of Chapter 13 (page 250), and write about it in four or more lines following a rhythm that seems suitable. Rhyme the lines if you wish. Be sure that neither the rhythm nor the rhyme distorts the meaning and the symbolism you want to convey.

A FEW VERSE FORMS

Through the centuries English poets have borrowed or developed several hundred verse forms. These are patterns of rhyme and rhythm. A few that you may find most useful or interesting will be described here.

Blank verse is unrhymed iambic pentameter: ˘´ ˘´ ˘´ ˘´ ˘´. As we have seen (page 255), the iambics may be varied. Shakespeare's plays are mainly in blank verse; Milton chose this form for *Paradise Lost;* thousands of other poets have used it.

Free verse, also unrhymed, is irregular in form. Most of Walt Whitman's poetry is in free verse, and so are most of the students' poems quoted in Chapter Thirteen. Free verse is successful only if it has some rhythm, even though uneven, and if the cargo of thought and feeling is considerable. Prose chopped up into uneven lengths does *not* constitute free verse.

A *couplet* consists of two rhyming lines of similar length and meter. Most lines in couplets are tetrameter or pentameter, though other lengths are possible. An especially polished form of the iambic pentameter couplet, called the *heroic couplet,* was perfected by Alexander Pope. The following student-written poem consists of only one tetrameter couplet:

The Poem

The freight train passed in perfect time,
Lacking only words and rhyme.

(Lowell Antenen)

Carol opened the next poem with a *triplet* (three rhyming lines similar in length and meter), continued it with couplets, and then repeated the triplet:

Song for a Very Young Heart

(Speak to me with the calico murmur of wind in the peach tree
    leaves;
Speak to me with the taffeta whisper of wind in the tall corn
    sheaves;
Speak to me with a velvety speaking; my heart knows what it
    believes.)
  Wind in my hair and sun on my face—
  Earth is a beautiful, close-to-God place.
  I have the rain and the sun and the sky
  And the lonely magic of a night bird's cry.
  Now I have you, and you are a song
  And a joy and a breathlessness; my love is strong
  In its faith in the simple, unbreakable rule
  That lives in the world bound up by the pool
  Of your eyes, brown and deep. I am lost in your eyes.
  You are my race and my goal and my prize. . . .

(Speak to me with the calico murmur of wind in the peach tree
    leaves;
Speak to me with the taffeta whisper of wind in the tall corn
    sheaves;
Speak to me with a velvety speaking; my heart knows what it
    believes.)

(Carol Hasely)

A *quatrain* is a poem or a stanza of four lines, with at least the second and fourth rhyming. Most ballads with which you are familiar are in quatrains rhyming *abcb,* with four iambic feet in the first and third lines, three in the second and fourth. "A Mystery" (page 237) follows a similar pattern. Other rhyme schemes are *abab* and *abba.* Darlene's whimsical little poem consists of three quatrains:

Undersea

Beneath the waters
Green and cool
The mermaids keep
A dancing school.

The oysters trot,
The lobsters prance,
The dolphins come
To join the dance.

But the jellyfish,
All rather small,
Can't seem to learn
The steps at all.

(Darlene Davey)

The name *cinquain* may be applied to any five-line stanza, although it is used especially for the particular kind that Adelaide Crapsey frequently used. Examples are on pages 246 and 249. Note the lack of rhyme, and the fact that the respective lines have two, four, six, eight, and two syllables.

Another five-line poem, almost invariably humorous or nonsensical, is the *limerick.* The first, second, and fifth lines rhyme and have three stressed syllables; the third and fourth lines rhyme and have two stresses.

Limerick

There once was a girl named Bet
Who kept a huge snake for a pet.
    Her friends heard a slurp,
    The snake gave a burp,
And they haven't found Bet as yet.

(Jim Solomon)

The *hokku*, a three-line poem, has been illustrated on page 245. The *tanka*, another imitation of a Japanese form, has five unrhymed lines, the first and third with five syllables each, the others with seven. It usually attempts a quick, significant comparison:

Tanka

Life is like a book.
You start at the beginning,
Progress to the end,
Living each precious chapter
Between preface and finis.

(Dorothy Kline)

Although both the hokku and the tanka are relatively uncommon forms, they provide help in learning brevity and precise diction.

A six-line verse is most often called a *sestet*. It has many possible variations of rhyme, line length, and rhythm.

A *heptastich*, of seven lines, or an *octave*, of eight lines, likewise may be of many varieties. One kind of octave, called a *triolet*, is rather amusing to write, though moderately difficult. Its eight lines rhyme *abaaabab*, but the first, fourth and seventh lines are the same, as are the second and eighth. Here is an example:

Triolet

As snow falls softly like a veil,
It hides the bush and bends the bough.
Our steps are cushioned on the trail
As snow falls softly like a veil
And slowly fills each river dale.
The frosted world is transformed now
As snow falls softly like a veil
And hides the bush and bends the bough.

(Evan Myers)

The *sonnet* is a fourteen-line iambic pentameter poem. In the Italian, or Petrarchan form, there is a clear break between the octave (the first eight lines) and the sestet. The octave states a question, a doubt, a thought, or a wish, and the sestet answers the question or says something else relevant about the content of the octave; in other words it provides a kind of solution. The octave rhymes *abba abba;* the sestet, usually *cdecde* or *cdcdcd* or *cdeedc.* The Shakespearean sonnet is less rigid in form, with the concluding couplet normally summarizing or answering or contrasting with the rest of the poem. Its rhyme scheme is usually *abab cdcd efef gg.* Many modern poets have written irregular sonnets, with shorter or longer lines and various other structural differences. Here is a student's version of a Petrarchan sonnet:

A Sonnet

The cold wind swirls around the trees. The bare
   And slender branches bend beneath its blow.
   The sky is threatening; clouds are filled with snow.
The wind is icy as a witch's glare.
The storm looms bleak above the hill to tear
   Across the countryside, to freeze the flow
   Of swiftly running streams that lie below.
The storm breaks and a chill hangs in the air.

And when at last the sun shines through the mist
Spreading its glow across the countryside,
Its light reveals some things that may seem odd
To us. We see a world the sun has kissed
With shining life, a world of things untried,
A pure world that has just been washed by God.

(Barbara Myers)

One other type of writing should be mentioned, although it is not a specific form. This is the *parody*, an imitation, humorous or serious, of a well-known poem or part of a poem. Bill's verse which opened Chapter 13 (page 231) is a parody, imitating the form and some specific lines of Joyce Kilmer's best-known poem. Students in one class enjoyed Edgar Lee Masters' *Spoon River Anthology* and attempted to write similar word portraits of men and women imagined as buried in the Spoon River cemetery. Here is one of the results:

Jake Hill

Some say I was worthless—no good to anyone.
Perhaps I was, for most of my life was spent in prisons and
reformatories.
Here, however, I had time to think,
And at long last I began to realize my obligation to society.
When I offered myself as a guinea pig for a scientific experi-
ment, the warden said I might gain my freedom.
There was a chance, though, that I could lose my life.
I took that chance—perhaps it was my gambling instinct—and
lost.
But I have no regrets
For above me I hear the footsteps of those who live because I
lost my greatest gamble.

(Marcia Dalbey)

Amused by Lewis Carroll's nonsense verse, Dorothy wrote a parody called "The Tale of the Jadioray," which started like this:

The Cadora was scrubby gibuous,
  And he went on his yilligy way.
But then he stopped in frufal surprise,
  When he saw the Jadioray!

                                        (Dorothy Carter)

EXERCISE TWO

1. In Exercises Two (3), Three, and Four of Chapter 13, you prepared what may be suggestions for poems. Choose one of those that you especially like, and try your hand at building it into a poem. Use any form you wish.

2. Choose another poem-idea, preferably an original one, but possibly related to Exercises Two, Three, Four of Chapter 13. Experiment with different forms for developing it. You may, for instance, want to say it in blank verse, free verse, couplets, or one or more quatrains. Which form seems to work out best for this particular idea? Why? Is it reasonable to conclude that a poem is best when the form and the idea are harmonious?

Section E

THE WRITER'S CRAFT

15

From Manuscript into Print

THE purpose of this chapter is to trace what happens to a writer's manuscript from the time he prepares it to the moment when the final printed version reaches him and he eagerly removes the wrapping. Although variations in procedure do exist, in general the steps involved are: preliminary revisions and preparation of the manuscript, submission of the manuscript, readers' reactions and editorial suggestions, further revisions, typesetting and art work, proofreading and corrections, and printing and binding. We shall use an imaginary nonfiction book as our example, and at the end shall note a few differences in treatment of magazine articles and news stories.

THE AUTHOR'S REVISIONS; PREPARATION OF THE MANUSCRIPT

We shall imagine that a teacher, Clarence McCoy, has written a manuscript for a book to be called *Student Activities in the High School*. He has done considerable research, interviewed many persons, and drawn upon his own experience in order to prepare a useful guide to the best ways of conducting worthwhile activities.

As we shall see in the next chapter, authors vary in their techniques of revision. Mr. McCoy, as it happens, writes his first draft in longhand, makes numerous revisions and deletions and additions and improvements in style, has his wife type the next draft, and then makes revisions in that until he is satisfied that the manuscript is as thorough and helpful and accurate as he can make it. These revisions are highly important, sometimes making the difference between acceptance and rejection.

Mr. McCoy's wife types the final manuscript, being sure to make a carbon copy for safety. (Thomas Carlyle once had to rewrite an entire book because his only copy was accidentally destroyed.) She types neatly, double-spacing everything. The lefthand margin is about an inch and a half wide, and the less regular righthand margin about three-quarters of an inch. The reason for fairly wide margins is to provide space later for the copy editor to put in necessary instructions for the typesetters. Mrs. McCoy indents extra the occasional long quotations that her husband has taken from other publications; when so indented, they do not require quotation marks.

At about this time, or more likely not until publication has been assured, Mr. McCoy writes to the publishers of the books and magazines from which he quotes, asking permission to use their material in his book. For short quotations, especially from prose, there is likely to be no charge, but for long ones a payment may be required. Such a payment may be made by the author (after he is sure of publication) or may be advanced by the publisher and perhaps deducted later from the author's royalties.

Mrs. McCoy starts each chapter on a new page. She numbers the pages in the upper righthand corner, consecutively through the manuscript. If graphs, tables, or illustrations are to be inserted, she notes the place they are to go, although page make-up may force some changes.

Mr. and Mrs. McCoy work together on proofreading the manuscript, watching for possible omissions and checking for possible typographical errors. They are doubly careful with quotations, making sure that they are exactly as in the original.

SUBMISSION OF THE MANUSCRIPT

If Mr. McCoy has already had an expression of interest from a publisher, or a commitment to publish, a brief note accompanies the manuscript, reminding the publisher of the previous correspondence. If the manuscript is being sent as one of the large number of unsolicited manuscripts that reach every publisher's desk, a brief letter will serve to explain why this particular publisher may find the book suitable for his firm, and to point out succinctly what kind of need the book will meet. However, the manuscript will inevitably be judged on its own merits, not on the eloquence of the accompanying letter.

Mr. McCoy knows that publishers have different specialties. Some publish only textbooks, some only religious books, some only plays, some mainly fiction, and some almost everything. Mr. McCoy has chosen a publisher who in the past has brought out books related in some way to Mr. McCoy's own.

READER'S REACTIONS AND
EDITORIAL SUGGESTIONS

When Mr. McCoy's manuscript reaches the publishing house, it is placed with others that have recently come in. In some houses manuscripts are divided into two groups, called rather irreverently the "rush pile" and the "slush pile." In the rush pile are the manuscripts from established authors, specially solicited manuscripts, manuscripts for which contracts have been signed, and manuscripts on topics of great current interest that should be published at once if at all. The slush pile consists mainly of unsolicited manuscripts from little-known authors.

Every large publishing house has a staff of readers who work steadily in a vain attempt to reduce the size of the two piles. Everything in the rush pile is given preferred treatment, and many of the manuscripts go directly to editors who will help to bring out the finished work. Manuscripts in the slush pile are all examined carefully by at least one reader, and in some houses by two, who must either agree on a recommendation or consult a third reader. However, it would be a mistake to assume that every word of every manuscript is read. Readers often apply what they call the "rotten-egg test," which is based on the theory that you don't have to eat a whole egg to realize that it is rotten.

Publishers are always looking for good manuscripts by previously unpublished authors, and they instruct their preliminary readers to reject only those manuscripts that are unquestionably poor. If a manuscript has more than a glimmer of merit and if it may fill a need, the readers are asked to submit it to an editor. Both the readers and the editors sometimes make mistakes, of course, and authors often console themselves with the knowledge that many excellent and successful books were rejected by several publishers before being accepted.

Mr. McCoy's manuscript survives the preliminary readers and is sent to the appropriate editorial department. There two or more persons read it and hold a conference about it. They have all noted ways in which they believe the manuscript can be strengthened, but they like many of its features. One of the editors says in effect, "I'll favor our publishing it only if this and this and that are changed." The others agree, and one of them draws up a recommendation to be sent with the manuscript to the editor in chief.

The editor in chief probably reads only parts of the manuscript, just enough to see that he agrees in general with the opinions of his subordinates. One member of the editorial staff writes a letter to Mr. McCoy, telling him that a contract will be forwarded to him if he agrees to make certain revisions.

FURTHER REVISIONS

Mr. and Mrs. McCoy are jubilant when the letter of acceptance arrives. Their joy subsides a little, though, when they realize the amount of work still to be done. Some additional research is needed for a couple of the chapters; two others need to be rewritten; minor changes must be made throughout the manuscript.

Some houses require that their authors work very closely with the editors in making revisions. Some textbook chapters, for instance, may be reworked a half-dozen or more times, the final version being almost completely different from the first draft and perhaps more a product of the editors than of the author. Other houses may give greater freedom. The author of a work of fiction is likely to have fewer restraints imposed upon him than is the writer of nonfiction.

Mr. McCoy spends the weeks or months necessary to make the changes, Mrs. McCoy retypes much or all of the manuscript, they proofread it again, and off it goes once more to the publisher.

TYPESETTING AND ART WORK

Meanwhile the editorial workers in the publishing house have not forgotten the existence of the manuscript. They have made many decisions about the typography and general format: page size, probable number of pages, weight and finish of paper, kind of binding, type size, style or styles of type, treatment of headings, and the like.

The art department has been consulted about cover design and also jacket design if the book is to have a dust jacket. The art department is also asked to help in preparing an attractive and clear layout of graphs and other illustrations, and perhaps to find additional photographs or other art that will help to brighten or clarify the copy. For some books the art department prepares special drawings or employs artists outside the firm to prepare them.

When Mr. McCoy's newly revised manuscript reaches the office, it goes directly to the editorial department. There someone makes sure that the recommended changes have been satisfactorily made. The manuscript now goes to a copy editor, who marks it to give the printer exact instructions, perhaps on every page, concerning typography.

Most of the copy is probably set on a linotype machine, although some other kinds of machines are now available. The linotype operator uses a keyboard something like that of a typewriter. His punching of the keys results in the setting of individual lines of type which are molded in hot lead. Headings and some hard-to-fit copy may be set by hand.

Meanwhile the art department has engravings prepared for the illustrations, choosing the proper size of screen according to the kind of paper to be used in the book.

PROOFREADING AND CORRECTION

The lines of type are assembled in long trays called galleys. The type is inked and a few proof copies are made, called galley proofs. These are read by two persons at the printer's, one reading aloud the manuscript, the other following the galley and attempting to find any printer's errors. The author may also be sent galley proof to read, although sometimes he is sent only page proofs. These are proofs with galley corrections made and with the type arranged page by page as it will appear in the book itself if no further corrections or other changes are made.

When Mr. McCoy receives proof, he is expected to read

it promptly and carefully, searching for any errors that may have escaped the notice of the other readers. The page proof affords the last opportunity to make any changes. However, alterations at this stage are expensive, and if he makes many of them, he may have to pay part of the cost.

You remember that the linotype sets complete lines. Any change, then, even a small one such as the addition or deletion of a comma, requires the resetting of an entire line. If a word or two are added or deleted in the first line of a paragraph, it may be necessary to reset the whole paragraph. If a line is added in page proof, it may be necessary to shift type in all the later pages of a chapter. These facts illustrate the importance of submitting a correct and polished manuscript so that very few alterations, exclusive of printer's errors, will be needed in the proof stage.

Proofreaders follow a system of marking that tells the printer very concisely what is to be changed. The place of correction is marked within the line, and the needed correction is shown in the margin of the proof. The usual proofreader's marks are shown here:

$\overset{\prime}{\vee}$	Insert apostrophe (or single quotation mark)
$\colon\mid$ or $\odot$	Insert colon
$\overset{\wedge}{,}$	Insert comma
$\overset{!}{/}$	Insert exclamation mark
$=\mid$ or $\mid=\mid$	Insert hyphen
$\odot$	Insert period
$\overset{?}{/}$	Insert question mark
$\overset{\prime\prime}{\vee}$	Insert quotation marks
$\overset{;}{/}$	Insert semicolon

$\|\frac{1}{en}\|$	Insert en dash (–)
$\|\frac{1}{em}\|$	Insert em dash (—)
$\|\frac{2}{em}\|$	Insert two-em dash (——)
	Used within the line, indicates insertion
$\wedge$	Delete (take out)
$\mathcal{J}$	Delete and close up
$\textcircled{\mathcal{J}}$	Turn an inverted letter
$\mathcal{I}$	Print as a ligature
$\downarrow$	Push down lead
$\|\|$	Straighten ends of lines
$\equiv$	Straighten lines
$\subset\supset$	Close up; reduce space
$\#$	Space (or more space)
$Eq\ \#$	Space evenly
$\square$	Indent one em
$\square\ \square$	Indent two ems
$\sqsubset$	Move to left
$\sqsupset$	Move to right
$\sqcap$	Move up
$\sqcup$	Move down
wf	Wrong font (size or style)
ld	Insert lead between lines
X	Broken type

ital Set in italic type (with _____ under text matter)

bf Set in boldface type (with ~~~~~ under text matter)

rom Set in roman type (with _____ under text matter)

cap Capitalize (with ≡≡≡ under text matter)

sc or scaps Small capitals (with ≡≡≡ under text matter)

lc Use lower case

sp Spell out

space out Spread words farther apart

tr Transpose (with ⌢ or ⌣ in text matter)

¶ New paragraph

no ¶ No paragraph

? or au Query to the author

stet Let it stand; change made was wrong

PRINTING AND BINDING

The printing process we are considering here, called letterpress, is the most widely used one. Others, such as offset, involve a somewhat different kind of typesetting and printing. In letterpress work, the type that has been set and corrected is fastened securely in forms, usually sixteen pages to the form. These forms are put directly on presses or sometimes are used instead as masters to produce curved plates carrying the typed matter; these plates may be used in high-speed rotary presses like those that turn out hundreds of thousands of newspapers daily.

The sheets of paper on which the book pages are printed on both sides are named broadsheets. After printing, these are folded by machines and gathered in groups called signatures. The first and last signatures are combined with the end papers that will appear in the book and are reinforced with muslin or other material. The signatures that will make up each copy of a book are assembled by a gathering machine and sewed together by a heavy-duty sewing machine. The book is mashed flat, glue is applied at the back, and the front, bottom, and top edges are trimmed.

Meanwhile covers have been made by cover-making machines, and printed with the title, author, and publisher. The cover and contents are brought together in a process known as casing-in. Finally the book is pressed again to make it lie flat, and inspected visually or electronically.

The editors supplied a copyright page, showing in whose name the copyright is held. Now that the book is off the press, one of the first acts is to send two copies to the United States Register of Copyrights, along with a small fee. Copyrighting the book makes it illegal for anyone except book reviewers to reproduce any part of it without permission.

Mr. McCoy is also sent several copies of his book. At last his long project is completed. Joyfully and yet with trepidation he and his wife open a copy, eager to admire the finished product but fearful that they may find some horrible mistake. Seeing none, they hold a private celebration and then wait patiently for the reviews.

TREATMENT OF MAGAZINE ARTICLES AND NEWSPAPER STORIES

The writer for magazines or newspapers is usually less intimately involved than the book-writer in seeing his brainchild through its printing. He must be no less careful in writing, checking, and revising, but often his task is ended when his final revisions are made. In fact, newspapers have rewrite desks where special writers may rewrite stories, shortening them or changing them in other ways to meet the demands of the next edition of the paper. Other specialists take care of the proofreading. This means that the reporter who wrote the original story will probably not see it again until it appears in print, and then may hardly recognize it.

Some magazines send proof to their authors for correction, but many do not. However, a magazine editor will normally not make drastic changes without consulting the author.

EXERCISE

1. If you have visited a printing establishment of any kind, be prepared to tell the class what you saw. Better yet, arrange either as individuals or as a class to visit or revisit a local printery.

2. Describe your own processes of revision of an important paper written for one of your classes. How do they differ from Mr. McCoy's (page 267)?

3. Here is a paragraph with many errors. It is the famous last paragraph of Patrick Henry's best-known speech. Copy it exactly, line for line, and then correct it as a proofreader would, using the symbols on pages 273–275.

> it is in vain, sir, to exstenuate the mat
> -ter. Gentlemen may cry, Peace, Peach
> —but thereis no peace The war is
> actully begun! The next gale that
> sweeps from hte north will bring to our
> ears that clash of resounding aLms!
> Our brethern are already in the feild!
> Why we stand hear idol? What is it
> that gentleman wish? What would
> they have, Is life so dear, or peace so
> sweet, as to be pur chased at the price
> of chains and sLAvery? Forbid it, Almighty
> God! i know not wat coarse others may
> take; but as for he, gibe me liberty
> or gve he breath!

16

Work Habits of
Professional Writers *

STUDY of the work habits of professional writers will by no means provide a formula for success. In fact, you will probably finish this chapter in greater puzzlement than you begin it, for, as you will discover, no two writers appear to plan and proceed in exactly the same way. Actually the purpose of the chapter is to reveal that creative writers do *not* follow formulas, that although some of them share a few characteristics, each of them must find the specific procedures that best suit his own temperament.

THE BACKGROUND FOR WRITING

Essayist and critic Bertrand Russell has said, "Shakespeare and Scott were read to me till I was about twelve, and after that I had to read them out loud. . . . Shelley and Keats I discovered for myself at the age of sixteen, and from then until I was twenty-one I read English poetry constantly, and learnt a great deal by heart. . . . I read Gibbon, Mill, Swift, Goethe, Heine, Racine, Corneille. . . ."

Many other twentieth-century writers avow their indebtedness to the great names of the past, not for ideas or plots or characters, but for style and ways of looking at life and hints of what creativity actually is. W. Somerset

---

* For many of the quotations in this chapter the author is indebted to Josephine K. Piercy, *Modern Writers at Work* (New York: The Macmillan Company, 1930) and Malcolm Cowley, ed., *Writers at Work: The Paris Review Interviews* (New York: The Viking Press, 1958), copyright 1957, 1958 by The Paris Review, Inc.

Maugham, for example, told of his copying out passages from the English classics, a half hour every day, and reading for another three hours. E. M. Forster refers to his "very literary childhood." William Faulkner said that he returned "as you do to old friends" to the books he "knew and loved" when he was a young man: the Old Testament, Dickens, Conrad, Cervantes, Flaubert, Balzac, Dostoevsky, Shakespeare, Keats, Shelley, and others, but he never read the psychologist Freud, who has influenced many modern writers. Italian novelist Alberto Moravia reveres Joyce, Dostoevsky, Manzoni, Voltaire, Balzac, de Maupassant, Shakespeare, Conrad, and Hardy. Robert Penn Warren says that he was only slightly interested in fiction before he finished college, but "I was reading my head off in poetry, Elizabethans and the moderns, Yeats, Hardy, Eliot, Hart Crane." Dorothy Parker imitated poems, and later commented, "The men you imitate in verse influence your prose, and what I got out of it was precision."

Novelist and essayist Meredith Nicholson likewise believed that "versifying is excellent preparation for prose as it gives practice in precision and brevity," and British essayist E. V. Lucas specifically recommended "8-syllable couplets in verse—the sense to conclude with each couplet." William Faulkner said, "I'm a failed poet. Maybe every novelist wants to write poetry first, finds he can't, and then tries the short story, which is the most demanding form after poetry. And, failing at that, only then does he take up novel writing." Short story writer Frank O'Connor wrote lyric poetry until he "discovered that God had not intended me to be a lyric poet."

In addition to emphasizing the importance of extensive reading and varied writing, modern authors refer to their need for what Aldous Huxley called an "apprenticeship," because "writing is exactly like any other skilled trade" (a comparison with which by no means all writers would agree). Ernest Hemingway said, "Everyone writes prose

badly to start but by continuing some get to write it well."
Humorist Irvin S. Cobb described his "system": "Practice,
hard work, reading the writings of real master-writers."
"A writer needs three things," said William Faulkner: "experience, observation, and imagination, any two of which,
at times any one of which, can supply the lack of the
others," and Nelson Algren says, "A writer doesn't really
live, he observes." Truman Capote comments, "Work is
the only device I know of. Writing has laws of perspective,
of light and shade, just as painting does, or music. If you
are born having them, fine. If not, learn them. Then rearrange the rules to suit yourself." Biographer Gamaliel Bradford once said, "A tremendous and undying persistence is
at least a very important part of the writer's equipment."
One of the best twentieth-century British writers about
the sea, William McFee, sums it up like this: "The phrase,
the paragraph, the chapter, grow in [the writer's] mind in
orderly and largely unconscious sequence, not because he
has had inspiration from on high, but because he has been
practicing the swing [like that in cricket or baseball] until
it has become second nature."

Although many writers serve as teachers or consultants
in summer writing conferences, some deny that writing
can really be learned in that way. Says William Styron, "A
writing course can only give you a start, and help a little.
It can't teach writing." In a humorous essay called "How
to Write Short Stories," Ring Lardner observed, ". . . you
can't find no school in operation up to date, whether it be
a general institute of learning or a school that specializes
in story writing, which can make a great author out of
a born druggist."

Sherwood Anderson, one of the most influential American short story writers of the century, emphasized knowledge of people as essential background, and others agree.
Anderson said, "We shall have to begin to write out of the
people and not for the people. . . . Your true novelist is a

man gone a little mad with the life of his time. As he goes through life he lives not in himself, but in many people." A Shakespearean critic missed this essential when a number of years ago he wrote *Shakespeare Apart,* a book in which he tried to show that the author of the plays was apart from and superior to the life of his time. The title should have been *Shakespeare a Part,* for Shakespeare shared deeply in the lives and thoughts of his Elizabethan contemporaries.

EXERCISE ONE

1. Of the authors named by Russell, Faulkner, Moravia, and Warren (pages 278–279), which are familiar to you? Members of the class may wish to dip into some of the unfamiliar ones and perhaps report informally on what they find.

2. In what ways, in your opinion, may the discipline of writing poetry improve one's prose?

3. How do you account for the fact that a few young writers burst into prominence without the "apprenticeship" that many established writers recommend?

4. From your own reading give examples of works that apparently grew, as Sherwood Anderson prescribed, "out of the people."

A WRITER'S REASONS FOR WRITING

Although some artistic writers admit that money is a major motive for writing, others have different explanations. Truman Capote claims to be "physically incapable" of writing anything he does not expect to be paid for. But in the eighteenth century, poet Thomas Gray, who found writing extremely difficult to do as well as he liked, said that his incentive was "self-realization." Alberto Moravia concurs, saying, "I write simply to amuse myself; I wish to entertain others and—and, well, to express myself. One has one's own way of expressing oneself, and writing happens to be mine."

Frank O'Connor says humorously that for a while it was a toss-up whether he would be a painter or a writer, but that when he was sixteen or seventeen he found that paints were expensive and pencils and paper cheap. A little more seriously, Thornton Wilder said, "I think I write in order to discover on my shelf a new book which I would enjoy reading, or a new play that would engross me." Much more seriously and more specifically, Robert Penn Warren declares, "Once you start illustrating virtue as such, you had better stop writing fiction. Do something else, like Y-work. Or join a committee. Your business as a writer is not to illustrate virtue, but to show how a fellow may move toward it—or away from it." William Faulkner played down the importance of the author: "The artist is of no importance. Only what he creates is important."

Two historians have summarized in different ways why dedicated writers write. In the nineteenth century William H. Prescott wrote: "The history of literature is the history of the human mind. It is, as compared with other histories, the intellectual as distinguished from the material, the informing spirit as compared with the outward and visible." And the twentieth-century Philip Guedalla has said: "[The historian's] business is to write about dead men; but if he is to do his duty, he should remember that they were not always dead. For he is not concerned to embalm them but to resurrect, to set them moving, catch the tone of their voices, tilt of their heads, and posture of the once living men."

EXERCISE TWO

1. In your own words explain the quotations from Warren, Faulkner, and Prescott on this page.

2. How do Guedalla's comments (above) relate to writings other than historical?

3. Why do *you* write?

SOURCES OF A WRITER'S IDEAS

Writers get their ideas from various sources. Joyce Cary said that it was impossible for him to base his characters upon people he knew, but E. M. Forster commented, "We all like to pretend we don't use real people, but one does actually. I used some of my family." French novelist François Mauriac gave credit to rediscovery: "I don't observe and I don't describe; I rediscover. I rediscover the narrow Jansenist world of my devout, unhappy, and introverted childhood." Mauriac thus goes back further in his life than did William Wordsworth on occasion; Wordsworth said that much of his poetry was the result of an often rather recent emotion "recollected in tranquillity."

Some writers have found it useful to keep notebooks in which they jot down story ideas, bits of description, almost anything. Others disparage this practice, E. M. Forster saying he thinks it "improper" and Dorothy Parker commenting that she once tried to keep a notebook but never could remember where she had put it.

It was Dorothy Parker, too, who remarked that her ideas came from sounds, not sights: "I haven't got a visual mind. I hear things." Frank O'Connor would agree: "I notice particularly the cadence of [people's] voices, the sort of phrase they'll use, and that's what I'm all the time trying to hear in my head, how people word things—because everybody speaks an entirely different language, that's really what it amounts to." O'Connor tries to reduce the main idea of each of his stories to four lines, to make sure that it is simple, compact, and unified.

François Mauriac attempts to recreate within himself the colors and smells of some place he has known. Faulkner said that his stories begin with a mental picture, an idea, or a memory, and added, "I don't know anything about inspiration, because I don't know what inspiration is—

I've heard about it, but I never saw it." Robert Penn Warren lets his ideas incubate slowly: "Something I read or see stays in my head for five or six years. I always remember the date, the place, the room, the road, where I was first struck."

Regardless of the source of their ideas most authors are like historian James Harvey Robinson in that they generally make one or more false starts before they gather momentum for the task. Said Robinson: "I have for many years used a typewriter before which I sit, making several false starts before I can bear to go on. A new start may be made later—or two or three. The wastebasket hides the shameful exposures of my incompetence."

EXERCISE THREE

Write a paragraph on "The Source of My Best Ideas."

A WRITER'S PLANNING

When Elliott Nugent and James Thurber collaborated on the play *The Male Animal*, Nugent attempted to plan everything in advance, even the positions of the characters on the stage. Thurber could not work in that way. He said that he had no idea of what any of the characters would say and do until he sat down at the typewriter and found out.

Nugent and Thurber illustrate the two extremes of careful planning and no planning, although Thurber admitted that sometimes he mentally "wrote" stories and sketches at the dinner table or at parties. H. L. Mencken probably typifies many authors in his comment, "I sometimes begin an article without knowing precisely where it will lead me, but that is not often." Truman Capote says that he thinks he has each story carefully planned but that in the writing "infinite surprises happen." E. M. Forster wrote: ". . . there must be something, some major object towards which one is to approach. When I began *A Passage to India* I knew that something important happened in the Malabar Caves, but I didn't know what it would be."

Among the writers who do or did little advance planning may be mentioned Carl Van Doren, John Middleton Murry, Joyce Cary, and Georges Simenon. Van Doren said that for him the pattern "largely takes care of itself, emerging from the details and not dominating them." Murry, describing his "theoretically abominable" procedure, said, "I am, apparently, incapable of thinking out even a brief essay beforehand. I make no plan and follow none. I have always, somewhere in my mind, a half-formed thought, which is always very elusive, and which I struggle to express." Cary declared, "You have to work out problems for yourself, on paper. Put the stuff down and read it—to see if it works. Construction is a complicated job." The prolific French novelist Georges Simenon, who ordinarily devotes only eleven days to one of his short novels, has said: "Unconsciously I probably always have two or three, not novels, not ideas about novels, but themes in my mind. . . . Two days before I start writing I consciously take up one of those ideas. . . . I know nothing about the events when I begin the novel. On the envelope I put only the names of the characters, their ages, their families. . . . On the eve of the first day I know what will happen in the first chapter. Then, day after day, chapter after chapter, I find what comes later."

In contrast, critic Irving Babbitt once asserted that too many modern writers have forgotten "the Horatian precept that the source of good writing is clear thinking," and urged less "spontaneous overflow" and more planning and "sustained effort." Social historian Henry Pratt Fairchild kept his mind busy on his current writing while he was riding on the train or subway or puttering in his garden, and while he was lying sleepless at night he would be "revolving the phraseology of various vital paragraphs." Novelist Angus Wilson makes detailed notes concerning his characters and their backgrounds and even draws maps of the places where the events occur. John Drinkwater summed up the case of those who plan in detail, saying, "The whole difference between good writing and bad writing is that in bad writing a man has not decided precisely what he wants to say and in consequence does not say it precisely, whereas in good writing he has decided down to the finest shade of meaning and has been able to find the exact words to express every subtlety of this thought."

EXERCISE FOUR

1. How do you account for the fact that writers who plan carefully and those who do not may both be successful?

2. In your own writing, have you usually been best satisfied with the results when you have planned carefully, planned in general but not in detail, or planned not at all?

THE PHYSICAL CIRCUMSTANCES OF WRITING

Don't be surprised if someday you meet an author who tells you that he does his best writing at midnight when seated in a tub of ice water. Explorer-author William Beebe said, "The things of mine people like best have been written in the treetops, or in ditches, or sitting on coral four fathoms down." Truman Capote can write only when lying down. He writes in longhand, often "obsessed with the placing of a comma, the weight of a semicolon." If Georges Simenon is ill for forty-eight hours, he loses the threads of whatever he is working on, throws away the completed chapters, and never returns to that novel. He gets a physical checkup before each novel, and clears his calendar completely for the eleven days it requires, for he cannot see anyone, speak to anyone, or receive a phone call. "All the day I am one of my characters. I feel what he feels."

Edna Ferber, according to Dorothy Parker, whistled as she typed. Miss Parker herself typed her own manuscripts with two fingers and no whistling: "I know so little about the typewriter that once I bought a new one because I couldn't change the ribbon on the one I had." James Thurber, handicapped by poor vision, either wrote in a huge sprawl, a few words to a page, or dictated for about three hours in the afternoon. William Styron does two or three pages in a five-hour day, writing in longhand on yellow sheets. "I seem to have some neurotic need to perfect each paragraph—each sentence, even—as I go along." Jack Kerouac endears himself to few editors by sometimes typing his manuscripts on long rolls of paper instead of on single sheets.

Nelson Algren works mostly at night, composing on a typewriter about five pages, which he then rewrites; ". . . the only way I could finish a book and get a plot was just to keep making it longer and longer until something happens," he belittles himself by saying. Ernest Hemingway expressed a distrust of typewriters: "I believe the typewriter is a curse of modern writing. It makes it too easy and the writing is solidified in type and it is hard to change when it might still be kept plastic and be worked over and brought nearer to what it should be before it is cast in type."

Hemingway is said to have sharpened twenty pencils before he started to write. Willa Cather used always to read a Biblical passage as a warm-up, for the sake of the style. Thornton Wilder warmed up with a long walk.

Such examples are given here not to add to the already prevalent theory that writers are eccentrics, but simply to show once more that they don't follow formulas. As a matter of fact, though, most of them are quite regular in their writing habits, as this representative list shows:

Sherwood Anderson: Wrote all morning.

Hamlin Garland: Wrote from 7 a.m. to noon.

Jane Austen: Wrote steadily with household noises all around her.

Angus Wilson: Writes from 8 a.m. to 2 p.m., "but if it's going well, I may go on to four." (He acts out his scenes, as Charles Dickens did.)

Elizabeth Bowen: Insists on writing something *every* day.

Alberto Moravia: Writes from 9 a.m. to noon.

H. L. Mencken: Worked as editor all day, wrote from 7 to 10 p.m. (But he couldn't write in New York, only in Baltimore.)

EXERCISE FIVE

What physical circumstances have you found conducive to your best writing? Have you given other circumstances an equally fair trial?

CONCERN FOR STYLE

Characteristic of all writers who aspire to be literary artists is a continuous concern for style, which often involves a relentless search for the exact word. Aldous Huxley deplores "long, pretentious, abstract words, lumped together in formless, doughy sentences." Gamaliel Bradford tried to "make it a life business to get rid of *clichés*, . . . those deadly worn counters of phrase that circulate with all of us like dirty dollar bills." Georges Simenon draws a pertinent analogy: "A commercial painter paints flat; you can put your finger through. But a painter—for example, an apple by Cézanne has weight. And it has juice, everything, with just three strokes. I tried to give my words just the weight that a stroke of Cézanne's gave to the apple."

Elizabeth Barrett Browning used to put pyramids of words in her margins as she sought the precise one, and Gustave Flaubert endured agony when the right word eluded him. Christopher Morley lamented the exaggerated diction of some journalistic writing, the sort that distorted "the pale and serene beauty" of an eclipse into "imaginary descriptions of green and orange flames shooting across the sky."

But writers know that style entails more than choice of words. A teacher in Sherwood Anderson's *Winesburg, Ohio* advises a young would-be writer: "You will have to know life. If you are to be a writer you'll have to stop fooling with words. . . . You must not become a mere peddler of words." Philosopher and essayist G. L. Dickinson said: "To write clearly means to think clearly. . . . The main point is to arrange your ideas in the right order, and connect your sentences rightly. This is difficult in English because there are so few connecting particles. Consequently, much has to be done by getting the right emphasis on the right word; and that is a matter of arrangement of the words." Truman Capote emphasizes finding "the most *natural* way of telling the story" and adds a note about the significance of the apparently inconsequential: "I believe a story can be wrecked by a faulty rhythm in a sentence—especially if it occurs toward the end—or a mistake in paragraphing, even punctuation." Rhythm and punctuation were important also to Hamlin Garland: "I strive for clarity, precision and the color and rhythm appropriate to the subject matter. In the use of punctuation I have but one rule: use only so many characters as are necessary to prevent a misunderstanding of the text."

Nelson Algren, whom Hemingway once paired with Faulkner as one of the two best writers in America, cautions that concern for style may be overdone: "You can get too fussy. I do find myself bogged down wondering whether I should use a colon or a semicolon, and I keep trying each one out. I guess you can overdo that. . . . I haven't consciously tried to develop [a style]. The only thing I've consciously tried to do was put myself in a position to hear the people I wanted to hear talk talk."

Stewart Edward White, for many years a popular novelist, said, "The technique of writing seems to me to depend first of all on a sense of balance and proportion. That is an innate sense," he declared, to the discomfort of those who do not have it. "It tells one what to put in and what to leave out, and exactly what high lights to place upon this and what obscurities to put upon the other."

How does one acquire a style? By wide reading, most authors would say, and by much writing, and fearless experimentation. Not, however, as the eighteenth century believed, by giving "your days and nights to Addison"—or anyone else. Gamaliel Bradford warned, "The worst thing that can happen to a young writer is to idolize any particular author and model himself upon him." François Mauriac echoes the thought: "A borrowed style is a bad style."

EXERCISE SIX

1. Look up *style* in two or more dictionaries. Do the dictionary definitions suggest the same ingredients of style as those named by the authors quoted in the section you have just read?

2. In a paragraph, attempt your own definition of *style*.

THE PAIN OF WRITING

Perhaps Joseph Conrad, in *A Personal Record,* has best revealed the strain of a literary career. This paragraph concerns the writing of his *Nostromo:*

For twenty months, neglecting the common joys of life that fall to the lot of the humblest on this earth, I had, like the prophet of old, "wrestled with the Lord" for my creation, for the headlands of the coast, for the darkness of the Placid Gulf, the light on the snows, the clouds in the sky, and for the breath of life that had to be blown into the shapes of men and women, of Latin and Saxon, of Jew and Gentile. These are, perhaps, strong words, but it is difficult to characterize otherwise the intimacy and the strain of a creative effort in which mind and will and conscience are engaged to the full, hour after hour, day after day, away from the world, and to the exclusion of all that makes life really lovable and gentle—something for which a material parallel can only be found in the everlasting sombre stress of the westward winter passage round Cape Horn.

More recent writers tend to agree with Conrad. Walter de la Mare said, "Writers so dissimilar as Dr. Johnson and Cardinal Newman have declared that literary composition is one of the most laborious of all human activities, and if my own very limited experience is of any value, it convinces me that the difficulties involved in the craft of writing by no means diminish with practice." Carl Van Doren once wrote: "I do not like to write. Invariably I put off whatever I have to do, dreading the strain, and turning to any possible diversion."

But there are dissenting voices. William Styron does not like to write, but admits to "a fine warm feeling when I'm doing well." Faulkner enjoyed the "point in the book where the characters themselves rise up and take charge and finish the job—say somewhere about page 275. Of course I don't know what would happen if I finished the book on page 274." Thornton Wilder reacted somewhat differently: "Once you catch the idea for an extended narration—drama or novel—and if that idea is firmly within you, then the writing brings you perhaps not so much pleasure as a deep absorption." But E. M. Forster declared: "I have always found writing pleasant, and don't understand what people mean by 'throes of creation.'"

EXERCISE SEVEN

In a couple of paragraphs (or stanzas of verse if you prefer) prove that for you either it's fun to write or it's no fun to write.

REVISION

Said Dorothy Parker: "It takes me six months to do a story. I think it out and then write it sentence by sentence —no first draft. I can't write five words but that I change seven." For Georges Simenon, revision is "cut, cut, cut." He takes out "adjectives, adverbs, and every word which is there just to make an effect." James Thurber rewrote up to fifteen times. Scott Fitzgerald once said to Thomas Wolfe, "You're a putter-inner and I'm a taker-outer." Hamlin Garland revised some pages of *A Son of the Middle Border* ten times. William Allen White wrote each piece over and over again. Frank O'Connor rewrites "endlessly, endlessly, endlessly." And Henry Seidel Canby, once editor of the *Saturday Review*, was not the only author to realize "if the idea is bad, nothing can be done except burn the manuscript."

Alberto Moravia compares his writing with the work of painters centuries ago, some of whom proceeded layer by layer: "The first draft is quite crude, far from being perfect, by no means finished; although even then, even at that point, it has its final structure, the form is visible. After that I rewrite it as many times—apply as many 'layers' —as I feel to be necessary."

Some authors, however, have their ideas so clearly in mind that they can write with only small revisions as they go along. Shakespeare was reported (probably inaccurately) as never having "blotted a line." Bertrand Russell said, "I now hardly ever make any corrections in a manuscript, beyond altering a word when there is unintentional repetition. I think over a book before beginning to write, and when I begin, the real work is finished. Of course, I always compose each sentence in full in my head before beginning to write it out." H. L. Mencken revised little, although when he found that a paragraph had got him "into muddy waters," he would tear up the whole page and do it over. Angus Wilson does only one draft of his novels, revising as he goes along.

EXERCISE EIGHT

What suggestions for revision of your own work have been called to your attention by any of the authors' comments you have read in this chapter?

AFTERMATH

When a work is once published, surprisingly few authors give it much more serious thought. True, a few, like Frank O'Connor, rewrite their stories even after publication, but most become absorbed instead in new projects. If the finished work is successful, some enjoy basking in their moments of glory, but others are halfway through the next book. If the finished work is unsuccessful, some shrug it off as Robert Penn Warren recommends: "When you fail at something you call it an 'experiment,' an élite word for flop."

And writers—at least they often say so—do not read reviews very religiously. Some profess disdain for the critics. Some are wryly amused by critics' far-fetched interpretations. Others say that they themselves are aware of more flaws in their work than anyone else can ever see. They would agree with Wilbur Daniel Steele, one of the best short story writers of our century: "There is a time when a tale is a fine and beautiful creature, a masterpiece without flaw, a drama calculated to move one beyond any drama yet written by man; and that is just before you sit down to write it." Each time a writer completes a piece and is ready to start another, he envisions such a flawless masterpiece. Hope springs eternal.

17

Writing as a Profession

ON "BEING A WRITER"

MANY young persons (and many not so young) dream of "being a writer." They picture themselves autographing their books, frequently seeing their names in magazines and newspapers, giving talks before admiring audiences, and traveling around the world on the fabulously large sums of money they receive.

Some of the dreamers keep on just dreaming. They are the ones who want to be writers but who do not really want to write. Writing is hard work. These dreamers would welcome the glory but are unwilling to perform the toil.

Some of the dreamers do try to write. They spend hours every day on the task. But, unhappily, they lack the innate ability, just as some would-be musicians lack what it takes to succeed on the concert stage. This inability is nothing to be ashamed of; success in another kind of work, for which they are better fitted, may come rapidly.

Some of the dreamers find that they can make a living from writing, or write to supplement another source of income, but that the kind of writing they can get paid for is different from what they dreamed about. They find themselves, for instance, working as newspaper reporters or as editors of "house publications" in industry; or they find themselves with a regular job that requires little writing but that permits them to use some spare time for composing magazine fillers or short stories for a church school publication.

Very few of the dreamers ever realize their dreams

fully. Even the successful writer cannot just "be a writer"; he must learn and think and write and write and revise and revise and learn and think and write and revise some more. He cannot make a career of parties and travel and stares of admiration.

The purpose of this chapter is to present as honestly as possible the pros and cons of the profession of writing. A student who is seriously considering a writing career should ask himself first the most basic question: Does he honestly want to write—hours and hours a day—or does he just want to be a writer?

EXERCISE ONE

Before reading any more of this chapter, write a short essay (perhaps two or three paragraphs) on "Why I Believe I Want (or Do Not Want) a Writing Career."

THE IMPORTANCE OF COMMUNICATION TODAY

Never before in man's history has so much use been made of communication, both oral and written. Never have printing presses reproduced so many millions of words each day. Never have business and industry written so many letters, made so many telephone calls, advertised so much. Never have the people, the word-consumers, been exposed to such barrages of communication.

Here are a few examples of the role and the cost of communication today. Two thirds of a railroad's payroll money is expended for communication. The nation's annual telephone bill is about six billion dollars. A business letter costs two dollars or more. About half the price of a new automobile goes for communication (if your father has a new three-thousand-dollar car, he is driving fifteen hundred dollars' worth of words). About half of all the money spent by all the branches of government goes for oral and written communication. If communication were to stop completely for a day, planes would cease flying, fires would rage unchecked, schools and factories and hospitals would cease functioning, government would stop, the world would be in turmoil.

But aside from its commercial importance, communication has other significance. Man makes progress through new ideas and through their transmission. Modern man would still be cave man if he had not found ways to transmit information, ideas, and ideals from one person's head to another's.

Always, out in front, are the interpreters, the analyzers, the dramatizers. These are the philosophers, the thinkers, the creators, the writers. Sometimes they put into words what no one else has thought or said; more often they try to write "what oft was thought, but ne'er so well expressed." Shelley said that they are "the legislators of mankind." If that claim is too tall, at least they are the men and women who do much to increase understanding of human motives, human strengths and weaknesses. Through their words they help us to know hundreds of persons whom we would otherwise not have known, and to undergo hundreds of experiences that we would otherwise never have encountered. They increase our sensitivity to beauty and to pain. They multiply each of us, making each not one man or woman, but a multitude.

EXERCISE TWO

1. In the second paragraph of the section you have just read are some rather surprising statements about the cost of communication. Discuss some of them, trying to discover the various items that make a business letter cost two dollars, the many kinds of communication that go into the manufacture and sale of an automobile (from iron ore pits through the dealer's showroom), and the kinds of communication in government.

2. Discuss: "Modern man would still be cave man if he had not found ways to transmit information, ideas, and ideals from one person's head to another's."

3. Galileo's studies in astronomy changed man's conception of the universe. Einstein's thinking in mathematics resulted in the release of atomic energy. Charles Dickens's *Oliver Twist* and Elizabeth Browning's "The Cry of the Children" helped to reform British child labor laws. Edwin Markham's "The Man with the Hoe" became an unofficial theme song that helped to bring about labor reforms in the United States. Upton Sinclair's *The Jungle* was instrumental in bringing about the United States Pure Food and Drug Act. Developing one or more such facts, write an essay called "Ideas Have Consequences."

WRITING OPPORTUNITIES IN MODERN AMERICA

The usual picture of a writer is of a person who sits in his study and spins from his imagination and his well-stocked mind the fine threads of his stories. Sometimes the picture is accurate, but more often not.

Journalism and publishing. Many of the nation's writers, instead of sitting in their studies, are leading the active lives of journalists. The United States has over 1700 daily newspapers, over 500 Sunday papers, and several thousand papers published weekly or at other intervals. Each of these papers has its own staff of writers and editors, consisting of from one person to several hundred persons. News bureaus such as the Associated Press have their own personnel.

Thousands of magazines are printed weekly, biweekly, monthly, or quarterly. Some forty of them have circulations exceeding a million, and editorial staffs large enough to carry such a responsibility. At the other extreme are specialized publications for welders, well-drillers, Poland China raisers, music teachers, and the like, with small circulations and small staffs.

Hundreds of companies publish books. Some specialize in religious books, plays, textbooks, or other varieties; some are general in their interests. In small companies one or two editors may do most of the work; large companies may have editorial staffs with a hundred or more persons on the payroll.

Some persons who work for newspapers, magazines, or book publishers have much opportunity to write; others, very little or none. Often, however, the person who enjoys working with words may find a pleasant niche for himself as a reporter, rewrite man, copyreader, proofreader, or member of an editorial staff, even though his writing activity may be limited.

A special kind of writing that may be considered journalistic is that done by certain employees of radio and television stations. Preparation of news broadcasts and special programs may be one of their responsibilities; another is called "continuity writing"—the preparation of the short noncommercial announcements giving station identification, special information, program notes, and the like.

Writing in business and industry. Advertising is the kind of writing most often associated with business and industry. The amount of money spent on advertising each year is approximately as great as the amount spent on public education. The billions of dollars' worth of advertisements must be prepared by someone, usually by specially trained writers.

But business and industry employ writers for other purposes, too. Some of them edit, or write and edit, what are called "house organs," usually small magazines or newsletters that are sent to dealers, agents, employees, and others especially interested in the work of the company. Reports to stockholders and sometimes magazines for stockholders are prepared for many corporations. Technical reports, sometimes translated into layman's language, are often circulated within a company or an industry. Special writing tasks sometimes arise, such as the preparation of a booklet for the information of the public, or the "ghost-writing" of speeches to be delivered by company officials.

Writing for the government. Branches of the federal government produce for wide or narrow distribution many thousands of articles, pamphlets, and books each year. Most of these are written by specialists and then edited by other persons to make them conform to prescribed style. For instance, a Department of Agriculture specialist may prepare a pamphlet on the care of peach trees; someone else will put it into final shape, and the government will print it. The U.S. Government Printing Office prints and distributes more material than any commercial publisher. State and local governments publish a relatively small number of pamphlets and books.

Free-lance writing. In the Middle Ages a free lance was a soldier who made his services available to anyone who would hire him. A free-lance writer, unlike the others so far considered in this chapter, writes for any periodical or publisher that will buy his words.

Most novelists, poets, authors of nonfiction books, short story writers, and writers of articles, as well as some writers for radio, television, and the movies, are free-lancers. They write what they think will sell, or perhaps what their natures make them write, and offer their wares in the marketplace. Sometimes they become regular contributors to one or a few magazines, or become firmly attached to a single publishing house, but they are still free-lancers unless they sign an agreement specifying that their work will be made available to only one publisher.

Most textbook authors are free-lancers, although they often make fairly definite long-term arrangements with publishers. Nearly all textbook writers are teachers first, writers second; the writing is a sideline. Some other free-lancers may also have regular employment, confining their writing to evenings or weekends.

Free-lancing is financially the most uncertain kind of writing. Many free-lancers have spent a year or much more on a book manuscript which no publisher would accept. If he has no other source of income, the free-lancer who makes no sales doesn't eat.

On the other hand, the word *free* in *free-lancing* is appealing. Few other persons are so devoid of restraint, so free to make their own decisions, as is the free-lancer.

EXERCISE THREE

1. List a dozen or two dozen kinds of printed material that you may see in your home, on newstands, in the school library, and in an office building. Include different kinds of materials in newspapers and magazines, as well as pamphlets, advertising brochures, and books. Decide which of these items were probably prepared by free-lancers, which by regular employees.

2. Discuss or write a paper on the subject "Free-lancing vs. Regular Employment." Tell which you would prefer and why.

TRAINING NEEDED FOR A WRITING CAREER

Unlike careers in medicine, in teaching, or even in a trade like bricklaying, no fairly standardized training for a writer is recognized. It is possible, though, to pick out some of the characteristics needed by most writers and thus to suggest indirectly the training needed.

1. *Knowledge of words.* Words are the writer's tools, just as brushes and paints are the artist's. The writer should be a student of words, their nuances, the results obtained from combining them in various ways.

2. *Writing skill.* The words make the sentences, the sentences make the paragraphs, and the paragraphs make

the articles and books. The writer needs to know the architecture of books, the structure of paragraphs, the infinite mosaics of sentences.

3. *Literary knowledge.* Most writers profit from a knowledge of how their great predecessors have clarified characters, depicted scenes, planned plots, explained ideas, and expressed emotions.

4. *General knowledge.* No writer can predict in advance what knowledge he may need for a particular purpose. Human knowledge is so vast, and is expanding so rapidly, that no one can carry more than a tiny fraction of it in his mind. Nevertheless, it is helpful if a writer has some conception of each of the major areas of knowledge, and especially useful if he knows where he can look for what he doesn't know. Someone once defined an educated man as "a person who knows where to find whatever he wants."

5. *Special knowledge.* The journalist, the advertising writer, the textbook writer, or the person who translates a technical scientific paper into layman's language obviously needs specialized knowledge. What is less generally recognized is that the free-lance likewise needs an area or areas of special competence. For example, Joseph Conrad and Rachel Carson were intimately familiar with different aspects of the sea, J. P. Marquand knew the habits and habitats of businessmen, and William Faulkner knew in infinite detail the people of a region.

6. *Knowledge of people.* Perhaps, as was just suggested, knowledge of people is specialized knowledge, but it is so important that it needs stressing. Most writers should know many persons from firsthand observation, and know more persons from their reading and still more persons *en masse* through their study of psychology and sociology. Writers need retentive ears and eyes and minds, so that they can recall and interpret the faint accent or other speech peculiarity, the twitching cheek muscle, the man-

nerisms that exist in thinking no less than in speech and action.

Not every successful writer has been a college graduate, but college perhaps affords the easiest way for most young persons to learn the things that may help most in a writing career. College courses and college life will not provide everything needed for success in writing; a long series of journalism courses will not insure a brilliant journalistic career, and a dozen courses in creative writing can't guarantee creativity. But college courses may provide some of the general knowledge and some of the literary and special knowledge, and may increase facility with words (and felicity too). If courses in journalism or creative writing can't tell a student exactly what he should do, they may help him to avoid a few things that he shouldn't do. Courses in a foreign language may simultaneously enrich understanding of one's own tongue. Study of sociology and psychology has apparent value. But one cannot say that any study is valueless to a prospective writer. One present-day writer, for instance, specialized in science and education; he taught science for a while, and then began writing children's books about science. His knowledge of science and of ways to present scientific facts interestingly to children, combined with his writing ability, has made his books fantastically successful.

EXERCISE FOUR

As a class project, each student may chooose one prominent American writer of the twentieth century and study his biography, particularly the parts dealing with his education. Questions like these should be answered in an attempt to see whether anything resembling a pattern exists in the education of modern writers:

Did the writer finish high school?

Did he begin writing at an early age?

Did he attend college?

THE WRITER'S CRAFT

If so, in what subjects did he specialize?

What early experiences probably did much to increase his knowledge of people?

What portions of his early career probably gave him other knowledge useful in his writing?

What early experiences probably were especially helpful in shaping his philosophy of life?

ADVANTAGES AND DISADVANTAGES OF A WRITING CAREER

A nineteenth-century sailor had been away from home for more than a year on a whaling vessel. He had endured cold, rain, snow, cramped quarters, low pay, and prolonged absence from his family. Yet his first act on returning to port was to sign up for another voyage. Why? Simply because he loved whaling.

For one who loves to work with words as well as this sailor liked his job, the chance to do that kind of work may outweigh all disadvantages. We usually are happiest in a job that involves what we do best and know most about.

Writing careers generally are careers of service, conveying information, ideas, and emotions to others. Those persons who like to serve find this a second advantage.

A free-lance writer may live almost anywhere he wishes and arrange his working hours to suit himself. For such a writer, his personal independence is a big advantage.

A few writers, much fewer than one per cent, become wealthy from their work. People who like big gambles consider advantageous the possibility of wealth, the possibility that at least one of their books will be a financial success, even though the odds against them are heavy.

The first disadvantage is related to the last-named advantage: Many writers live in poverty, uncertain from day to day and week to week whether they can pay the grocer and the landlord. Only a few thousand free-lance writers in the whole United States earn a dependable comfortable income. A novel that takes a year or more of the writer's time and that sells five thousand copies (a fair average) pays only about two thousand dollars in royalties.

Another disadvantage, not confined to writing, is that many persons overestimate their ability and dejectedly must seek another kind of work when they fail.

Rejection slips, often one after another, cause heartaches. Every writer gets them; as one boasted, "I've had my stories refused by the very best magazines!" Few other kinds of work (acting is one) result in such frequent turndowns. Usually the rejection slip contains no real explanation, and the writer soon begins wondering, heartsick, whether an acceptance will ever come.

Finally, the life of the writer, especially the free-lance, is lonely. The person who works best in a crowd, or in cooperation with others, should not think of free-lance writing, which requires seclusion for hours each day.

Writing, then, like every other occupation, has both advantages and disadvantages. A young person should think seriously of a writing career only after weighing carefully such pros and cons as have just been summarized. Particularly, as was suggested at the beginning of this chapter, he must be certain that his goal is to write and not just to "be a writer."

EXERCISE FIVE

For Exercise One (page 296) you were asked to write two or three paragraphs on "Why I Believe I Want (or Do Not Want) a Writing Career." Using what you have learned in this chapter, rewrite that essay.

18

Style Index for Quick Reference

This Index will help you solve problems of style that you may meet in your writing. In marking your papers, your teacher may want to use some of the symbols which are arranged alphabetically. When you find one of these symbols on your paper, turn to this Index and study the explanation given after the symbol; try to understand clearly the principle involved, and then make the necessary correction.

Ab *Abbreviation.* Ordinarily, use few abbreviations in connected writing. Acceptable before proper nouns are *Dr., Mr., Mrs.,* and *St.* (Saint). Acceptable after proper nouns are *Jr.,* and *Sr.,* as well as abbreviations of college degrees such as *A.B., A.M., Ph.D.* Avoid abbreviations for *and.* Avoid overuse of *etc.*

Ad *Confusion of adjectives and adverbs.* The purpose of adjectives is to modify nouns or words used as the equivalent of nouns. Adverbs generally modify verbs, although words like *very* or *too,* which are sometimes called "intensifiers," modify adjectives or other adverbs. A major trouble spot is illustrated in this sentence: *The new mower worked good.* Use *well* instead, because a verb (*worked*) should be modified by an adverb.
In summary, an adjective fits into slots like these:

A very _____ thing.
The thing is _____.

An adverb fits into a slot like this:

He walks _____.

An intensifier like *very, rather,* or *extremely* fits into a slot like this:

The _____ good man.

306

C *Case.* Errors in case almost always involve the pronouns *I, me, we, us, he, him, she, her, they, them, who, whom.* Most of the difficulties arise when the pronoun is used with another pronoun or a noun. That is, no one has trouble with *Give me the bracelets,* but *Give Marcia and _____ the bracelets* causes confusion. The solution is simple: Use the form you would use if the other pronoun or noun weren't there. *Give Marcia and me the bracelets.*

After the verb *be* (*am, is, are, was, were, being, been*) formal English prefers the nominative case *I, we, he, she, they,* as in *This is she speaking.* For some expressions, informal English occasionally uses *me, us, him, her, them*—for example, *It's me.*

Who is used as the subject of a sentence or clause, *whom* as any kind of object: *Who came? The man who came was Mr. Terry. You saw whom? Whom did you see? The man whom you saw was Mr. Terry. He is the man who I think will be elected next week.*

The possessive case of a pronoun or noun is generally used before a gerund (an *-ing* verb used as a noun): *I had not remembered his dancing. I had not remembered George's dancing.*

Cap *Capitalization.* These suggestions concern the major trouble spots; they do not cover all the rules.

1. In a direct quotation, capitalize the first word if it begins a complete sentence: *He replied, "You saw it yourself."* [BUT: *He referred to the "equitable" settlement.*]

2. In a letter, capitalize the first word of the salutation and of the complimentary close: *Dear Henry, My dear Mr. Martin, Yours sincerely.*

3. Capitalize the first and last words and all other important words in a literary title: *"Ode to the West Wind," A Dictionary of Modern English Usage, All Quiet on the Western Front.*

4. Capitalize names of persons, groups, and organizations, and words derived from such names, but not nouns like *doctor. president, lieutenant, company,* and *sophomore,* unless they are parts of proper nouns: *John Milton Miltonian, Future Teachers of America, Americanism, President L. R. Meigs, the Acme Company, a corporation president, a small company, a sophomore.*

5. Capitalize names of historical periods or major historical events: *the Dark Ages, the Battle of Hastings.* Either capitals or

lower case may be used with centuries: *the Twentieth Century*
or *the twentieth century.*

6. Capitalize names of days, months, and holidays, but not
names of seasons: *Tuesday, July, Labor Day, summer.*

7. Capitalize nouns or pronouns meaning *God* or *Jesus,* and
names of sacred books: *Jehovah, the Almighty, He who died on
the cross, the Bible, the Book of Numbers, the Talmud.* Do not
capitalize *god* or *gods* when referring to pagan deities: *the gods
of Greece, the goddess of wisdom.*

8. Capitalize personified abstract nouns: *O Justice, where
art thou?*

9. Capitalize titles preceding names, but not following: *Vice-
president Fairless; L. M. Fairless, vice-president in charge of
sales; Superintendent Prentice Wright; Prentice Wright, superintendent of schools.*

10. Capitalize names showing family relationships when they
are used with proper nouns or as substitutes for proper nouns;
but not after possessives like *my* or *Frank's: Aunt Matilda; then
Father spoke; my aunt; Frank's father.*

11. Capitalize names of specific places: *Thirtieth Street, the
Atlantic Ocean, the South (part of the country).* NOTE: Newspapers now usually do not capitalize words like *street* and *ocean*
in the examples, but magazines and books generally do.

12. Do not capitalize names of directions unless they refer
to specific parts of the country: *Head west; do not turn toward
the south. We live in the South.*

13. Capitalize names of school subjects if they are languages
or if a number accompanies them, but not otherwise: *Spanish,
Mathematics 2, a course in mathematics, a science course, book-
keeping.*

14. Capitalize nouns or their abbreviations when they are followed by designating numbers, except the nouns *page* and *line:
Highway 12, Chapter V, Room 416, Act IV, page 12, line 2.*

Clr *Clearness.* Each sentence should reveal its meaning readily
enough that a reader will not be confused even momentarily. If
the teacher frequently has to mark Clr on your paper, form the
habit of reading your sentences aloud, one by one, and asking
yourself, "Could anyone possibly be confused by this?"

Coh *Coherence.* Sometimes your teacher may use the symbol Coh instead of Clr. Faulty coherence leads to lack of clarity. It means that some of your sentences do not form smooth paragraphs. Sometimes transitions (see Trans) are inadequate or poorly chosen.

Com *Comparison.* 1. Most adjectives and adverbs exist in three forms: the *positive,* the *comparative,* and the *superlative.*

Positive	*Comparative*	*Superlative*
small	smaller	smallest
candid	more candid	most candid
quickly	more quickly	most quickly

In formal writing the comparative degree is used in comparing two things, the superlative in comparing three or more. *The boy is the smaller of the two children. The boy is the smallest of the three children.*

2. Do not omit necessary words in stating a comparison. Say "Alaska is larger than any other state"; do not omit *other,* because Alaska is a state and it is therefore nonsense to say "Alaska is larger than any state." These other examples show in italics the words that only careless writers would omit:

The lieutenant worked harder than anyone *else.*

London is closer to New York than Buenos Aires *is.*

The expense for labor is greater than *that for* materials.

She likes Frank more than *she does* Bill.

The story was so interesting *that I read it all in one sitting.*

3. If you write a comparison using *as . . . as,* or *as . . . as . . . than,* or *one of the . . . if not the,* finish the comparison at the earliest possible moment: *He was as lucky as his brother, if not luckier.* [NOT: *He was as lucky, if not luckier, than his brother.*] *This is one of the largest redwood trees, if not the largest.* [NOT: *This is one of the largest, if not the largest, redwood trees.*]

Con *Connectives.* Avoid misuses of the following connectives:

1. *while* Since *while* generally refers to time, a sentence like this is confusing: *While oranges are grown in California, they are consumed in the East.* Sometimes *although, but,* or *and* should replace *while.*

2. *because* In formal English avoid: *The reason is because . . .*
Say: The reason is that . . .

3. *when, where* Avoid defining a thing as a *when* or a *where.*
NOT: *Zoology is where* [or *when*] *you study animals.* BETTER:
Zoology is the study of animals.

Also, avoid expressions like "I saw in the paper where," or "I
read where." NOT: *I read where a new carburetor has been invented.* BETTER: *I read that . . .*

4. *so* Avoid excessive use of *so.* Sometimes *so that* is preferable. Often a *so . . . so* sentence needs revising.

5. *like* Many persons still prefer not to use *like* to introduce
a clause, favoring *It looked as if it would snow* rather than *It
looked like it would snow.*

6. *nor* After *neither,* use *nor,* not *or: Neither the chimneys
nor the gutters were damaged.*

D *Diction.* If your teacher uses this symbol, it means either that
you have not chosen the most effective word or that you have
used a word with the wrong meaning.

Dict *Dictionary.* This symbol means that you should look up
in the dictionary a word that the teacher has marked. Perhaps
you have used an incorrect form, or maybe the teacher wants
you to be sure you know the exact meaning.

Dng *Dangling modifier.* A dangling modifier is a word or group
of words that does not clearly modify anything in the sentence.
For instance, in *Climbing to the top of the barn, the distant
smoke could be more clearly seen,* the clause starting with *Climbing* has nothing to modify. BETTER: *Climbing to the top of the
barn, we could see . . .*

Emph *Emphasis.* Emphasis in a composition is attained by de-
voting most space to that which is to be emphasized, and by
putting especially important elements near the beginning or the
end. Within a sentence, observing the following suggestions will
improve emphasis.

1. Put the most important idea into the main clause. NOT: *It
was a bright, sunny afternoon and Grandpa was strolling in the
woods when a bear killed him.* BETTER: *When Grandpa was stroll-*

ing in the woods one bright, sunny afternoon, an angry female bear set upon him and killed him.

2. Use the active voice, not the passive, for emphasis. NOT: *The winning touchdown was scored by Jim Leonard.* BETTER: *Jim Leonard scored the winning touchdown.*

3. Avoid straggly sentence endings. NOT: *He is in the Latin room, maybe.* BETTER: *He may be in the Latin room.* NOT: *The abuse of this privilege will lead to abuses of other privileges, in time to come, in all probability, it seems to me.* BETTER: *In time to come, the abuse of this privilege is likely to lead to abuses of other privileges.*

4. In a series, build up to the most important item. NOT: *I respect him for his character, his habits, and his clean-cut appearance.* BETTER: *I respect him for his clean-cut appearance, his habits, and his character.*

5. Use both loose and periodic sentences. A loose sentence is one in which the main idea is revealed before the end: *The prisoners escaped from their cell at 11 p.m., although the usual precautions had been taken.* A periodic sentence retains the main idea until the end: *At 11 p.m., despite the fact that the usual precautions had been taken, the prisoners escaped from their cell.*

Eu *Euphony.* Good writing is generally pleasant to the ear. Bad writing is often grating and unpleasant. Particularly to be avoided are unintentional rhymes and a long series of hissing sounds. POOR: *Feeling that he was a sinner, he nevertheless ate his dinner.* POOR: *Several succulent, savory stalks still stood beside the stream.*

Exc *Excessive coordination.* When two or more ideas are joined in a sentence, often one is more important than the others. (See **Emph,** page 310.) If so, it should be placed in the main clause, with the others reduced to phrases or dependent clauses. In other words, complex sentences are often better than compound. This is particularly true when the parts of a compound sentence go on and on, strung together with *and*'s and *so*'s. POOR: *I am looking forward to college life, and I believe it will be exciting and intellectually stimulating.* BETTER: *I am looking forward to college life, because I believe . . .* [OR: *. . . which, I believe, will be . . .*] POOR: *My old Mercury is a good old car, and I have done a lot of* *work on it, and it has cost me a great deal of money, so I really should enjoy it, and I do.* BETTER: *I really enjoy my good old Mercury, even though it has required a great amount of work and money.*

Fig *Figure of speech.* For a discussion of effective figures of speech, see pages 37-42.

Frag *Sentence fragment* (sometimes called a *period fault* or an *incomplete sentence*). Writing usually requires the consistent use of complete sentences. Fragments may be justified in reporting conversation and for a few other specialized or stylistic purposes, but ordinarily complete sentences are preferable. Particularly to be avoided is the fragment which belongs logically with an adjacent sentence. NOT: *He closed his left eye and shaded the right with his hand. A habit he had recently acquired.* BETTER: *He closed his left eye and shaded the right with his hand, a habit he had recently acquired.* NOT: *The elephant lowered his trunk into the stream and then jerked it back. Because, to his surprise, the water was hot.* BETTER: *The elephant lowered his trunk into the stream and then jerked it back because, to his surprise, the water was hot.*

H *Hackneyed expression. Hackneyed* means "trite" or "worn-out." Many good, colorful expressions have been used so often that it is generally best to avoid them. Among the hundreds of such phrases are these: *busy as bees, view with alarm, Father Time, crack of dawn, rustling grass, every waking hour, sterling character, walk on air, off the beaten track, eat one's words, quick as a flash, pretty as a picture, streamlined efficiency, trackless ocean.*

Ital *Italics.* In writing or typing, underline to indicate italics. Printers of books and magazines set in italic type anything that has been underlined in a manuscript. Newspapers rarely use italics.

Italics are used chiefly for the following purposes:

1. To indicate foreign words which have not become standard English: *al fresco, à la belle étoile.*

2. To indicate titles of books, long plays, newspapers, maga-

zines, and long musical compositions: *For Whom the Bell Tolls, Twelfth Night,* the *Louisville Journal,* the *Saturday Review, Il Trovatore.*

3. To indicate words and letters used as the names of words and letters: the *i* before the *b* in *intelligible.*

4. To indicate names of ships (less often used now than previously): the *Independence.*

5. Rarely, to emphasize: I said *hot* water, not *cold.*

K *Awkward.* Your teacher may use this symbol when a sentence or an expression is not actually wrong but seems awkward. The symbol *Awk* is also used.

Log *Logic.* This symbol means that the teacher believes your thinking is faulty.

M *Margin.* Unless your teacher gives other instructions, the lefthand margin should be about one and one-half inches, the righthand about a half inch. The lefthand margin should be straight except for paragraph indentions. Margins for poetry, of course, are often wider and less regular.

Mood *Mood.* Most English verbs are in the indicative mood. A few, giving commands or requests, are imperative. The chief problems arise in the third mood, the subjunctive, which in formal English is used in these ways:

1. To express a condition contrary to fact: *If he* were *here, he would paint the barn himself. If I* were *you, I should read the telegram.*

2. To express a wish: *I wish Jeanette* were *here.*

3. In statements showing necessity, request, or urgency: *It was essential that he* be *discharged. I propose that he* be *discharged. I urge that he* be *discharged.*

4. After *as if* or *as though* to show uncertainty: *The boy looked as if he* were *lost.*

N *Number.* Sometimes a writer does not know whether to spell out or use figures for certain numbers. The following principles are generally followed by magazine and book publishers. Newspaper practice makes more use of figures, and some magazines are beginning to follow newspaper usage.

1. In most writing, spell out numbers that can be expressed

in one or two words, and use figures for the rest: *twelve; twenty-two; one thousand; 284; 1,632.* (Most newspapers use figures for numbers greater than ten.)

2. Use figures for dimensions, scores, and exact sums of money: *a 2 by 8 plank; a 14 to 0 score; $17.26; about two thousand dollars.*

3. Use figures to represent things in sequence: *page 23; Chapter X; 18 Van Buren Street; Act II; scene i, line 14.*

4. When several numbers appear in the same paragraph, use either words or figures for all.

5. Avoid beginning a sentence with a figure.

6. Use figures for dates except in formal social writing.

7. Generally avoid *st, nd, rd,* and *th* in giving dates or ordinal numbers.

8. With *a.m.* and *p.m.* use figures; do not add *o'clock: 7:30 p.m.; 9:00 (or 9) a.m.* BUT *nine o'clock.*

9. Insert commas to set off figures in groups of three, counting from the right. Exceptions: dates, street and telephone numbers, serial numbers. *3,684; 4,627,842; the year 1972; 1843 North Main; telephone 367-4329; social security number 327-06-0912.*

Om   *Omission.* The teacher's use of this symbol means that you have left out some word or words desirable for clearness or conformity with modern usage. For example, in reference to our country, *the* should precede *United States* used as a noun. Other examples: POOR: *I plan to attend University of Michigan.* [Insert *the.*] POOR: *She ate the pie and half the cupcakes.* [Insert *of.*] POOR: *Alice concealed Nancy had been in the next room.* [Insert *the fact that* before *Nancy.*] POOR: *A whippoorwill was calling and the crickets chirring.* [Insert *were.*]

Par cst   *Parallel construction.* The same grammatical forms are needed in the related parts of each of the following constructions.

1. In a series: *She detests swimming, boating, and fishing.* [NOT: *She detests swimming, boating, and to go fishing.*]

2. In comparisons: *He likes to bowl better than to play tennis.* [NOT: *He likes to bowl better than tennis.*]

3. With *both . . . and, either . . . or, neither . . . nor, not only . . . but also*: *He likes both bowling and boating. Not only the exercise but also the excitement appeals to him.*

Pred *Predication.* Avoid using a sentence or a clause when a phrase or a word can do the work equally well. POOR: *She objected to the question on the grounds that it was irrelevant and that it had been asked before.* BETTER: *She objected to the question as irrelevant and repetitious.* POOR: *Standing under a tree which is large is dangerous when it is stormy.* BETTER: *Standing under a large tree is dangerous in storms.*

Pron *Pronoun shift.* Observe the following principles in using pronouns, in order to avoid undesirable shifts.

1. In formal English, the pronouns *anybody, anyone, anything, each one, everyone, everybody, everything, no one, nobody, nothing, one, someone, somebody,* and *something* are regarded as singular. If another pronoun or a possessive is needed to refer to one of these words, it should be in a singular form. RIGHT: *Everybody did his* [not *their*] *share.* RIGHT: *If anyone has an objection, he* [not *they*] *should offer it now.* RIGHT: *Everyone felt sorry for himself* [not *themselves*]. RIGHT: *One should do his best work if he possibly can.* [OR, MORE BRITISH: *One should do one's best work if one possibly can.*]

2. Avoid shifting from *I* to *you* or *he,* or any similar shifts in person, unless there is good reason for the change. Also avoid such shifts in number as using *they* to refer to *a person.* POOR: *When one has a difficult assignment, you should begin to work early in the morning.* [Change *you* to *he.*] POOR: *If a person took this advice seriously, they would spend half their income on insurance.* [Change *they* to *he, their* to *his.*]

P ' *Punctuation: Apostrophes.* 1. Use an apostrophe to show possession. It goes before the *s* in singular nouns. For plural nouns ending in *s,* it goes after the *s.* Note that the possessives *his, hers, its, yours, ours, theirs,* and *whose* have no apostrophes. *A horse's hoof, the horses' heads, Mr. Davis'* [or *Davis's*] *house, the Joneses' house.*

2. Use an apostrophe to show omission of letters or figures: *hasn't, weren't, he'd, it's* [meaning *it is*], *who's* [meaning *who is* or *who has*], *standin'* [*standing*], *the class of '68.*

3. Use an apostrophe to show the plurals of figures, signs, or letters, and to show the plural of words referred to as words: *His 5's look like s's; several so's in one sentence; #'s.*

4. Do not use apostrophes in forming other plurals (despite the practice of many amateur sign painters).

P [ ]   *Punctuation: Brackets.* Observe that brackets are square-cornered. Their use is rare, being chiefly the indication that the writer has inserted a comment of his own in something he is quoting.

Herbert Hoover wrote: "It [the term *rugged individualism*] has been used for over a half-century in eulogy of those God-fearing men and women of honesty whose stamina and character and fearless assertion of rights led them to make their own way in life."

P :   *Punctuation: Colons.* 1. Use a colon before a direct, formal quotation. (See the quotation from Herbert Hoover, above, as an example.)

2. Use a colon before a formal enumeration or list, especially after such expressions as *the following* or *as follows.*

3. Use a colon to separate hours and minutes and to separate chapter and verse in a Biblical reference. (A centered period is sometimes used instead.) *4:26 a.m., John 3:16*

4. Use a colon after the salutation of a business letter. *Dear Sir:*

P, c   *Punctuation: Commas with coordinate expressions.* In a series, use commas to separate the items. The comma before *and* in a series is optional; follow your teacher's preference. *The blue, yellow,* (or no comma) *and red kites tugged gaily at their strings. We searched in the corridor, in the English room, and in the history room. Why he went, when he went, and where he went are all unknown.*

2. Separate two coordinate words (usually adjectives) with a comma. *A flickering, dwindling light shone for a few minutes.*

3. Use a comma to separate the two independent clauses in a compound sentence, if the second clause is introduced by *and, but, for, or, nor, yet,* or *so. In the Salem witch trials most of the accused denied their guilt, but fifty-five confessed that they were indeed witches.*

P, i *Punctuation: Commas with interpolations.* Interpolations are words, phrases, or clauses that provide additional facts or emphasis but that are not essential to the grammatical completeness or the central meaning of the sentence. Such interpolations are set off with two commas if they occur within the sentence, or with one comma if they occur at the beginning or end.

DATES: On August 14, 1961, the apparition was seen again.

PLACES: In Ogden, Utah, a serious fire broke out.

NAMES OF PERSONS BEING ADDRESSED: Then, Margaret, I began to worry.

INTERRUPTED DIALOGUE: "At the end," Wilmer concluded, "we had killed nearly forty groundhogs."

EXPLANATION OR QUALIFICATION: The inauguration, at that time held on March 4, was a memorable one.

CONTRAST: The deputy, not the sheriff, made the arrest.

EXPRESSIONS FOR EMPHASIS: This charge, I insist, is false.

TRANSITIONS: We know, moreover, that Brown had a police record.

APPOSITIVES: Adams, the second President, had long been known as a statesman.

MILD EXCLAMATIONS: Oh, I suppose so.

NOMINATIVE ABSOLUTES: The moon having risen, we could see the general shape of the cliff.

NONRESTRICTIVE CLAUSES: The Jonathan apple, which is bright red and very juicy, is my favorite.

P, m *Punctuation: Commas to prevent misreading.* Although a bad sentence cannot be made readable by the insertion of a few commas, often a comma or two will add to the clarity of a well-constructed sentence. *While I was shooting Bill Martin waited for his turn.* [Insert a comma after *shooting.*] *After spading the soil should be pulverized.* [Comma after *spading.*] *Progress was slow but steady gains were made.* [Comma after *slow.*]

P— *Punctuation: Dashes.* A dash is an informal mark of punctuation, most useful in showing a somewhat violent interruption of sentence structure. *While the team was—where are you going, Jim? Marybellissima—that's really her name—is now about eight-*

een. Avoid overusing dashes. In writing or typing, use two short lines to distinguish the dash from the hyphen.

P ! *Punctuation: Exclamation points.* Use an exclamation point after a short expression showing strong emotion or surprise. Use only one. Do not employ exclamatory sentences frequently, or the effect will be weakened. *Help! How sure he was of himself!*

P- *Punctuation: Hyphens.* Hyphens are actually spelling devices, but it is customary to treat them as punctuation.

1. In dividing a word at the end of a line, use a hyphen. Divide only between syllables. (see **Syl.**)

2. Use a hyphen to connect two or more words used before a noun as a single adjective: *a two-fisted man; a happy-go-lucky attitude; twenty five-dollar bills.*

3. Use a hyphen in compound numbers from twenty-one to ninety-nine, and in fractions used as modifiers. Do not hyphenate a fraction used as a noun: *twenty-five dollar bills; a two-thirds vote* (but *two thirds of the vote*).

4. Use a hyphen after a prefix followed by a capitalized word: *pro-Russian; un-American.*

5. Use a hyphen if a prefix or a suffix results in repetition of the same vowel or in a triple consonant: *anti-intellectual; a bell-like sound.*

6. Consult your dictionary when in doubt as to whether other words should be hyphenated, written solid, or written as two words.

P ( ) *Punctuation: Parentheses.* 1. Use parentheses to enclose a parenthetical expression not closely related to the rest of the sentence. *My cousin (the one I wrote you about last week) has now gone home. The Locarno Pact (see page 526) was signed in 1925.*

2. Be careful to use both halves of the parentheses.

3. If you find yourself using large numbers of parentheses, examine your sentences to see whether some of them should not be rewritten. Parenthetical expressions tend to slow the reader and sometimes become annoying.

P . *Punctuation: Periods.* 1. Use a period after a declarative sentence or an imperative sentence unless it can be considered exclamatory. A sentence that expresses a request in the form of a question is also usually punctuated with a period: *Will you please turn out the light.*

2. Use a period after an abbreviation. (See **Ab.**)

P ? *Punctuation: Question marks.* 1. Use a question mark after a direct question, but not after an indirect question. DIRECT: *When will he arrive?* INDIRECT: *I asked when he would arrive.*

2. Use a question mark (in parentheses) to show doubt about the accuracy of information: *Shakespeare was born on April 23 (?), 1564.*

3. Do not use a question mark to indicate humor or irony. POOR: *Let me tell you about our warm (?) trip through Canada.*

P " " *Punctuation: Quotation marks.* Enclose a direct quotation in quotation marks, but not an indirect quotation. DIRECT: *Jack asked, "Where did the plane land?"* INDIRECT: *Jack asked where the plane had landed.*

2. For a quotation within another quotation, use single quotation marks. *The sergeant reported, "The captain said, 'Move straight ahead.'"*

3. In formal writing, enclose slang expressions and highly technical terms in quotation marks. Do not overuse this device, though, as the quotation marks seem rather apologetic.

4. When closing quotation marks are used with other punctuation, put periods and commas inside the quotation marks; put colons or semicolons outside; put question marks and exclamation points inside when the quotation is a question or an exclamation but not otherwise.

"The team won easily," he reported.

He reported, "The team won easily."

The child began to recite "Little Boy Blue"; then she burst into tears.

He said concerning his "temporary indisposition": "It was a severe abdominal pain."

Ray asked, "Where is the compass?"

Did Ray say, "The compass is lost"?

Greta shouted, "Turn to the right!"
Imagine his calling it a "simple mistake"!

5. In paragraphing conversation, start a new paragraph with
each change of speaker. When the same person speaks two successive paragraphs, put no quotation marks at the end of the first
paragraph, but use them at the beginning of the second.

P ; *Punctuation: Semicolons.* 1. In a compound sentence, separate the independent clauses with a semicolon unless the second
clause starts with *and, but, for, or, nor, yet,* or *so.* (See **P,c** 3.) *The
Senate voted 82 to 6 for the bill; in the House, however, considerable debate seemed certain.*

2. It is sometimes, but not often, desirable to use a semicolon
in a place where a comma might cause misreading. The situations
in which semicolons are most often justified are in series with internal punctuation: *We chose Hunnicutt Mallow, a senior; Ger-
aldine Wozarth, a junior; Jay Wright, a sophomore; and Glenna
Trimmer, another senior.*

Ref *Reference of pronouns.* The pronouns *he, she, it, they, him,
her, them, who, whom, which, that, this, these,* and *those* should
always refer unmistakably to an antecedent.

POOR: They had a heavy snow in Colorado. [Who are *they*?]
POOR: Jim declared that he had seen Freda in the theater,
which seemed doubtful to us. [*Which* seems for a moment to
refer to *theater.*]
POOR: After you have bathed the baby, pour it down the drain.
[What is *it*?]
POOR: After the halfback plunged through Greg's guard position, he resolved to stop him next time. [Avoid using a pronoun
to refer to a possessive.]

Rep *Repetition.* Avoid purposeless repetition of a word or an
idea.

RS *Run-on sentence.* Two sentences should not be run together
without punctuation or with only a comma between them.

Sp *Spelling.* Keep a list of all words you misspell in any of your
courses. Study this list frequently, perhaps once a week, so that

you never need misspell a word more than once.

Ss *Short sentences.* Although short sentences are sometimes useful for either a staccato or a childish effect, in general a long succession of short sentences should be avoided. If your teacher places this symbol on a paper of yours, see how the sentences may be sensibly combined.

Syl *Syllabication.* In dividing a word at the end of a line, make the division only between syllables. A word of only one syllable should not be divided. It is undesirable to have only a single letter or two letters on either line. Place a hyphen at the end of the line to show that the word is completed on the next line.

If you are not sure where the division between syllables is, consult your dictionary.

T *Title.* The title of a composition or story should suggest the content without giving away any important sercets. Center the title on the first page, about an inch and a half from the top. Capitalize the first and last words and all other important words. Do not use quotation marks unless the title is a quotation. Do not use end punctuation unless a question mark or an exclamation point is needed. Leave a blank line or space between the title and the first line of the composition.

Trans *Transition.* In moving from one idea to another, you often need a word, phrase, clause, or sentence to show the relationship of the two ideas. Examples of transitions are *however, moreover, later, for this reason, granted that, while the suitcase was being packed,* and *in addition to.*

Va *Verb agreement.* 1. A verb should agree with its subject even when other words separate the subject and verb: *The reasons for this decision* are *numerous.*

2. The introductory *there* is not the subject. The verb agrees with the subject, which follows: *There* are *two robins in the cherry tree.*

3. The pronouns *anybody, anyone, anything, each, either, everybody, everyone, everything, neither, no one, nobody, nothing, one, somebody, someone,* and *something* take singular verbs.

4. A compound subject with the parts joined by *and* requires a plural verb: *The monkey and the squirrel* are *scolding each other*.

5. Two subjects joined by *or* or *nor* require a plural verb only if the last subject is plural.

The monkey or the parrot is *constantly chattering.*
The monkey or the parrots are *constantly chattering.*
The parrots or the monkey is *constantly chattering.*

6. The verb with a collective noun is normally singular. However, if individual activity is suggested, the verb is plural. *The band* was *marching. The band* were *leaving for their homes.*

Var *Variety.* Reduce sentence monotony by using sentences of different lengths and by avoiding several consecutive sentences following the same pattern. Begin your sentences in different ways.

Vpp *Verb principal part.* The past tense of certain verbs is used without a helper (auxiliary). The past participle is used as a verb with a helper such as *is, was, has, have,* or *had.* PRESENT: *begin;* PAST: *began;* PAST PARTICIPLE: *(has) begun.* For the principal parts of a verb, look in the dictionary under the present tense of that verb.

Vs *Verb shift.* Avoid unnecessary shifts in tense, voice, or mood of verbs.

We started to unload the furniture from the truck, only to discover that the large mirror is broken. [Change *is* to *was* to avoid the shift in tense.]

We started to unload the furniture from the truck, and soon the task was completed. [Change the last part to *and soon we completed the task,* to avoid the shift from active to passive voice.]

Start to unload the furniture, and you should put it into the bedroom at once. [Change the last part to *and put it into the bedroom at once,* to avoid the shift in mood.]

W *Wordiness.* Use no more words than are necessary to express your ideas clearly and effectively.

WORDY: There are many individual persons who have had the good fortune to be as satisfactorily endowed mentally as was our first President, George Washington, but it seems relatively safe and incontrovertible to assert and declare that few have attained a greater degree of success, as a result of possessing this endowment, in the affairs which they have undertaken than the father of his country met.

BETTER: Many men have been as intelligent as George Washington, but few have used their mental ability more successfully.

Index

Since the items in the "Style Index for Quick Reference" (pages 306-323) are arranged alphabetically, they are not included in this index.

Acquaintances, as subject, 14-15
Adjectives, in description, 29-31
Adverbs, in description, 31-2
Alliteration, 254
Amphibrachic foot, 256
Analogy, 41
Anapestic foot, 255-6
Apostrophe, 42
Argumentation, 58-9, 104-9
Art work, in books, 271-2
Article, 93-118, 276-7
Assonance, 254
Autobiography, 80-6

Begging the question, 106
Binding, of books, 275-6
Biography, 86-92
Blank verse, 258
Book review, 109-12, 128
Bunner, Henry C., 43

Causal relationship, 106
Characterization, 137-56
  in literary plays, 224-5
  in playlets, 217-20
  in short stories, 178-85, 200-1, 210
  nine methods, 141-52
Characters, 137-56
  background, flat, rounded, 154
  growth in, 153-4
Chekhov, Anton, 182
Chemistry game, 153
Cinquain, 246-7, 248-9, 260
Class calendar, 22
Class projects, 21-2

Coherence, 54-7, 62, 77
Columns, 129-30
Communication, importance of, 296-8
Comparison, 40-1, 102
Compositions, 47-68, 93-118
Concreteness, in poetry, 239-42
Conflict, in plot, 162-9, 224
Conrad, Joseph, 30, 290-1
Content, 59-63
Conversation, 146
Couplet, 258-9
Creativity, usefulness of, 4-5
Curiosity, 66-7

Dactylic foot, 256
Darwin, Charles, 97
Deduction, 101-2, 105-6
Depth, 61-2
Description, 23-32, 33-44, 58
  factual, 33-5
  figurative, 37-9
  interpretive, 35-7
Development, 62, 103-4
Diagrams, 61-2
Diction, 23-32, 64-5, 76, 78-9, 85-6, 173, 288-90
Dimeter, 256
Dos Passos, John, 38

Editorials, 129
Emerson, Ralph Waldo, 36
Emotion, as subject, 17
Emphasis, 77
Episode, 162-5, 171-5